natural English

pre-intermediate teacher's book
Ruth Gairns & Stuart Redman

OXFORD
UNIVERSITY PRESS

contents

introduction pp.6–12   **writing** syllabus chart p.13   **pronunciation** syllabus chart p.14   **extended speaking** feedback sheet p.15

in unit one ...
pp.16–25

life with Agrippine
cartoon happy families
natural English asking people to be quiet

listening how to ... ask questions
natural English What's ... like?
grammar question forms
listening stories about meeting famous people
natural English showing a lot of interest

wordbooster
relatives
talking about you and your family

reading relationships
natural English possessive 's
reading Special delivery
grammar past simple
natural English both

extended speaking
is your family like mine?
collect ideas
natural English How about you?
prepare a questionnaire
have a conversation
write about your families

test yourself!
revision and progress check

one review p.25
revision activities

one wordlist p.130

in unit two ...
pp.26–33

reading family meals
natural English have + noun
vocabulary food
reading What do we eat?
grammar countable and uncountable nouns
natural English a lot of, much, many, any

wordbooster
restaurant language
extreme adjectives

listening how to ... be the perfect guest
natural English saying sorry
listening friends having dinner together
natural English offering food or drink
grammar adjectives and adverbs

extended speaking
restaurant scene
collect ideas
invent a conversation
natural English talking about a picture
write the conversation
act out your conversation
listen

test yourself!
revision and progress check

two review p.33
revision activities

two wordlist p.131

in unit three ...
pp.34–41

reading a strange place to live
natural English the best / worst thing about ...
grammar present perfect and past simple
natural English once, twice, etc.
reading Man in a suitcase

wordbooster
describing towns
distance and time
natural English a five-minute walk

listening how to ... get around town
vocabulary prepositional phrases
natural English asking where things are
listening a visitor asking for directions
natural English a great / horrible place

extended speaking
this is where I live
collect ideas
talk about your area
write about your area

test yourself!
revision and progress check

three review p.41
revision activities

three wordlist p.132

in unit four ...
pp.42–49

reading shop till you drop
natural English this / that (one); these / those (ones)
reading Drop that price
natural English can / can't afford
grammar will for spontaneous decisions and offers

wordbooster
clothes
natural English wear / carry
phrasal verbs (1)

listening how to ... buy clothes
vocabulary shopping
natural English talking about size
listening a shopping story
writing re-write a story using link words
grammar too / very, too much / many

extended speaking
shoe shop scene
collect ideas
invent a conversation
act out your conversation
listen

test yourself!
revision and progress check

four review p.49
revision activities

four wordlist p.133

units one to eight

in unit five ...
pp.50–57

life with Agrippine
cartoon spelling
natural English *How do you spell ...?*

listening how to ...
use a study centre
vocabulary study centre
listening a teacher explains how to use a study centre
natural English asking for permission
grammar *can / can't; have to / don't have to; had to / didn't have to / did you have to?*

wordbooster
verb + noun collocation
school and university
natural English *what / when you like*

reading taking exams
natural English saying if things are true
reading *How to do well in exams*
natural English giving instructions / advice
writing write a list of instructions

extended speaking
education
collect ideas
listen
discussion on schools
prepare a survey
interview other people

test yourself!
revision and progress check

five review *p.57*
revision activities

five wordlist *p.134*

in unit six ...
pp.58–65

listening how to ...
compare things
vocabulary parts of a country
grammar superlative adjectives
listening people comparing different parts of their countries
grammar comparative adjectives

wordbooster
weather conditions
climate and temperature
natural English *a bit (of) ...*

reading looking ahead
natural English guessing
reading *The tomorrow people*
natural English *what sort / kind of ...?*
grammar *will, be going to, might* for prediction

extended speaking
a weather forecast
collect ideas
plan a weather forecast
write the forecast
natural English vague language: *around, about* or *so*
present your weather forecast

test yourself!
revision and progress check

six review *p.65*
revision activities

six wordlist *p.135*

in unit seven ...
pp.66–73

listening how to ...
tell a story
listening a romantic story
natural English *anyway, so anyway*
vocabulary phrases with *go*
writing write about a great day out
natural English link words and phrases

wordbooster
irregular verbs
phrasal verbs (2)

reading we had a terrible time
natural English *have a good / bad time*
reading *A honeymoon to forget*
natural English uses of *get*
grammar past simple and past continuous

extended speaking
stop thief!
collect ideas
natural English asking how to say things
invent the story
tell the story
listen
write the story

test yourself!
revision and progress check

seven review *p.73*
revision activities

seven wordlist *p.136*

in unit eight ...
pp.74–81

life with Agrippine
cartoon holidays
natural English suggestions

reading free time
natural English *it's popular / common*
reading *Free time in Ecuador and Hong Kong*
grammar *be going to, might, would like to*
natural English *be going to* + verb

wordbooster
time phrases
natural English *all day / night / week / the time*

listening how to ...
make arrangements
vocabulary verb + noun collocation
natural English invitations
listening people making an arrangement by phone
natural English making arrangements
grammar present continuous for future
writing write an e-mail invitation

extended speaking
plan a night out
collect ideas
plan a night out
talk about your plans

test yourself!
revision and progress check

eight review *p.81*
revision activities

eight wordlist *p.137*

contents

in **unit nine** ...
pp.82–89

listening life changes
natural English *still*
grammar present perfect with *for* and *since*
listening people talking about changes
natural English use of *long*

wordbooster
homes
natural English *there's .../there are .../it's got ...*
adjectives describing homes

reading how to ...
give opinions
grammar *should / shouldn't*
reading *Meanwhile back in the fifties*
natural English vague language *thing(s)*
writing write a list of rules for husbands

extended speaking
from home to home
collect ideas
prepare an interview
do the interview
discussion on homes
write about your home

test yourself!
revision and progress check

nine review *p.89*
revision activities

nine wordlist *p.138*

in **unit ten** ...
pp.90–97

reading sleepwalking
vocabulary sleep
reading *Do you sleepwalk?*
grammar *-ed /-ing* adjectives
natural English *really*
writing write a dream sequence

wordbooster
aches and pains
natural English *What's the matter?*

listening how to ...
make an appointment
grammar verb patterns
listening people making appointments by phone
natural English accepting and refusing suggestions
natural English fillers in conversation

extended speaking
nightmare!
collect ideas
prepare a story
tell the story
listen
write the story

test yourself!
revision and progress check

ten review *p.97*
revision activities

ten wordlist *p.139*

in **unit eleven** ...
pp.98–105

life with **Agrippine**
cartoon concert
natural English leaving out words

reading how to ...
describe office life
reading *What can you do in your office?*
natural English *I (don't) agree / it depends*
vocabulary work and working conditions
natural English uses of *work* (n)

wordbooster
office jobs
relationships

listening can my girlfriend come too?
listening people discussing a problem
grammar conditional sentences with *will / might*
natural English *What if ...?*
writing write a postcard

extended speaking
24.com
collect ideas
discuss problems between workers in a company

test yourself!
revision and progress check

eleven review *p.105*
revision activities

eleven wordlist *p.140*

in **unit twelve** ...
pp.106–113

listening how to ...
describe the past
vocabulary activities
natural English *me too / me neither*
listening people talking about how they made friends abroad
grammar *used to* + verb

wordbooster
life events
professions

reading friends reunited
natural English showing surprise
reading *Friends reunited*
grammar present perfect and past simple revision
natural English greeting old friends

extended speaking
school reunion
collect ideas
invent a character
natural English asking about the past and present
role play
write a profile for a website

test yourself!
revision and progress check

twelve review *p.113*
revision activities

twelve wordlist *p.141*

units nine to fourteen

in unit thirteen ...
pp.114–121

reading speed dating
natural English have (got) sth in common
reading Speed dating
grammar conditional sentences with would

wordbooster
describing character
natural English quite/not very + adjective
likes, dislikes, and interests

listening how to ...
describe people
natural English asking about people
vocabulary describing appearance
natural English describing age
listening people describing somebody at work
grammar defining relative clauses
writing write your own speed dating profile

extended speaking
find your perfect partner
collect ideas
create profiles
find a perfect partner

test yourself!
revision and progress check

thirteen review *p.121*
revision activities

thirteen wordlist *p.142*

in unit fourteen ...
pp.122–129

reading where shall we stay?
natural English when/where was that?
reading Staying in Japan
grammar present and past passives
writing a letter of complaint to a hotel

wordbooster
hotel rooms and bathrooms
natural English another / some more
verbs often confused

listening how to ...
get through an airport
vocabulary airports
natural English requests
listening at an airport check-in desk
natural English taking time to think

extended speaking
hotels
collect ideas
prepare the role play
role play
listen

test yourself!
revision and progress check

fourteen review *p.129*
revision activities

fourteen wordlist *p.143*

teacher development chapters

how to ...
do pair and group work
p.146

how to ...
practise grammar
p.153

how to ...
motivate low level learners to write
p.160

how to ...
use the learners as a resource
p.167

how to ...
help learners understand natural speech
p.174

language reference key
pp.181–183

natural English website
www.oup.com/elt/teacher/naturalenglish
Extra class activities and resources and links to the student's site.

also available

test booklet
Unit-by-unit tests for grammar, vocabulary, and *natural English* plus seven skills tests. Common exam-style questions in 'exam focus' sections throughout.

reading & writing skills resource book
Complements the *natural English* reading and writing syllabuses.
– an extra reading lesson for every unit of the student's book
– material related to the student's book by topic
– develops real life reading and writing skills useful for work or study
– advice on text types and skills

5

introduction

how we wrote this course

Before we established the language syllabus for the **natural English** course, we wanted to be sure that what we set out to teach pre-intermediate learners corresponded to what they actually needed to learn at that stage in their language development. So, instead of starting with a prescribed syllabus, we began by planning a series of communicative activities with certain criteria:

- they should be achievable, engaging, and purposeful
- they should be language rich in that they would push learners into extensive and varied language use, and could not be accomplished with a very limited range of expression
- they should range across different time frames (past, present, and future)
- they should have different topics and themes
- they should include different activity types, e.g. role play; discussion; giving, justifying, and reacting to opinions; planning and negotiating; exchanging information; presenting ideas; sharing experiences; telling stories, etc.

We then wrote the activities. Initially, we produced more than we needed, and after trialling, we eliminated those which did not work as well as we had hoped, or that overlapped with others which were richer in language or more successful. Those that remained became the **extended speaking** activities and role plays which you will find in the **student's book** in a much refined and reworked form, thanks to the learner data and feedback received from teachers during piloting of the material. Here are two examples from the pre-intermediate level:

you're going to:	you're going to:
collect ideas talk about picnics; tell the beginning of the story and check vocabulary	**collect ideas** listen to someone talking about the homes they've lived in
invent the story prepare the story and decide on the ending	**prepare an interview** plan questions and think about your answers
tell the story tell the story to a new partner	**do the interview** talk about your home history and your present home
listen listen to someone telling the same story	**discussion** talk about your family with a partner
writing write your story	**writing** write about your homes
but first ... Look back at the **don't forget** boxes in this unit. You can use this language in the activity.	**but first ...** Look back at the **don't forget** boxes in this unit. You can use this language in the activity.

from pre-intermediate **student's book, unit seven** p.70 and **unit nine** p.90

trialling and recording the activities

We asked teachers to use the activities with their pre-intermediate and selected elementary classes and record small groups doing the activities. We also piloted them ourselves with small groups. In all, we recorded almost two hundred learners from over a dozen different countries. In our earlier research (at intermediate and upper intermediate levels) we had done a limited amount of piloting of native speakers doing the relevant activities, but at this level we didn't think it would be of great benefit. However, following on from our experience at the higher levels, we did pilot the activities with learners above the target level, so we recorded intermediate level students as well.

analysing the learner data

After transcribing the recordings, we had a considerable amount of data at pre-intermediate level, but also data at the levels just above and below pre-intermediate. As with the previous levels, the comparisons were fascinating, and knowing what could be achieved just above and below the target level was very informative in helping us to identify the most useful, relevant and achievable target language for pre-intermediate learners. At that point we were able to start writing the **student's book**.

To summarize, the development of the course involved the following stages:

1 devise the extended speaking activities / role plays for trialling
2 trial and record elementary, pre-intermediate and intermediate level learners
3 transcribe and analyse the data
4 select appropriate language for the syllabus
5 write the learning materials in each unit leading up to the extended speaking and role plays (and refine them).

what is natural English?

Throughout the course we have tried to identify language relevant to the needs of learners at each respective level. For the most part, that has meant the inclusion of high-frequency language used naturally by native speakers and proficient users of the language: if a word or phrase is used frequently, it is likely to be useful in a range of everyday communication.

However, not all language used naturally by native speakers is necessarily suitable for many foreign learners, and that includes some high-frequency language. Our own classroom experience has taught us that many learners find it difficult to incorporate highly idiomatic language into their own interlanguage, and a word or phrase which sounds very natural when used by a native speaker can have the opposite effect when used by a foreign learner - it sounds very unnatural. We have, therefore, tried to focus on language which is used naturally by native speakers or proficient speakers of the language, but also sounds natural when used by foreign learners. So, at this pre-intermediate level for example, we want learners to use high-frequency and relatively informal ways of thanking people such as *thanks* and *thanks a lot*; but we have not introduced the more colloquial phrases such as *cheers* or *ta*.

the natural English syllabus

How does anyone decide exactly what language will fulfil these criteria? It is, of course, highly subjective. As yet, there isn't a readily available core lexicon of phrases and collocations to teach pre-intermediate learners on the basis of frequency, let alone taking into account the question of which phrases might be most 'suitable' for learners at this level. Our strategy has been to use our own classroom knowledge and experience to interpret our data of pre-intermediate and intermediate level language use, in conjunction with information from the *Longman Grammar of Spoken and Written English*, a range of ELT dictionaries and data from the British National Corpus and the Oxford Corpus Collection. In this way, we arrived at an appropriate language syllabus for pre-intermediate learners.

what else did we learn from the data?

These are some of the general findings to emerge from our data, which influenced the way we then produced the material.

level of confidence

Many learners at this level (but by no means all) lack the confidence to experiment with language. This showed up in the trialling with some learners treating communication activities as language drills. Of course, learners need controlled practice to help them to produce language accurately and more automatically, but they also need opportunities to use language freely – to develop fluency by thinking more about what they are saying than how they are saying it. For this reason, we felt that the **extended speaking** activities were just as relevant to this level as they had been to higher levels.

When learners engage in genuine communication they will inevitably make mistakes. Throughout the notes in the **teacher's book**, we have tried to anticipate errors and minimize these; but at the same time we believe that mistakes are part of the learning process and should be viewed constructively in the classroom, i.e. what can we learn from them for future productive use?

reacting emotionally

Not surprisingly perhaps at this level, learners were so involved in finding the right words to express an idea that they were sometimes completely disengaged from the emotional content of what they were saying, e.g. responding in totally matter-of-fact ways to content that warranted enthusiasm or sympathy. We have included simple but appropriate ways of making relevant emotional responses (e.g. showing interest, enthusiasm, sadness, sympathy, etc) but also highlighted the need throughout the material for learners to consider how they respond and react to incoming information.

length of turns

Throughout the data we saw evidence of very short turns (again shorter than at the intermediate level). This is to be expected, but we have tried to extend utterances by building into activities a lot of planning and rehearsal time. In addition,

we feel that structuring speaking activities is essential to ensure that learners have plenty to talk about. Listening models or teacher models which show students how they can develop topics are also instrumental in encouraging more output and longer turns and so we have included these where appropriate.

grammar

Many pre-intermediate learners have 'studied' grammar such as the past simple and present perfect, but it was clear that productive use is still exceedingly difficult. There was a lot of simplification throughout the data, and many learners at this level are only truly comfortable when operating in the present simple.

We also found that learners were uniformly poor at asking questions, and their use of modal verbs was extremely limited; *can* being the only notable exception.

In response you will find considerable attention is paid to all of these areas.

vocabulary

The most obvious shortcoming was the lack of familiarity with high-frequency phrases in a number of everyday situations. For example, we didn't find many learners who were familiar with questions commonly used in restaurants such as: *Are you ready to order?* And we heard many inaccurate apologies (*I'm sorry for the late* / *I'm sorry if I'm arrive late* / *I'm sorry I'm too late* / *I'm sorry for be late*), but very few students who were able to produce *I'm sorry I'm late.* at the appropriate time. The language in the **natural English** boxes is the most obvious way we have tackled this shortcoming, but you will find a number of common lexical chunks throughout the **wordboosters** and other vocabulary development exercises.

how to use the key features of natural English

- life with Agrippine
- **natural English** boxes
- wordbooster
- test yourself!
- listening booklet
- language reference and practice exercises
- reviews
- workbook
- teacher's book
- skills resource book
- test booklet

life with Agrippine

Selected units in the course (1, 5, 8, and 11) begin with a section including a Bretécher cartoon called **life with Agrippine**. Each cartoon begins with personalized speaking practice, followed by the cartoon with **natural English** features derived from the reading or listening input.

why cartoons?

They provide a light-hearted and engaging lead-in to the theme of the unit through reading for fun. The Bretécher cartoons raise recognizable and universal issues to do with contemporary life, and although aimed at adults, they are also appealing to younger adults.

how to ... use the cartoons

With the **Bretécher cartoons**, there will be a temptation for learners to read ahead to the next cartoon strip if they like them. If they do so, at least it will mean that learners are very motivated.

- You could do the first speaking activity in the cartoon section with books closed, either by telling learners orally what to do or by writing the questions / prompts on the board. This will prevent learners from reading the cartoon before you want them to. The speaking activity can be done in pairs, groups, or as a whole class.
- You can then tell learners to look at the pre-set questions and read the cartoon. In the first one, point out the glossary so that learners can read quickly and understand the humour. Avoid getting involved in a detailed study or word-for-word translation at this stage: as a text, it has been written to be read for pleasure.
- Decide whether you want to use the recording. It will help your learners get a feel for natural sounding English, although some teachers may prefer not to use it, as the cartoon was originally written as a text to be read, not listened to.

Once you have dealt with the **natural English** focus, you could consider other activities:

- The cartoons lend themselves well to reading aloud or acting out in pairs or small groups. This could either be done in a very controlled way, or learners could read the conversations a couple of times, then shut their books and improvise them.
- We think all four cartoons are based around aspects of everyday life that might stimulate discussion.
- You may find other well-known cartoon strips in the local culture which you could take into class and learners could translate, or you could blank out the mother tongue dialogue and write an English version yourself, or ask your learners to write the dialogue.

natural English boxes

Most of the **natural English** boxes consist of natural English phrases. They normally occur four or five times in each unit, with one or two boxes in each main section and often one in the **wordbooster**.

what do the natural English boxes contain?

These boxes focus on important aspects of everyday language, some of which fall outside the traditional grammatical / lexical syllabus. They include:

- familiar functional exponents: e.g. saying sorry (*I'm sorry I'm late*) and asking for permission (*Is it OK if I ... ?*)
- communication strategies: e.g. inviting people to speak (*How about you?*) and showing a lot of interest (*Really? How interesting.*)
- high-frequency words in spoken English, e.g. *get, still, quite*
- common features of spoken English: e.g. vague language (*thing*), qualifying (*a bit*), leaving out words (*don't know; see you later*)
- lexical chunks: e.g. *it's a great place, I can't afford it, What's the matter?*

The language here is presented in chunks, with each box containing a limited number of phrases to avoid memory overload. The phrases are practised on the spot, and then learners have the opportunity to use them later in freer activities, (e.g. in **it's your turn!**) and the **extended speaking** activity at the end of each unit.

how to ... use the natural English boxes

These boxes have been positioned at a point within each cycle where they are going to be of immediate value, and many of the phrases are recorded to provide a pronunciation model. There is an instruction before each **natural English** box providing learners with a task to highlight the forms and / or focus on meaning, e.g. *listen and complete the gaps in the phrases*; or *match the questions and answers (in the box)*. Beneath each box there is a controlled practice exercise to focus on pronunciation and consolidate meaning, and in many cases this is followed by a personalized practice activity. In the classroom, you could vary the presentation of the language in the following ways:

- If the target phrases have been recorded, you could ask learners to listen to them first. They could do this with books shut and treat it as a dictation, then compare their answers with the **student's book**; or they could listen and follow in the **student's book** at the same time, and then repeat from the recording or the model that you give them yourself.
- You can read the phrases aloud for learners to repeat; alternatively, you can ask individual learners to read them out as a way of presenting them.
- You can ask learners to read the box silently, then answer any queries they have, before you get them to say the phrases.
- You could write the phrases on the board or OHP for everyone to focus on. Then ask learners about any problems they have with meaning and form of the examples before practice.
- You could sometimes elicit the phrases before learners read them. For instance, ask them how they could ask for permission, or what they would say when offering food and drink. Write their suggestions on the board, and then let learners compare with the **natural English** box. In some cases learners will know some important phrases, but they may not be very accurate or know the most natural way to express these concepts.
- Once learners have practised the phrases, you could ask them to shut their **student's book** and write down the phrases they remember.
- If you have a weaker class, you might decide to focus on only one or two of the phrases for productive practice; for a stronger group, you may want to add one or two phrases of your own.
- For revision, you could tell learners they are going to be tested on the **natural English** boxes of the last two units you have done; they should revise them for homework. The next day, you can test them in a number of ways:
  - give them an error-spotting test
  - fill gaps in phrases or give stimuli which learners respond to
  - ask them to write four-line dialogues in pairs.
- The **workbook** provides you with a number of consolidation and further practice exercises of **natural English** (and, of course, other language presented in the **student's book** – see below for more details).
- Because the phrases are clearly very useful, you may want to put some of them on display in your classroom. You could also get learners to start a **natural English** and vocabulary notebook and record the phrases under headings as they learn them. You should decide together whether natural (rather than literal) translations would be a useful option for self-study.

wordbooster

Wordbooster is a section in each unit devoted to vocabulary development. It is almost always divided into two parts, each one focusing on a different lexical area: at least one is topic-based, the other may be based or focus on the grammar of vocabulary, e.g. phrasal verbs.

why wordbooster?

Throughout the other sections in each unit, you will find vocabulary input which is practised within the section, and is often needed for the **extended speaking** activity. The **wordbooster** sections have two main aims:

– they present much of the key vocabulary that learners will need in the **extended speaking** activity at the end of the unit;
– they also cover topic areas and linguistic areas which sometimes go beyond the immediate requirements of the fourteen units and so help to provide a more comprehensive vocabulary syllabus.

The **wordbooster** section is designed to have a different feel from the other more interactive sections in the course, and it provides a change of pace and activity type.

how to ... use wordbooster

Each **wordbooster** will take approximately 30 to 40 minutes to complete, and it can be used flexibly.

– In some units, you can do the **wordbooster** activities earlier or later than they appear in the unit. This will be highlighted in the teacher's notes.
– You don't need to do the whole **wordbooster** in one session. As it is divided into two sections, you can do one part in one lesson, and the other part in a later lesson. In other words, you can use this section to fit in with your own teaching timetable. For instance, if you have 15 minutes at the end of a lesson, you can do one of these sections.
– You can do some of it in class, and some of it can be done for homework.
– Encourage learners to record the language learnt in these sections in their **natural English** and vocabulary notebooks.

test yourself!

Test yourself! is an end-of-unit test or revision activity enabling learners to assess their progress, and consider how they performed in the **extended speaking** activity. It is a short, easily administered test covering lexis, **natural English** phrases, and grammar from the unit in a standardized format:

– producing items within categories
– transforming sentences
– correcting errors.

how to ... use test yourself!

You can use it either before the **extended speaking** activity, for revision purposes, or afterwards, as an end-of-unit test. You may want to give learners time to prepare for it, e.g. read through the unit for homework, or make it a more casual and informal revision activity. Make it clear to learners that their answers in the test should only include new language from the unit.

The test can be used in different ways:

– A formal test. Ask learners to complete it individually, and then collect in their answers to mark.
– An informal test. Ask learners to complete it individually, then go through the answers with the whole class.
– A more interactive test. Ask learners to complete it in pairs. Go through the answers with the class, or ask a pair to mark the answers of another pair.
– You could get learners to complete the test individually or in pairs, then they can check their answers by looking back through the unit. Asking learners to search for answers in this way may not give you as much feedback on their progress, but it may be more memorable for them as learners.
– You could give the test for homework. Learners can then use the unit material as they wish.

Refer learners back to the checklist of the language input at the beginning of the unit. They can then tick which areas they feel more confident in. This is an important way for you to discover which areas they feel they need to revise. You may still have **workbook** exercises, **language reference** and **practice** exercises and **review** units which you can use for this revision.

why ask learners to mark their performance?

Asking learners to give themselves a mark for their performance in the **extended speaking** activity may seem an unusual thing to do. Clearly the precise mark is irrelevant, but we have found it a useful way to encourage learners to reflect more generally on their ability to communicate, and their contribution to the activity, without getting too involved in minor errors, grammar mistakes, etc. It also gives you a chance to have a one-to-one chat with learners, and provide them with some positive feedback and encouragement. It may take several units before learners are able to do this effectively, so your support will be essential in the early stages.

listening booklet

The **listening booklet** is a separate booklet in the back cover pocket of the **student's book**. It provides:

– complete tapescripts for all of the **student's book** listening material
– tapescript-based exercises
– optional listening and pronunciation activities
– the phonemic chart on the back cover, with example words for each sound.

The activities and exercises focus on:

– features of natural English
– pronunciation in context, including focuses on individual sounds, word stress, sentence stress, and intonation
– development of listening sub-skills.

why a separate booklet?

Until recently, tapescripts have often been buried in the back of coursebooks and largely under-exploited. In **natural English**, listening is a very important part of the syllabus, with the majority of recorded material being improvised, unscripted, and delivered at natural speed. It is, therefore, an invaluable source of natural spoken English, so we have set out to exploit the material as much as possible, both for acquiring new language and developing listening sub-skills. Following the tapescript after one or two attempts at listening is a valuable way for learners to decode the parts they haven't understood; it is not only useful, but also a popular activity.

Learners should find the separate booklet very convenient, and it also allows them to make greater use of the listening material.

how to ... use the listening booklet

Within the main listening cycle in each unit, the **student's book** indicates the best point at which to go the **listening booklet** and make use of the tapescript and further exercises. For each unit there are two exercises in the listening booklet based on the main listening, but we generally think it is better to do just one in class (more might affect the pace of the lesson) and one for homework, so that each learner has the opportunity to learn from the tapescript in their own way.

Further exercises are included for many of the other recordings. These are not specifically signposted in the **student's book** as we feel you should make use of them at your discretion, and when it is most convenient in your teaching programme.

You will find at least one exercise on individual sounds in each unit, so by the end of the **student's book**, your learners should be very familiar with phonemic script. If you would like to know more about teaching the phonemic script yourself, follow up the reference below:

> Want to know more? Go to ... how to teach phonemic script in **natural English** intermediate **teacher's book**, *pp. 168-171*.

You might also wish to devise your own activities around the listening material, along similar lines to those already provided in the **listening booklet**.

language reference and practice exercises

The **language reference** section contains more detailed explanations of the key grammar and lexical grammar in the units, plus a large bank of **practice exercises** which have been included for two main reasons:

- they make the language reference much more engaging and interactive
- they provide practice and consolidation which teachers and learners can use flexibly: within the lesson when the grammar is being taught, in a later lesson for revision purposes, or for self-study.

Most of the exercises are objective with a right-or-wrong answer which makes them easy for you to administer.

how to ... use language reference and practice exercises

- Use them when the need arises. If you always tell learners to read the **language reference** and do all the **practice exercises** exercises within the lesson, you may have problems with pace and variety. Rather, use them at your discretion. If, for instance, you find that the learners need a little more practice than is provided in a grammar section, select the appropriate exercise (e.g. unit one: questions end with prepositions: do exercise 1.4 in **practice**). Areas of grammar are not equally easy or difficult for all nationalities. The **practice exercises** provide additional practice on all areas; you can select the ones which are most relevant to your learners.
- The **practice exercises** are ideal for self-study. Learners can read the explanations on the left, then cover them while they do the exercises on the right. Finally, they can look again at the explanations if necessary. You can give them the answers to the **practice exercises**, which are at the back of this teacher's book, *p.181* to *p.183*.
- If learners write the answers in pencil or in a notebook, they will be able to re-use the exercises for revision. Some learners also benefit from writing their own language examples under the ones given in the **language reference**. They can also annotate, translate, etc.

reviews

Review sections occur after every two units in the **student's book**. Each section is two pages, so there is a page of three or four activities for each unit. These activities revise the main grammar, vocabulary and **natural English**. Some of them can be done individually, but there is an interactive element in most, which is designed to help learners to consolidate their understanding and ability to use the language productively. They have not been constructed as objective tests.

how to ... use the review

You have several options:

- you could use the **review** sections as they occur, i.e. review two units at a time when you have completed them
- you could use the **review** section for a unit immediately after you have finished it
- you could use individual activities within a **review** section at different times, e.g. use a review grammar activity after you have completed the grammar section in the unit, but possibly save the **natural English** review activity for a later lesson
- you could do some activities in class and set others for homework

In other words, the **review** sections have been designed so that you can use them flexibly to fit in with your teaching programme.

workbook

The **workbook** recycles and consolidates vocabulary, grammar, and **natural English** from the **student's book**. It also provides language extension sections called **expand your grammar** and **expand your vocabulary** for stronger or more confident learners. These present and practise new material that learners have not met in the **student's book**. Another important feature of the **workbook** is the **say it!** sections, which encourage learners to rehearse language through prompted oral responses. There are two other regular features: **think back!** (revision prompts) and **write it!** (prompts for writing tasks). You can use the **workbook** for extra practice in class or set exercises for learners to do out of class time. The **with key** version allows learners to use the **workbook** autonomously.

teacher's book

This **teacher's book** is the product of our own teaching and teacher training experience combined with extensive research carried out by Oxford University Press into how teacher's books are used.

lesson plans

The teaching notes are presented as flexible lesson plans, which are easy to dip into and use at a glance. We talk you through each lesson, offering classroom management tips (**troubleshooting**), anticipating problems (**language point**), giving additional cultural information (**culture note**), and suggesting alternative ways of using the material (**ideas plus**). In addition, each lesson plan provides you with the exercise keys, a summary of the lesson contents, and the estimated length of the lesson.

At the end of each teacher's book, there's a photocopiable wordlist of **natural English** phrases and vocabulary items for each unit of the **student's book**. This is a useful reference for you, and a clear, concise record for the learners, which they can annotate with explanations, translation, pronunciation, etc. and use for their own revision.

teacher development chapters

You'll find the teacher development chapters after the lesson plans, starting on *p.146*. These practical chapters encourage reflection on teaching principles and techniques. At pre-intermediate level the areas covered are:

- how to ... do pair and group work   *p.146*
- how to ... practise grammar   *p.153*
- how to ... motivate low level learners to write *p.160*
- how to ... use the learners as a resource   *p.167*
- how to ... help learners understand natural speech *p.174*

The chapters are regularly cross-referenced from the lesson plans but you can read them at any time and in any order.

Each chapter contains the following features:

- **think!** tasks for the reader with accompanying answer keys (see *p.154*)
- **try it out** boxes offering practical classroom ideas related to the topic of the chapter (see *p.157*)
- **natural English student's book** extracts to illustrate specific points (see *p.162*)
- **follow-up** sections at the end of each chapter providing a short bibliography for further reading on the topic (see *p.166*).

This **teacher's book** also contains a photocopiable key to the **student's book language reference** section (*pp.181–183*).

For reference, a pronunciation chart on *p.14* shows the pronunciation syllabus across the pre-intermediate **student's book** and **listening booklet**. There is also a chart on *p.13* showing the writing skills and tasks that are covered in the pre-intermediate **student's book** and the **reading and writing skills resource book**.

skills resource book

what's in the reading and writing skills resource book?

The 64-page photocopiable resource book contains 14 reading lessons and 14 writing lessons, i.e. one reading lesson and one writing lesson for each unit of the pre-intermediate **student's book**, on a similar theme. Each lesson lasts between 30 and 60 minutes and is accompanied by easy-to-use teacher's notes.

The reading lessons are based around a range of authentic texts from website and newspaper articles to fables, recipes, menus, and quizzes. The aim is to expose students to a number of different and accessible text types whilst giving them practice in 'real world' reading skills. It includes the basic reading skills on a regular basis but slightly more challenging ones are also introduced. Here are some of the skills you will find:

- predicting
- activating background knowledge
- reading for gist
- understanding the main points
- reading for specific information
- reading for details
- inferring
- assessing the writer's purpose
- responding to the text

The writing lessons are based around model texts which students then analyse for relevant features of language and style. Students are helped with ideas and planning, and each lesson culminates in a **writing task** that can be done in class time or set for homework. Regular **tip** boxes give advice to students on how to approach the various skills and tasks.

The writing lessons are divided into two sections:

Units one – seven train students in the skills of writing. Each unit focuses on one skill starting with broader skills and moving towards more detailed skills. Isolating the individual skills in this way should give students confidence in using them in the second half of the book. The skills that are covered are:

- how to ... write in an appropriate style
- how to ... organize ideas
- how to ... develop ideas
- how to ... link ideas
- how to ... make a text more interesting
- how to ... improve punctuation
- how to ... correct and edit your work

Units eight – fourteen give students practice in writing short exam- and work-related texts. The focus here is on relevant functional language whilst also giving students practice in using the writing skills learnt in the first seven units. The lessons focus on the following:

- how to ... write a letter of enquiry
- how to ... write a detailed note
- how to ... make and break arrangements
- how to ... describe yourself in a letter of application
- how to ... write a film review
- how to ... compare and contrast two places
- how to ... write a story

In addition, students are encouraged to assess their own progress in reading and writing by using the **self-assessment** chart at the back of the book. There are also **vocabulary diaries** for students to keep a record of new words they have encountered in the reading and writing lessons.

The interleaved **teacher's notes** are set out in a simple grid with **answer keys** and **guidance notes** clearly visible at a glance. There is advice on particular text types and how to help students develop their reading and writing skills. The **ideas plus** boxes give suggestions on how to exploit the material further.

how to ... use the skills resource book

The **reading and writing skills resource book** is designed to be used in class to supplement the **natural English** pre-intermediate **student's book**. It can be used to build on and extend the reading and writing skills already covered in the **student's book**, or as a stand-alone reading and writing course. It is also intended that the pre-intermediate level will prepare students for the kinds of reading and writing skills that they may meet in the intermediate and upper-intermediate **skills resource books**.

test booklet

The pre-intermediate **test booklet** provides photocopiable unit-by-unit tests for the grammar, vocabulary, and **natural English** syllabus, and skills tests every two units. The skills tests cover reading, writing, speaking and listening. The listening tests reuse the **student's book** material but exploit it using different tasks. 'Live' dictation tests are also provided if you wish to use listening material which will be entirely new to the students.

The **test booklet** also contains exam-style question types in regular **exam focus** sections. These appear at the end of each unit test and throughout the skills tests. The aim is to give students practice and confidence in tackling common exam-style questions. An answer key is provided at the back.

writing in natural English — pre-intermediate

	student's book	skills resource book how to ...	skills / tasks
unit one	write a paragraph comparing families p.15	write in an appropriate style p.6	identifying text type and purpose, using prepositions of time and place, noticing style, using appropriate language, generating ideas **writing task:** an invitation to a celebration
unit two	write a restaurant dialogue p.23	organise ideas p.10	understanding writer's purpose, organizing ideas, planning your writing, generating ideas **writing task:** an information leaflet on food
unit three	write a paragraph about where you live p.33	develop ideas p.14	generating ideas, developing a text, developing your ideas, organizing ideas **writing task:** a description of a favourite place
unit four	re-write a story using link words p.39 write a shop dialogue p.41	link ideas p.18	generating ideas, understanding linking words, using linking words, planning your writing **writing task:** a report on a shopping centre
unit five	write a list of instructions p.51 write a True / False survey p.53	make a text more interesting p.22	generating ideas, increasing range, improving a text, giving details and examples **writing task:** a description of a favourite teacher
unit six	write a weather forecast p.61	improve punctuation p.26	generating ideas, identifying punctuation, using punctuation, checking punctuation **writing task:** a letter to a friend coming to visit
unit seven	write about a great day out p.66 write about a picture story p.71	correct and edit your work p.30	generating ideas, checking for mistakes, correcting frequent mistakes **writing task:** a description of an important day
unit eight	write an e-mail invitation p.79	write a letter of enquiry p.34	generating ideas, organizing ideas, asking for information politely **writing task:** a letter of enquiry for a holiday course
unit nine	write a list of rules for husbands p.89 punctuate a paragraph and write about your home history p.91	write a detailed note p.38	generating ideas, recognizing structures and functions, understanding language in context, using functional language **writing task:** a note giving instructions to someone staying in your home
unit ten	write a dream sequence p.94 write a picture story using link words / phrases p.99	make and break arrangements p.42	generating ideas, understanding language in use, making and breaking informal arrangements, breaking formal arrangements **writing task:** an e-mail to cancel an arrangement
unit eleven	write a postcard p.109	describe yourself in a letter of application p.46	generating ideas, giving information about yourself, focusing on plans for the future, writing about plans for the future **writing task:** a letter applying for a job in a summer camp
unit twelve	write a character profile p.119	write a film review p.50	generating ideas, expressing opinions, describing a film, connecting ideas in longer sentences **writing task:** a film review
unit thirteen	write your own speed dating profile p.127	compare and contrast two places p.54	generating ideas, focusing on pros and cons, understanding language in use, comparing and contrasting, organizing ideas **writing task:** an e-mail comparing two flats to rent
unit fourteen	write a letter of complaint to a hotel p.132	write a story p.58	generating ideas, focusing on the sequence of events, using narrative tenses, organizing ideas **writing task:** a description of an amazing journey

pronunciation in natural English — pre-intermediate

	student's book	listening booklet
unit one	possessive 's p.11	sentence stress p.5 sounds: /θ/ and /ð/ p.6
unit two	intonation in questions p.16 word stress p.17 sentence stress p.20 sentence stress p.21	sounds: same or different p.7 schwa /ə/ p.9
unit three	sentence stress p.26 sentence stress p.29	weak forms p.11 sounds: the letter *i* p.11 syllables p.13
unit four	*this* /ðɪs/ and *these* /ðiːz/ p.34 *I'll* /aɪl/ p.36 linking p.37 sentence stress p.38	sounds: /ɪ/ and /iː/ p.15 sounds: the letter *r* p.15 sounds: /eə/ and /ɪə/ p.15
unit five	word stress p.46 intonation p.47 word stress p.49 sentence stress p.49 contractions p.50	sounds: the alphabet p.17 *want to* /ˈwɒnə/ and *going to* /ˈgʌnə/ p.17 intonation p.19
unit six	*there'll* /ˈðeərəl/ and *it'll* /ɪtl/ p.57 sentence stress p.58	missing syllables p.21 weak forms p.21 sounds: the letter *w* p.22
unit seven	irregular verbs p.67 sentence stress p.68 weak forms p.69	linking p.23 sounds: the letter *o* p.24
unit eight	intonation in suggestions p.72 word stress p.77 sentence stress p.77 sentence stress p.78 intonation p.78	sounds: /ʊ/ and /uː/ p.25 word stress p.27 sounds: /ɔː/ and /əʊ/ p.27 intonation p.27
unit nine	*for* /fə/ and *since* /sɪns/ p.85 word stress p.87 *there's* /ðeəz/ and *there are* /ˈðeərə/ p.87 *should* /ʃʊd/ and *shouldn't* /ʃʊdnt/ p.88	consonant groups p.29 sounds: /g/, /dʒ/, and /tʃ/ p.29
unit ten	sentence stress p.94	sounds: /ɜː/ and /e/ p.31
unit eleven	sentence stress p.105 word stress p.106 *it'll* /ɪtl/, *won't* /wəʊnt/, and *might* /maɪt/ p.108	sounds: /s/, /z/, and /ʃ/ p.35 sounds: /ʌ/ p.37
unit twelve	intonation p.112 *used to* /ˈjuːstə/ p.113 word stress p.115 intonation p.115 sentence stress p.117	sounds: /ɒ/ and /əʊ/ p.39
unit thirteen	*I'd* /aɪd/ and *wouldn't* /wʊdnt/ p.124 sentence stress p.126	linking p.41 schwa /ə/ p.41 silent *t* p.41 sentence stress p.41
unit fourteen	sentence stress p.130 phonemic spelling p.133 intonation p.134	sounds: /æ/ and /ʌ/ p.43 sentence stress p.43

extended speaking — feedback checklist

During the **extended speaking** activity at the end of each unit, note down examples of …

- **good language use**

- **effective communication strategies**
  (turn-taking, interrupting, inviting others to speak, etc.)

- **learner errors**
  (vocabulary, grammar, pronunciation, etc.)

- **particular communication problems**

Make sure you allow time for feedback at the end of the lesson. You can use the notes you make above to praise effective language use and communication or, if necessary, to do some remedial work.

Photocopiable © Oxford University Press 2005

one

in unit one ...

life with **Agrippine**
p.16

listening
how to ... ask questions
p.16

wordbooster
p.20

reading
relationships
p.22

extended speaking
is your family like mine?
p.24

test yourself!
p.25

review
p.25

wordlist
p.130

life with Agrippine   30 mins

reading for fun
natural English asking people to be quiet

happy families

Want to know more about using **life with Agrippine?** Go to the **introduction:** *p.7.*

- You could do **exercise 1** in small groups or as an open class. Alternatively, see **ideas plus** on the right. With learners from the same country, they can just give the names of the programmes in their first language. However, you may want to take this opportunity to feed in the names of certain popular types of programme, e.g. *soap opera, drama series, quiz, chat show,* or *documentary.*

- Before doing **exercise 2**, show them the **glossary**. These are provided to make it easier for learners to read quickly and therefore enjoy the humour of the cartoon. You'll see phonemic script here (and throughout the book) for words which students often find difficult to pronounce. You could check students' pronunciation after the accompanying listening activity. The part of speech (**n** for *noun*, **v** for *verb*, etc.) is also provided for many of the words so that students can include this type of information in their own vocabulary record-keeping. Finally, you will see the ☺ symbol for informal language next to some words and phrases. See **language point** on the right.

- After you have explained the **glossary**, students can read the cartoon and talk briefly about it in small groups or as an open class in **exercise 2**. Play the recording of the cartoon in **exercise 3**. This is largely for pleasure, but also to provide a model for when they act out the cartoon themselves.

- In **exercise 4**, go through the **natural English** phrases from the less polite to the more polite. With a monolingual group, it might be a useful concept check to ask them for equivalents in their language before practising the pronunciation with the class.

- **Exercise 5** is an opportunity for learners to work on the rhythm and intonation of whole sentences, from the animated sentences at the beginning and middle, to the low-key sentences at the end.

listening how to ... ask questions   90 mins +

discuss typical questions we ask about other people

talk about people and places using **natural English** phrases

focus on the grammar of question forms

listen to people describing famous people they've met

practise showing interest using **natural English** phrases

interview others about their best friend

lead-in

- You could introduce **exercise 1** yourself on the board so that students don't have their heads buried in their books before they compare in **exercise 2**. For **exercise 3**, direct students to the **natural English** box and play the recording. Play it again if necessary. Check the answers before they go on to **exercise 4**.

- **Exercise 5** checks meaning <u>and</u> form. This is necessary because *like* has different meanings and can operate in different parts of speech. See **language point** on the right. **Exercise 6** provides controlled practice and an opportunity to focus on the contractions and intonation in the questions, which you can monitor.

- Before students begin **exercise 7**, you could take this opportunity to explain the use of *their* in the rubric. We often use this form to refer to someone whose sex is not mentioned or not known – it is shorter and easier than repeating *his* or *her* all the time. **Exercise 7** is designed for practice of the target language, but it can be exploited further. Demonstrate the communicative potential of this activity by asking a confident student the first question, then <u>follow up their answer with further relevant questions</u>, e.g. *Which floor is it on? What's the building like? Does it have a garden? What's it like? Do you have a garage or parking space?* etc. They shouldn't feel compelled to follow up every topic, but they should have the freedom to follow up topics of genuine interest. As a follow-up, see **workbook, expand your vocabulary,** describing things, *p.5.*

16

friends and family

exercise 4
Shh!
Quiet!
Be quiet!

ideas plus speaking

This cycle starts with personalization to motivate and relax the learners. Alternatively, you could use these questions below in a mingling activity:

What do you do when you're watching TV? (Have dinner? Talk to the family? Study? Read? Eat chocolate? Watch in silence? etc.) Find what people in your class do most when watching TV.

In your country, do you have pop music TV programmes? If so, do you watch them? What are they like? / What do you think of them?

language point informal language

Here and throughout the course, you will find informal language highlighted with a ☺ symbol, which you will need to point out to your learners. Note that informal language and slang are not the same thing. Informal language is used in normal conversation, but may not be suitable in certain formal contexts. Slang is very informal language, which is often restricted to certain groups of people and may be offensive to some others.

exercise 3
go to **listening booklet** *p.4*
exercise 4
1 d   2 a   3 b   4 c
exercise 5
What's he like? – a   What's she like? – a

language point *like*

Learners at this level probably need to be able to distinguish three different uses of *like*:

1 Used here 'to ask someone's opinion of someone or something',
  e.g. *What's he like? What was the film like?*

2 Used as a preposition with the meaning 'similar to',
  e.g. *She's like her father. This computer is like mine.*

3 Used as a verb with the meaning 'to enjoy an activity' or 'to find a person or thing pleasant / attractive',
  e.g. *I like skiing. They liked Hungary very much. Does he like his new boss?*

17

one

grammar question forms

- Before you start this section, see **culture note** on the right.
- Divide the class into As and Bs to complete the questions. In fact, the questions are the same but with different parts removed, so when students get together in **exercise 2**, they will be able to correct each other as necessary. Move round and monitor the pairs at this stage and help with pronunciation.
- There are no trick questions in **exercise 3**. They are simply designed to check grammar that the learners should already know, but as a pairwork activity it gives them a chance to demonstrate their knowledge which you can monitor. If necessary, you can go to the **language reference** and **practice exercises** *pp.150* and *151* for further controlled practice.
- In **exercise 4**, you could invite specific students to ask you the questions, or just let them shout out questions randomly (make sure one or two students do not dominate). Ask them to listen to and note down all of your answers. At the end, put them back in pairs to test each other on what they have learnt:
  e.g. *When did (name of teacher) first meet (name of best friend)? What's he / she like?*
  As an extra activity, students could use the information as the basis for a guided writing activity, with the questions serving as the framework for the writing.

listen to this

- When you test students on the pictures in **exercise 1**, you could ask them to think of celebrities in their own country they would like to meet.
- The first listening extract in **tune in** is very short. It is designed to give learners a chance to tune into / adapt to the speakers' voices, and be in a position to tackle with confidence the longer extract which follows. Make sure students are comfortable with this first extract. If necessary, play it a few times.

Want to know more? Go to **how to ...** teach listening **intermediate teacher's book**, *p.152*.

- For **exercise 3**, make sure students read and understand the statements before they listen. They could put K for Kylie or J for Jennifer next to each statement as they listen – this reduces the burden of writing and allows you to go round and monitor their answers. If some are wrong, play the recording again. Students can go on to answer the questions in **exercise 4** at this point. After they have listened, put them in pairs to compare answers. The value of this is that their conversations may indicate why someone hasn't understood a particular part of the passage.

Want to know more? Go to **how to ...** help learners understand natural speech (testing vs. teaching) *p.177*

- The **listening challenge** in **exercise 5** provides extra listening practice, after which you could make use of the **listening booklet**. We feel that listening with the tapescript is a very valuable post-listening activity – it can help learners to identify a specific listening problem – and you will also find additional pronunciation and / or vocabulary exercises there based on the listening extracts.
- For **exercise 6**, direct learners to the **natural English** box then play tapescript **1.4** again for students to order the phrases, but more importantly, they get a model of how the phrases need to sound in order to show real interest. Practise the phrases in pairs or with the whole class in **exercise 7**.
- Remind students that they are practising 'showing a lot of interest' in **exercise 8**, so the information they respond to needs to be reasonably interesting. This may not happen unless the activity is prepared carefully. See **troubleshooting**.

speaking it's your turn!

- This final activity gives learners a chance to practise question forms again along with the language from both **natural English** boxes. And as with **exercise 7** in the **lead-in** *p.8*, you should encourage students to see the communicative potential of the activity and move beyond the questions they practised earlier when interviewing their teacher. You could brainstorm a few additional questions with the class or put learners in pairs to think up more questions before they do the activity.
- During the activity, monitor and make notes. Bring the activity to a close with a feedback session on both the content of their conversations (the ideas and ability to keep the conversation going), and the language used (successful examples of language use as well as errors).

Want to know more? Go to **how to ...** monitor and give feedback **intermediate teacher's book**, *p.156*.

friends and family

exercise 1
see **student's book** for answers

exercise 3
1 because it is *you* (second person singular), not *he / she / it*.
2 because it is *he / she / it* (third person singular), not *you*.
3 because it is the past tense and therefore we need *did* not *do*.
4 because it is the verb *be* and we don't use *do / does* with *be*.
5 because it is the verb *have got*, and we don't use *do / does* with *have got*.
6 because it is the full verb *have*, not *have got*. Therefore we use *do / does* not *have / has*

culture note giving personal information

We have included the activity of asking the teacher about their close friend because we feel it is more motivating for the learners than asking about a fictional character; we also think that most native speakers would be quite happy to answer questions as part of a classroom activity. They are free to self-censor, i.e. give as much or as little information as they choose, and they can refuse to answer a question. However, if you are not happy with this type of activity or feel it is inappropriate in the culture where you teach, please omit or adapt it.

Attitudes to personal information may vary from culture to culture. In the UK for example, we feel it would normally be acceptable to ask someone their job, their religion, or whether they are married. It would not be acceptable to ask someone how much they earn, and we wouldn't normally ask someone their age unless we had a legitimate reason for doing so. Is this similar or different in the country you work in?

exercise 1
1 Brad Pitt, Donatella Versace, Jennifer Aniston, Kylie Minogue, Luciano Pavarotti, Ralph Fiennes, Tiger Woods

exercise 2
1 Kylie Minogue   2 Jennifer Aniston

exercise 3
2, 4, 5 Kylie Minogue 1, 3 Jennifer Aniston

exercise 4
The first speaker spent two weeks with Kylie Minogue. The second speaker spent an evening with Jennifer Aniston.
They don't see these people now.

exercise 5
1 Ralph Fiennes   2 when she was 23
3 He's lovely / really nice / normal / ordinary.
4 Ralph Fiennes had a phone call from Steven Spielberg. He wanted Ralph Fiennes to be in his film, 'Schindler's List'.

exercise 6
1 Wow!
2 Fantastic.
3 Ah, interesting.
4 Wow!
5 Really?

troubleshooting generating ideas

On the spur of the moment some learners find it difficult to come up with ideas for this type of activity. Make sure that doesn't happen by setting it up carefully. Here are three things you could do to help:

1 Give some examples yourself to start learners thinking, e.g. *I once found a wallet with €300 in it; I worked in a Safari park in Kenya two years ago; I saved a little girl who fell into a lake; I can stand on one leg with my eyes closed for a minute (it's incredibly difficult to do this); I can count from one to ten in Maori; I can write with both hands;* etc.

2 Give learners time to think and plan what they are going to say.

3 Adapt the activity. For example, tell learners to think of one true idea and two false ones. They tell their partner, who reacts with real interest, and then the partner must say which sentence they think is true and which two are false. This avoids the problem of students thinking up a lot of interesting and true information about themselves.

one

wordbooster

30–45 mins

This **wordbooster** is best used at this point in the unit as the vocabulary is useful for the reading section which follows.

glossary

collocation Two or more words frequently used together, e.g. *a close friend, spend money, terribly sorry*

relatives

- This is an area of vocabulary where it is difficult to predict what learners might know. If you think students will struggle with **exercise 1** as it stands, see **ideas plus**.
- We have included a phonemic transcription for the items as they all have problems of one sort or another, but especially the pronunciation of *-ther* / ðə / in *father* and / ʌ / in *son*. If your students are not familiar with phonemic transcriptions, we would certainly recommend that you introduce important symbols on a gradual basis. After checking the answers, practise the pronunciation with the class.

Want to know more? Go to **how to ...** teach phonemic script **intermediate teacher's book** *pp.168-71*.

- **Exercise 2** tidies up several other items of vocabulary, e.g. *parents* and *relatives*, which are false friends for certain nationalities and therefore potentially problematic. The pronunciation of the diphthong in *parents* /ˈpeərənts/ is also a common problem.
- **Exercise 3** is just a bit of fun to consolidate the vocabulary. If you think your learners won't know the people referred to on the recording, you could omit it or think of examples your students will be familiar with.

talking about you and your family

- Some of the lexical items here will be new, others are items which learners know but commonly get wrong, e.g. *My brother has twelve years old* instead of *My brother is twelve years old*. You could put students in pairs or small groups to pool their knowledge, and let them use bilingual and / or monolingual dictionaries to help them. Check the answers and clarify any problems, e.g. the difference between *argue* and *discuss* (if you *argue*, you *discuss something angrily*). See also **language point**.
- **Test your partner** is an opportunity for students to get intensive controlled practice while you listen. This exercise type is repeated throughout the book, so after several examples, learners should be able to get into pairs, look at the example and get on with it themselves. For this first one though, demonstrate the activity with a confident student , perhaps three examples; and you could also teach the correct phrase for learners to say if someone gets an answer wrong, i.e. *I'm sorry, that isn't right* or *I'm sorry that's wrong*. This type of exercise is much more successful if it keeps up a good pace and momentum, so get students to repeat the exercise and swap until they can do it clearly and fluently. After **test your partner**, keep **exercise 2** quite brief. The reason for this is that the students are going to do a similar activity but on a larger scale during the **extended speaking** activity at the end of the unit.

friends and family

exercise 1
sister, daughter, aunt, grandmother, sister-in-law, daughter-in-law, niece, cousin, stepmother

exercise 2
parents, grandparents, relatives

exercise 3
1 Kylie Minogue
2 Michael Schumacher
3 Enrique Iglesias
4 David Beckham
5 Queen Elizabeth II

ideas plus adapting an activity

Here are two possibilities:
1 Draw a family tree on the board and insert pictures of male relatives. See if you can elicit the correct names for the relatives from the learners; if not, provide them and check pronunciation.
2 Direct students to the exercise in the **student's book** and let them use bilingual dictionaries to find any items they don't know.

exercise 1
2 family
3 own
4 strict
5 a lot
6 with my sister
7 old
8 celebration
9 parent
10 married

language point collocation

You will notice that some of the items in **exercise 1** are in **bold**, e.g. *only* and *close*. We have done this to highlight the fact that the words in the box regularly co-occur with the words in **bold** – that is to say, they are common ***collocations*****, e.g. *an only child, a close family*, etc.

We have included common collocations throughout the vocabulary input in the **student's book** and we believe it is important for learners to notice these collocations, learn them, and write them down as phrases in their notebooks.

one

reading relationships

75–90 mins

talk about how people are related using possessive 's

read and discuss an amusing anecdote

study and practise the past simple

practise the use of *both* with the past simple to find things in common with a partner

lead-in

- The focus of the **lead-in** is the use of the possessive 's, which is a problem for many nationalities. You could start, however, by asking the class to describe Robert in their own words: age, clothes, looks, etc. When the pairs discuss Mary's possible relationship to Robert in **exercise 1**, move round and listen to their answers; this will give you an indication of their knowledge and grasp of the possessive 's. Listen to the students' suggestions as to who Mary might be, but don't give the answer just yet.
- Direct the group to the **natural English** box and discuss **exercise 2** with the class (see **troubleshooting** on the right). For **exercise 3**, play the recording and ask students to listen carefully to the pronunciation. Practise the phrases with the class.
- When learners discuss the pictures and relationships in **exercise 4** and then **exercise 5**, encourage them to practise using the possessive 's, e.g. *I think this is Robert's sister*, and don't let them get away with just saying, *I think this is the sister*. Monitor the discussion, but don't confirm any of their answers.
- Play the recording in **exercise 6** so they can listen and find out if they were right. For further work on possessive 's, refer students to the **language reference** and **practice exercises** *p.151*.

read on

- **Exercise 1** is a slight shift in topic away from relatives to relationships, and it introduces the theme of the reading text. Do class feedback on the additional reasons learners have come up with.
- The question in **exercise 2** is quite straightforward, but they can't be sure of the correct answer until the last line, so it is a way of propelling them through the text. This is what you want for a first reading of this type of text, so try to discourage learners from turning to their bilingual dictionaries at this stage – you can reassure them there will be an opportunity to use their dictionaries later. In fact, the **glossary** explains most of the new vocabulary here.
- **Exercise 3** demands a more detailed understanding, so give students time to read the text more carefully. After you have checked their answers, it is worth highlighting and, if necessary, clarifying the items in the **glossary** – they are not only very useful high frequency lexical items, but several are recycled in **exercise 5**, so learners will need to understand them. If you want to make use of the text for some pronunciation work, see **ideas plus** on the right.
- **Exercise 4** gives learners the chance to react to the story and discuss their attitude to the two central characters, and it is followed by a further personalized discussion in **exercises 5** and **6** in which students talk about their own punctuality and reliability. In fact, *punctual* is an item learners may want for these exercises, so you could pre-teach it.

grammar past simple

- **Exercise 1** makes the link between the story of Robert and Harriet and the grammar in this section. The True / False statements are quite tricky and most of the students will probably have to return to the text to get them all correct.
- We are assuming that learners will be familiar with the form and meaning of the past simple, so **exercise 2** is really for you to check that understanding and possibly fill in one or two gaps in their knowledge, e.g. with irregular verb forms. **Exercise 3** offers further practice, including a number of other irregular verbs, and you can also go to the **language reference** and **practice exercises** on *p.152* for further consolidation if you wish. Refer students also to the irregular verbs list on *p.174*.
- The students will be returning to practise negative forms and questions in the past simple in **exercise 6**, but first there is a focus on the meaning of *both* and how it is used in different syntactic patterns in **exercise 4**. See **language point** on the right. Recording **1.8** gives learners a chance to hear the pronunciation of *both*: the 'th' sound / θ / is difficult for some nationalities. After **exercise 5**, you could go to the **listening booklet** *p.6*, which has a further exercise contrasting / θ / of unvoiced 'th' and / ð / of voiced 'th'.
- If you feel it is necessary, you could suggest some additional prompts for **exercise 6** to get students started, e.g. *What did you have for breakfast? What time did you have dinner? What time did you go to bed? Did you do any homework?* etc. They may find it hard to remember all six things they both did, so suggest they write them down as they go along. They should write complete sentences, e.g. *We both came to school by bus*, and the winners are the first pair to shout 'finished!' and hold up their paper with six completed sentences. See also **workbook**, **expand your grammar** *neither p.8*.

22

friends and family

exercise 6
1. Mary is Robert's mother.
2. Kathy is Robert's sister.
3. Sally is Robert's new girlfriend.
4. Harriet is Robert's ex-girlfriend.
5. Anna is Robert's boss.

troubleshooting using the mother tongue

Some teachers are reluctant to introduce discussion of translation equivalents between English and the students' own language. Our own feeling is that learners do this automatically most of the time and, provided the teacher is very familiar with the students' mother tongue, such a discussion can be harnessed to their advantage. If you know that there is a clear equivalent, it is often a quick and effective way of checking whether the students have understood something. And if there isn't a clear equivalent for a particular word, phrase or structure, it can be equally valuable to point this out in order to demonstrate the limitations of translation.

With a multilingual group, translation equivalents cannot be used as a check on understanding, but they can often lead to very interesting and genuinely communicative discussions on the differences between languages.

exercise 1 possible answers
One of them falls in love with someone else.
They don't like each others' friends / family.
They have different attitudes / opinions.
They are from different backgrounds.

exercise 2
It's about the end of their relationship.

exercise 3
1. Harriet   3. Robert   5. Harriet   7. Robert
2. Robert   4. Robert   6. Robert   8. Harriet

ideas plus acting out a dialogue

Part of the story recreates the conversation that Robert had with Harriet when she forgot to turn up for his party. You could put learners in pairs to practise the dialogue from 'Where are you?' to 'Oh, you're impossible!'. They will need to add a couple of lines at the beginning to start it off. The student playing 'Robert' should sound extremely angry, but it might add more humour to the conversation if you suggest to the student playing Harriet that she sounds very casual – to the point where she obviously doesn't care about Robert at all. Monitor and perhaps suggest that the best pair acts out their conversation for the rest of the class.

This is probably not the ideal activity if your class is mostly of the same sex!

exercise 1
1. true   2. false   3. true   4. false

exercise 2
1. The past simple is used for things that are finished.
2. yesterday, last week, ten days ago, in 1995
3. regular verbs: worked, started
   regular verbs ending in *e / y*: arrived, received, carried, married
   irregular verbs: found, saw, got, rang, spent, forgot
   negative: didn't see
   question and short answer: Did you see; did, didn't

exercise 3
see the original article in the **student's book** *p.12* for answers

exercise 4
go to **listening booklet** *p.6*

language point *both*

Notice the different patterns and forms here:

auxiliary verb + *both*, e.g. They **are both** Spanish.

both + full verb, e.g. They **both work** in an office.

This second idea can also be expressed using *both of* + object pronoun:

Both of them work. (NOT Both of ~~they~~ work.)

Notice that when *both* is followed by an article or possessive adjective + noun, the preposition is optional:

I like **both (of) the children**; **Both (of) my sisters** *are married*.

23

one

extended speaking is your family like mine?

60–75 mins

listen to people talking about their families

talk about your own family with a partner

write down similarities and differences between your families

- It is important at the beginning of this activity to let learners read the left-hand column, or tell them what they are going to do in the lesson or put it on the board. This will enable them to get the whole picture. You should also give them time to look back at the **don't forget!** boxes which appear at the end of each section in the unit.

collect ideas

- **Exercises 1** and **2** provide listening practice, but they also serve as models for the activity the students will be doing in **exercise 8**.
- For **exercise 3**, explain the key phrases in the **natural English** box and play recording **1.9** again. Make sure the learners know that they have to shout out STOP as soon as they hear the phrases; this makes it more fun. In **exercise 4**, get learners to practise the conversation in the **natural English** box using using both phrases (*How about you? / And you?*).

prepare a questionnaire

- In the trialling we found that, occasionally, conversations in **exercise 8** tailed off quite quickly. This was almost always when learners treated the activity simply as a language exercise and didn't follow up intial questions in the way one would in a real-life situation. It is essential learners are aware that this is intended as a genuine communication activity in which it is their objective to find out as much as possible about their partner's family. For this to happen, and for the activity to retain its momentum, learners need a range of possible follow-up questions so that they can concentrate more on the content of the conversation, and less on having to assemble too many new questions from scratch. Therefore, as preparation for the main activity in **exercise 8**, give students plenty of time to generate some follow-up questions in **exercise 6**.

Want to know more? Go to **how to ...** use the learners as a resource (task performance) *p.170.*

exercise 1
1. David's got a brother and a sister.
2. His sister's a television director; his brother's a medical student.
3. Lynne's got a brother and a sister.
4. Her brother's an engineer, and her sister's a secondary school teacher.

exercise 2
1. Seema's family went to Delhi to see her grandmother.
2. A 40th birthday party for Roger's brother.

have a conversation

- Monitor the conversations in **exercise 8** carefully and make notes for later feedback. If the activity works well, you could repeat it; if not now, then at a later date.
- Finish the conversations with a feedback session with plenty of support and encouragement. Students gain a lot of confidence from knowing they have used language correctly and performed well.

writing

- You could follow the instructions in the student's book for **exercise 9**, or try a different way. Ask each student to write down two similarities and two differences on their own before comparing with a partner.
- When you explain how they can link their ideas in **exercise 10**, the main focus will obviously be on *however*, which is likely to be the one new item here. You can explain that the meaning is really the same as *but*, the difference being that we commonly use it to link one sentence with another, and not to join two clauses within a single sentence (where we use *but*). If you wish, you could also use this opportunity to explain one common form of *ellipsis*: see **language point** on the right. It occurs in the examples (*but I don't; but Dagmar hasn't*).
- If you have time, do the writing activity in class; you can then move round and give individual help where necessary, as some classes appreciate time devoted to writing. If there is no time available, it would be suitable for homework. An alternative homework suggestion is to ask students to write a letter to their teacher about their family with the ideas and language they have used in the lesson.

friends and family

one review student's book p.24   45 mins

Want to know more about how to use the reviews? Go to the introduction p.10.

grammar past simple

- We expect learners to know these verbs, but irregular past tenses are a common source of error. Monitor while they are writing in **exercise 1**.
- Demonstrate what they have to do in **exercise 2** by doing the first example or two with a student in front of the class. After the pair work, you could check the answers quickly with the whole class.
- For the rhymes in **exercise 3**, point out in the example that although they are spelt differently, the words *said* and *red* rhyme. You can use the recordings as a check in **exercise 4** if you wish. You can also highlight the main stresses which fall on the last words of each line.

> **exercise 1**
> brown circle: read /red/, told, broke, spent, sang, made, cost, cut, thought, began
> white circle: bought, ran, paid, went, sold, said, spoke, rang, lost, shut
> **exercise 2**
> read / said; told / sold; broke / spoke; spent / went; sang / rang; made / paid; cost / lost; began / ran; cut / shut; thought / bought
> **exercise 4**
> go to **listening booklet** p.10

vocabulary family and relationships

- This activity could be done for homework if you prefer. If you use it in class, students could do it in pairs as a race. You can also adapt this activity and produce your own word square to test other topics of vocabulary, or students can even produce their own word squares on different topics, and then they give them to each other to solve.

> **Down:** stepmother, niece, son(-in-law), relatives
> **Across:** nephew, married, only child, cousin, granny, parents

grammar question practice

- Encourage learners to produce a range of questions, i.e. using different question words and tenses. Monitor carefully and correct errors.

natural English

- All the **natural English** exercises in the **review** sections are designed so that learners can check their answers by looking back at the **natural English** boxes in the appropriate unit. This encourages learners to use the course book as a revision tool and resource, and to discourage the idea that newly learnt language doesn't need to be revisited.
- When students have checked their answers, you can extend the activity by asking them in pairs to incorporate each sentence into a natural dialogue. For example:
  1 A What's he like?   B He's very nice.
  2 A Do you know Mary?   B Yes, we both go to the same school.

> **exercise 1**
> see **natural English** boxes in **unit one** for answers

go to wordlist p.130

> **language point** ellipsis
> We often leave out words to avoid repetition, or when they aren't really necessary because the meaning is clear without them. We refer to this as *ellipsis*, and one common example is the omission of a verb and often other words that follow it, after *be* and *have* (used as auxiliary or non-auxiliary verbs).
> *Did she see it?*   *No, she didn't (see it).*
> *Are you going to phone him?* *Yes, I am (going to phone him).*
> *Has she got any brothers?*   *No, she hasn't (got any brothers).*

test yourself!

Encourage learners to use **test yourself!** to reflect on their progress as well as doing the test activities. Give them a few minutes to mark the line before they do the **test yourself!** activities and to go back to the unit contents and tick the language they can now use confidently. This should motivate learners and will help them to be analytical about their own learning.

Want to know more? Go to the introduction p.9 for ways of using the test yourself!

> 1 son / daughter, uncle / aunt, grandfather / grandmother, son-in-law / daughter-in-law, nephew / niece, cousin, stepfather / stepmother, parent, grandparent
> 2 found, spent, rang, forgot, met, saw
> 3 shut up; quiet; be quiet; could you be quiet, please?

> 1 only
> 2 get
> 3 about
> 4 both

> 1 I went with **David's father**.
> 2 What**'s it** like?
> 3 Where **did** you meet her yesterday?
> 4 She lives **on** her own.

two

in unit two ...

reading family meals
p.26

wordbooster
p.28

listening
how to ... be the perfect guest
p.30

extended speaking
restaurant scene
p.32

test yourself!
p.33

review
p.33

wordlist
p.131

reading family meals

talk about family meals using **natural English** phrases

focus on food vocabulary

read and talk about family food shopping in different countries

focus on countable and uncountable nouns

discuss your family eating habits

glossary

zero article when an article is <u>not</u> used in English, e.g. have ~~a~~ dinner

skimming and scanning skimming means reading for gist, to understand the main points of a text as in **read on exercise 1** below; scanning means reading to find specific information, as in **read on exercise 2**.

ellipsis where words are left out in a sentence deliberately, often to avoid repetition. e.g. *I'm busy today, but Daisy isn't.* NOT ~~but Daisy isn't busy~~.

lead-in

90+ mins

- In the **lead-in** we focus on the common use of *have* + noun in spoken English. Many learners use less common collocations, e.g. *eat breakfast, take a coffee*; and they often have problems with the zero article in phrases such as *have lunch*. For more practice, go to the **language reference** and **practice exercises** on *p.153*.

- First check that students understand the vocabulary in the questionnaire, e.g. *do the shopping* means 'shopping for food / things you need regularly', not for clothes, books, etc. There are two useful lexical patterns to highlight in this exercise: *do the* (*washing / cooking*, etc.) and *have* (*breakfast / dinner*, etc.). For an alternative start to the lesson, see **ideas plus** on the right.

- After going through the questionnaire together, you could ask students to report back at the end of **exercise 2** on one similarity or difference in their group.

- You can use the recording in **exercise 3** to focus on the intonation at the end of the questions in the **natural English** box. At the same time, point out the collocations with *have* if you haven't already done so. Use the recording or your own model for students to practise the intonation. Listen and correct where necessary during **exercise 5**.

vocabulary food

- Learners can collaborate on **exercise 1** to share their knowledge, then work with another pair if there are still items they don't know. Ask them to write the words on the board (or write them yourself) so that they can correct any spelling errors. If appropriate, you could also highlight *jar, packet, bowl*, and *bunch*, although it is not necessary for this lesson. You could elicit the plural form *loaf / loaves*, since *loaves* comes up in the reading text that follows.

- Many of the food items in the **glossary** present pronunciation problems for learners, with both sounds and stress. For this reason, you could approach **exercise 2** diagnostically and see how learners think items are pronounced / stressed. When you play the recording in **exercise 3**, pause the tape and check any items which you may have heard them mispronounce. You could use phonemic script for sounds which cause particular problems, e.g. *spinach* /ˈspɪnɪtʃ/.

- For extra vocabulary development, see **ideas plus** on the right.

read on

- In **exercise 1** learners are given a simple pre-reading task to encourage them to *skim* the text. If your learners are reading very slowly, look at the **troubleshooting** box on the right.

- **Exercise 2** gives students practice in *scanning* for specific information in the texts. Do the first example with the class, then tell them about the time limit. After two minutes, tell them they have a minute left (but if everyone needs more time, be prepared to be flexible). Notice that there are examples of *ellipsis* in the exercise, e.g. *The Celiks eat fresh fish, but the Cavens <u>don't</u>*. This came up before in the writing activity in **extended speaking** in **unit one**, so if you dealt with it there, you could point it out again here.

- After students have compared in **exercise 3**, go over the answers with the class.

something to eat

exercise 3
The voice goes down on the three *Wh-* questions.
It goes up on the Yes / No question.

What time do you have breakfast? ↘

What did you have for dinner last night? ↘

Where did you have lunch yesterday? ↘

Shall we have coffee? ↗

ideas plus teacher talk
Before students look at the questionnaire, you could tell them about your shopping and eating habits, using the questionnaire as a framework. As you talk, you can explain the new vocabulary. Try to keep it natural, and avoid reading from a script if you can. Talk for a couple of minutes; this will be useful listening practice for the students. Before you start, tell them to try and remember as much as possible. When you finish, put students in pairs to try to recall what you said, or to make notes together if you prefer. Then bring the class together and ask different students to tell you something that they remember. At the end, write the new vocabulary items on the board for students to copy.

exercises 1 and 2
1 onion
2 pasta
3 spinach
4 aubergine
5 (a bowl of) rice
6 chick peas
7 courgette
8 carrots
9 (a bunch of) grapes
10 (a packet of) frozen peas
11 (a loaf of) bread
12 red pepper
13 olives
14 instant coffee

ideas plus bringing in pictures
With some topic areas, it is not easy to decide exactly which vocabulary items to teach learners at each level; food is a good example of this. For this lesson, we have chosen items which tie in with the reading activity, but one way in which you can involve learners in the selection of vocabulary items is to ask them to find pictures of food from magazines and newspapers to bring to the next lesson. They should choose about 6-8 items, and use a dictionary to check the spelling and pronunciation before the lesson. In class, put students in small groups to show the items they have found, and see if others in their group know how to say them in English: if not, they can teach them. You will need to monitor carefully to check pronunciation, but this can be one way of giving learners control, and you can adapt it for other topics. They can also pin the items to a noticeboard and label them for reference.

exercise 1
1 The Celiks buy their food at the (open-air) market; the Cavens shop mainly in supermarkets.
2 The Celiks eat more fresh food.

exercise 2
1 vegetables
2 fish
3 beer
4 bananas
5 frozen food
6 cola
7 beef
8 instant coffee and orange juice

troubleshooting reading quickly
It is important to observe exactly how your learners read a text. Do they read slowly, following the text with their fingers, or saying the text aloud to themselves? Do they stop all the time to look up new words in a dictionary? If so, they are probably reading word-for-word, rather than *skimming*. At this point, you want your learners to be able to read for gist to encourage natural reading habits, so make it clear that they don't need to read and understand every single word. It may help to set them a time limit. Noise is also distracting, so make sure there is peace and quiet, and avoid reading the text aloud yourself when they read for the first time. If many of your class read slowly, you can build up speed with short speed-reading activities. An OHP is a useful tool: copy a text onto a transparency, and as students start reading, cover the text gradually from the top downwards (without making it too demanding!).

two

grammar countable / uncountable nouns

- Students will have met some countable and uncountable nouns at elementary level, so the concept should not be new, but errors are still common. You could use visual aids or board drawings to show that apples are countable, and things like sugar or bread are not. See also the **language point** on the right. Check the answers to **exercise 1** together before going on to the rules in **exercise 2**.

- To provide more challenge for learners, they should cover the rules in **exercise 2** as suggested; if they need more support, they needn't do this. Answer the first rule together, then let them work alone or in pairs.

- **Exercise 3** is a peer teaching activity. Divide the class into As and Bs, and if you like, let A students work together on their correction exercise at the back of the book; ditto for B students. Regroup students into A/ B pairs. Students read the original (uncorrected) sentences to their partner, who have to listen and correct and learners can teach / correct each other. Monitor to check this is happening.

> **Want to know more?** Go to **how to** ... do pair and group work (peer teaching / testing) *p.147*.

- For more controlled practice of this grammar point, go to the **language reference** and **practice exercises** on *pp.153* and *154* and **workbook**, **expand your grammar** making uncountable nouns countable *p.11*.

speaking it's your turn!

- The **natural English** box reinforces the previous grammar point, but also highlights the fact that we use *a lot of* in questions, negative and positive sentences. Go through the information in the box, then play the recording for students to check the pronunciation in **exercise 1**. This language will be useful in **exercise 4**.

- For **exercise 3**, be prepared to help with any extra vocabulary that is needed to talk about their family's eating habits. If students don't spend much time with their family, they can talk about themselves.

- Monitor the group activity in **exercise 4**, making sure students are on the right track. You could note down examples of good language use or errors for feedback after **exercise 5**.

wordbooster

30–45 mins

> This **wordbooster** is best done at this point in this unit as the vocabulary feeds into the listening section and **extended speaking** activity.

restaurant language

- The language in **exercise 1** will be essential for the **extended speaking** activity at the end of this unit. Some phrases will be familiar to students, but they are unlikely to use some of the very common formulaic expressions. When you have checked the answers with the class, you could point out the use of *Would you like / I'd like* NOT ~~I like~~; and *I'll have ...* NOT ~~I have~~.

- You can elicit the answers to **exercise 2** to check understanding, and then do **exercise 3** orally.

- Before students practise the dialogue, check their pronunciation, e.g. m<u>e</u>nu /ˈmenjuː/, soup /suːp/ NOT soap /səʊp/, strawberries /ˈstrɔːbriːz/, dess<u>er</u>t /dɪˈzɜːt/. Also, rising intonation on the questions below:

  Would you like to see the wine list as well?   Are you ready to order?

  Is everything all right?   Could I have the bill, please?

extreme adjectives

- Students could work in pairs on **exercise 1**, using dictionaries if possible. Alternatively, write each word on a flashcard, put a 'positive' and 'negative' column on the board, and let students discuss where the words should go. Elicit answers, stick the words in the table on the board, and check pronunciation.

- Some of the items have a broad range of meaning, e.g. *awful / horrible / fabulous*; others are more specific, e.g. *disgusting / gorgeous / delicious*. For this reason, **exercise 2** focuses on the more specific meanings of four of the adjectives.

- **Exercises 3** and **4** provide controlled practice, but for extra personalized practice, ask students to write down the name of a book, film, place, person, item of food, and a drink which they could describe using the adjectives, e.g. *The Lord of the Rings*. They then ask their partner why they have written the items, and the partner may reply, *I think Lord of the Rings is absolutely brilliant*.

- For the difference between extreme and gradable adjectives, see the **language point** on the right and for further practice see **workbook**, **expand your vocabulary** gradable and extreme adjectives *p.12*.

something to eat

exercise 1
<u>countable nouns</u>: onion, carrot, aubergine, chick peas, courgette, grapes, peas, red pepper, olives
<u>uncountable nouns</u>: pasta, spinach, rice, bread, instant coffee

exercise 2
Uncountable nouns don't have a plural with 's'.
Uncountable nouns are used with a singular verb.
Uncountable nouns are usually used with 'some'.
'Much' is usually used with uncountable nouns in questions and negatives.
'Many' is usually used with countable nouns in questions and negatives.

language point nouns which can be countable and uncountable

Many items listed in a dictionary as uncountable are also given as a countable form. *Coffee, tea, beer*, etc. fall into this category when used in the sense of *a cup of coffee / tea* or *a glass of beer*, e.g. *We'll have a coffee and two beers, please*. We have highlighted this feature in the **language reference** on *p.154* in a **natural English** box, and you might like to point it out.

---

exercise 1
You don't hear the /t/ sound in 'don't'.

---

exercise 1
| 1 starter | 3 wine list | 5 dessert | 7 bill | 9 main course |
| 2 menu | 4 order | 6 all right | 8 meal | |

exercise 2
<u>waiter</u>: Here's the menu. Would you like to see the wine list as well? Are you ready to order ? Is everything all right? Enjoy your meal.
<u>customer</u>: I'd like mushroom soup for my starter. I'd like strawberries with ice cream for dessert. Could I have the bill, please? I'll have the lobster for my main course.

exercise 3 possible order
b   Here's the menu. Would you like to see the wine list as well?
c   Are you ready to order ?
a   I'd like mushroom soup for my starter.
h   I'll have the lobster for my main course.
g   Enjoy your meal.
e   Is everything all right?
d   I'd like strawberries with ice cream for dessert.
f   Could I have the bill please?

---

exercise 1
<u>extreme positive</u>: wonderful, delicious, gorgeous, fabulous, brilliant
<u>extreme negative</u>: awful, horrible, disgusting, terrible

exercise 2
1 delicious   2 gorgeous   3 brilliant   4 disgusting

exercise 3 possible answers
1 This student is absolutely brilliant.
2 The weather was absolutely awful.
3 His girlfriend is absolutely gorgeous.
4 This ice cream is absolutely delicious.
5 My holiday was absolutely fabulous.
6 This is absolutely disgusting.

language point extreme and gradable adjectives

To help students with the difference between gradable adjectives, e.g. *good, nice, pleasant*, and extreme adjectives, e.g. *wonderful, delicious, terrible*, you can draw a cline across the board, like this:

☺   ☺   ☹

wonderful   good, nice, pleasant   terrible

You can also tell them that *wonderful* includes the idea of *very*, i.e. it means very good. For this reason, we don't say ~~very wonderful / very awful~~ but we can say *absolutely wonderful / awful*. All the adjectives in **exercise 1** are extreme adjectives, so they can be used with *absolutely*.

29

two

listening how to ... be the perfect guest

75–90 mins

talk about cultural norms to do with visiting people

practise making apologies and excuses using **natural English** phrases

listen to conversations at the dinner table

offer food and drinks using **natural English** phrases

focus on adjectives and adverbs

role play dinner conversations

lead-in

- **Exercise 1** asks learners to think about cultural norms in their country. In monolingual groups, there will be some consensus, but also differences based on age, personality, etc. In multilingual classes there are likely to be a lot of differences. See the **culture note** on the right.
- Direct students to the **natural English** box in **exercise 3**. Pause and replay the recording as necessary, then use the recording again for students to listen and repeat. To focus on sentence stress, you could ask them to go to the **listening booklet** for **exercise 4** and notice the underlined stresses. Play the recording again if necessary to reinforce this. Monitor the pairs and help students with pronunciation.
- Before doing **exercise 5**, you could ask students to brainstorm reasons for being late in pairs: the ones given in **exercise 5** are useful to learn (or have on a wallchart in your class for latecomers to use!). At the end students can record all the reasons in their notebooks. You can do **exercise 6** as a class mingle, with students giving a different reason / excuse each time.

listen to this

- Use the photos of Clare and Mike to set the scene, and clarify the information in **exercise 1**.
- Make sure they have read the summary in **exercise 2** before listening to the second part of the conversation; check that they understand *taste* (v). Students can listen for the answers the first time, complete what they can at the end, then listen again for the gaps they missed. Alternatively, ask students to work with a partner and predict the answers before they listen; this will throw up a number of possibilities in advance, and may help weaker learners. While they are writing, monitor and decide whether you need to replay the recording, or replay and pause it.
- Use the photo to set the scene for the final recording in the **listening challenge** i.e. Gerry, Clare's husband, joins the dinner party. Then proceed to **exercises 4** and **5** (see **ideas plus** on the right).

grammar adjectives and adverbs

- For **exercise 1**, check students can recognize adjectives by doing the first example or two together. Students can compare their answers to this exercise after **exercise 2**. Ask students to think about their own language: Do adjectives go before nouns? Do they use adjectives after the same verbs as in the rule box? Bear in mind this can be a difficult grammar area for many learners. See the **language point** on the right. Note also that *smell, taste, look* + adjective will be useful in the **extended speaking** activity at the end of the unit.
- **Exercise 3** recycles some of the extreme adjectives from the **wordbooster**, but students will need to use other adjectives as well. Monitor and help where necessary, before they read their new sentences to a partner in **exercise 4**. This activity should generate some useful vocabulary and common collocations, so after **exercise 4**, you could put their answers on the board for everyone to copy.
- **Exercise 5** looks at how adverbs can qualify a verb or an adjective. Use the examples with arrows to explain the difference. *Very, really, incredibly,* and *absolutely* intensify or emphasize the meaning of the adjective they precede; *quickly, well,* and *carefully* answer the question 'how?', e.g. How do you eat?
- After feedback on **exercise 6**, students could read the text aloud for consolidation and pronunciation practice. You could also use this text as a dictogloss for revision.

Want to know more about dictogloss? Go to **intermediate teacher's book**, *p146*.

speaking it's your turn!

- This role play gives students the opportunity to practise the **natural English** phrases and grammar they have learnt in this lesson in a freer way. You may need to start by teaching the meaning of certain verbs included in the role cards. See the **troubleshooting** box on the right.
- Students can plan what they are going to say, with a partner of the same role as this will give them confidence. Then reorganize the groups so there is an A, B, and C in each group. As the A and B students start the conversation, C students can wait at the side until it is time for them to join in. Monitor the role plays carefully and pick out some examples of good language use and some errors to go over on the board at the end. You can ask students to swap role cards and do the activity again.

something to eat

exercise 3
go to the **listening booklet** *p.8*

exercise 5
My train was late again.
I couldn't find your flat.
I had a meeting.
I had a problem at work.
I missed the bus.

culture note visiting friends
If your learners are interested in British culture, the answers are broadly as follows:
- Most people try to arrive reasonably near the time they are invited. It is normal to arrive up to ten minutes late and not apologize; however, after about fifteen minutes, many people would apologize. It isn't common to arrive earlier than the time agreed, as the friend will be busy preparing food, etc.
- People usually take a bottle of wine or flowers or chocolates.
- After the meal, most people sit and chat for an hour or two.
- It is normal to thank the friend within a couple of days, either by phone, e-mail or letter / card. For more cross-cultural activities see the reference below.

Want to know more? Go to **People Like Us** unit 16, '**Gift Giving**' or **People Like Us Too** unit 2 **Home Visits**. Both books by Simon Greenall and published by Macmillan.

exercise 1
1 The traffic was terrible.
2 She didn't have time to get him a present.

exercise 2
1 red wine   4 onions   7 fabulous
2 chicken   5 Maria   8 bread
3 peppers   6 wonderful

exercise 3
1 No, because he had   2 white wine
   a big lunch.   3 Mike's ex-girlfriend, Lucy.

ideas plus role play
The phrases *something to eat / drink* in the **natural English** box are very common in spoken English and transparent in meaning, but rarely used by learners at this level. After **exercise 5**, you could set up a quick role play: students sit in groups of four, and take turns at being the host in their home, using the language in the box and any other language they like.

exercise 1
1 delicious   4 late   7 wonderful
2 Australian   5 disgusting   8 cold
3 strong   6 lovely

exercise 2
before nouns; after certain verbs; *taste, smell, look*

exercise 3 possible answers
1 wonderful / awful   5 strange / terrible
2 cheap / French   6 fantastic / strange
3 weak / white   7 great / interesting
4 big / an early   8 delicious / burnt

exercise 5
1 verb   3 verb   5 adjective
2 adjective   4 adjective   6 verb

exercise 6
1 great   4 terrible   7 wonderful
2 incredibly   5 quickly   8 delicious
3 good   6 carefully   9 absolutely

language point adjectives and adverbs
In a number of languages including French, Italian, Portuguese, Spanish, and Arabic, adjectives follow the noun, e.g. *a chair green*. In some languages, e.g. Greek, Turkish and German, adjectives are used as adverbs, e.g. *she speaks quick*. In French, Spanish, Italian, Portuguese, and Greek, adjectives are inflected, e.g. *two blues cars*. In Japanese, *look / taste*, etc. are followed by an adverb, e.g. *It looks tastily*. Many foreign learners confuse *good / well* and *bad / badly*. In other words, there are many pitfalls for learners with adjectives and adverbs, and you will no doubt have experience with other nationalities who have some of these problems. It's essential to be aware of typical problems if you are teaching a monolingual group to help you focus on particular rules and provide more practice. You can use the **practice exercises** in the **language reference** *pp.154* and *155* and the **workbook** exercises *p.13*.

Want to know more? See *Practical English Usage* (OUP) by Michael Swan for a detailed analysis.

troubleshooting function verbs
Verbs such as *greet, invite, offer*, and *accept* are useful for learners to understand as they describe common functions. However, it is important they recognize that they won't be used in the role play itself. For example, if they said, 'Can I offer you a drink?', they would sound too formal. You can check that they understand the meaning of the verbs by writing them on the board and then 'performing' the verb yourself, e.g. point to *greet* and say *hello* or *good morning*, or by asking students to *greet* you, *offer* you a drink, etc. Do this before they plan what to say.

31

two

extended speaking restaurant scene

60–75 mins

talk about your favourite restaurant/ café

invent a conversation in a restaurant

describe pictures using **natural English** phrases

write the conversation

act it out for other students

listen to English speakers acting the same conversation

- It is important at the beginning of this activity to let learners read the left-hand column or tell them what they are going to do in the lesson, or put it on the board. This will enable them to get the whole picture. You should also give them time to look back at the **don't forget!** boxes which occur at the end of each section in the unit.

collect ideas

- The activity in **exercises 1** and **2** should work with students who are studying in their own country, as they may be interested to know about different places in their own town / city. In an English-speaking country, learners can either talk about their home country (which may provide cross-cultural information), or restaurants / cafés in the place where they are studying. Make sure everyone has thought of a place to describe, then proceed to **exercise 2**. At the end, ask the class if any of their answers were similar, and if so, why? As a follow up, see the **ideas plus** on the right.

invent a conversation

- In **exercise 3**, give students sufficient time to study the picture story – people can interpret illustrations in different ways, no matter how simple they may appear. When the pairs have finished, go over the answers as a class to check understanding. The exercise also revises *look* + adjective.
- Before they invent the conversation together in **exercise 5**, point out the language in the **natural English** box in **exercise 4**. This transactional language will help them with the activity. Notice that the present continuous is used here to describe the actions in the picture happening 'at the present moment'.

writing

- Inventing the conversation in the picture story proved to be very interesting during the piloting of this activity. We found that students spent a considerable amount of time discussing what to write in the speech bubbles, and were very keen to improve their efforts. They frequently asked each other about the accuracy and the appropriateness of what they wrote. The various groups produced different dialogues but they weren't radically different, as they had to keep to the scenario suggested, but enough to make it worthwhile for students to compare with other groups. If you have a large class, you could ask students to write the conversations on paper so that you can collect them in (see below).
- **Exercise 5** does require teacher support. You need to be circulating, helping and correcting at the appropriate times, but resist the temptation to step in and help too much. Remind groups when they reach the end of the writing to go back and see if they can put in contractions as suggested in **exercise 6**. You can also ask students to check particular errors they always make.
- For **exercise 7**, try to get round quickly and check that all the writing is accurate: students shouldn't go away with written work which is seriously wrong. They won't get it right at first, but you can guide them with corrections. With large classes, it may be impractical to correct all the groups, in which case you could stop the lesson at this point, collect the written work, and hand it back to groups in a future lesson with a correction code. They can carry on with the rest of the lesson (acting out and listening).

act out the conversation

- Most students will be happy to practise their conversations together in **exercise 8**, and it will work best if they can rearrange the seating to reflect the pictures. Groups of four will enable them to take a role each, and swap round to practise it again, then do the other pair's conversation. Monitor and help with pronunciation, and encourage students to have fun with this; it doesn't need to be word perfect.
- For **exercise 9**, students can act in front of the class, or put pairs of groups together to act for each other. Monitor and give feedback at the end: praise their efforts and feed in corrections.

listen

- Students should be able to follow the gist of the listening in **exercise 10**; you can ask them to tell you any differences with their conversation rather than writing them down if you prefer.

exercise 10
go to **listening booklet** *p.8*

something to eat

two review student's book *p.25*   45 mins

ideas plus class survey
For some classes, a class survey on local restaurants / cafés could be motivating. Each pair could carry out a survey on, say, two particular places in their town and produce a chart to record other people's views on service, food, atmosphere, and value for money. They should ask for comments (e.g. *the food is fantastic, it's very expensive, the waiters are friendly*) rather than scores (e.g. 8 out of 10) so that plenty of language is generated. At the end, the pairs could present their findings to the class orally, or each pair could write a short report on their restaurants to go into a class booklet or for the noticeboard.

Want to know more about how to use the **reviews**? Go to the **introduction** *p.10*.

natural English

- Make it clear to students that for **exercise 1**, they have to write down the actual words spoken, e.g. *I'm sorry I'm late. It doesn't matter.*
- Students may write answers which are different from those given in the **natural English** boxes. In this case, simply check that what they have written is correct.

exercise 2
see **natural English** boxes in **unit two** for answers

exercise 3 possible answers
1 I'm sorry I'm late; Don't worry. / It doesn't matter.
2 I'm sorry I'm late, the traffic was terrible; Don't worry. / It doesn't matter.
3 Would you like something to drink? / How about something to drink?
  No, thanks. / That would be lovely. I'll have an orange juice, please.
4 Are you ready to order? Yes, I'd like / I'll have tuna salad for my starter and roast beef for the main course.
5 Could I have the bill, please?

vocabulary food / uncountable nouns

- You can go over the answers to **exercise 1** before proceeding to the listening activity. During the listening, you'll probably need to pause the tape to give students a few seconds to find / discuss the answers.

exercise 1
onion [C], courgette [C], can [C] of cola [U], carrots [C], frozen peas [C], green pepper [C], spinach [U], rice [U], bread [U], aubergine [C], tuna [U], grapes [C], chick peas [C], olives [C], instant coffee [U]

exercise 2 (students should delete these in this order)
1 pepper
2 grapes
3 cola, tuna
4 olives
5 peas
6 courgette, carrot, chick peas, coffee
7 bread
8 (an) onion, (an) aubergine
9 rice
10 spinach

vocabulary adjectives

- When students have completed **exercises 1** and **2**, they could work with a new partner to practise the dialogues, and see if their answers are different.

exercise 1
brilliant, disgusting, gorgeous, horrible, terrible, awful, fabulous, delicious

exercise 2 possible answers
1 awful / terrible
2 gorgeous / awful
3 terrible / awful
4 brilliant / awful / terrible
5 delicious / awful / terrible
6 disgusting
7 fabulous
8 awful / brilliant

go to **wordlist** *p.131*

test yourself!

Want to know more? Go to the **introduction** *p.9* for ways of using the **test yourself!**

1 onion, aubergine, courgette, spinach, peas or (red) pepper
2 positive adjectives: fabulous, gorgeous, wonderful, brilliant, delicious
  negative adjectives: horrible, awful, disgusting
3 pasta, rice, bread, coffee, toast

1 I'm; worry
2 course
3 absolutely
4 something

1 When do you usually have ~~the~~ lunch?
2 We eat **a lot of** meat in our family.
3 My teacher speaks **perfect** English / **English perfectly**.
4 We had **spaghetti** for dinner last night.

33

three

in unit three ...

reading a strange place to live
p.34

wordbooster
p.36

listening how to ... get around town
p.38

extended speaking this is where I live
p.40

test yourself!
p.41

review
p.41

wordlist
p.132

---

talk about living in certain places using **natural English** phrases

study and practise the present perfect and past simple

read and talk about a man who lives in an airport

talk about things you've done using **natural English** phrases

glossary

elision when certain sounds are 'dropped' in connected speech, e.g. *last Friday* /lɑːs fraɪdeɪ/

---

reading a strange place to live

90+ mins

lead-in

- Although **exercise 1** could be interpreted as a hypothetical situation where 'unreal' conditionals are required, it is quite natural to reply to the initial question (which learners already know as a fixed phrase rather than a conditional) in the present tense:

  A *Would* you *like* to live on this boat?   B *No, it's too small.*

- The students will have further practice later, so keep **exercise 2** quite brief.

- After students have completed **exercises 3** and **4**, they can practise their pronunciation. As well as working on the correct stress pattern, you could highlight the *elision*, in this case the omission of the 't' in the *best thing* /ðə bes θɪŋ / and *the worst thing* /ðə wɜːs θɪŋ/, and the pronunciation of the /ɜː/ sound in worst /wɜːst/.

grammar present perfect and past simple

- This section starts with familiar grammar, the past simple, before moving on to the present perfect, which is difficult for most nationalities. See the **language point** on the right. The listening in **exercise 1** sets the time frame clearly in the past simple, and the questions in **exercise 2** consolidate this.

- **Exercise 3** introduces the present perfect. We assume that learners have seen the tense before, and many will have heard the name 'present perfect'; but we are not assuming any more than that. You could put learners in pairs or small groups to pool their knowledge, and their discussions may reveal to you how much or how little they know. Bring the class together for the answers. For **questions 2** and **3** you could ask for a show of hands (e.g. *Put your hands up if you think the questions are about past time.*); this will give you some indication as to students grasp of the concept at this stage.

- The table in **exercise 4** gives learners a clear written record of the grammar, and filling it in will give them some time and space to let the information sink in.

- In **exercise 5**, learners have to choose time expressions which are compatible with the concept of either past simple or present perfect, while **exercises 6** and **7** return to a focus on form. **Exercise 6** is a substitution drill which students can repeat two or three times (one hopes gaining in confidence and fluency each time), and many find it very enjoyable, especially if they can do it in pairs and go at their own pace. Repeat the example with a confident student and possibly add one or two more so that students are absolutely clear what they have to do. Monitor while they work in pairs. You could finish with a quick round of drilling the whole class together. It needs to be well orchestrated – a ragged drill is frustrating – but it can generate a lot of fun.

Want to know more? Go to **how to ...** practise grammar (substitution drills) *p.156*.

- **Exercise 8** is a further opportunity for reflection and consolidation. Students could check their answers in pairs.

- For more practice with present perfect, go to **language reference** and **practice exercises** *p.155* and *156* and see **workbook**, **expand your grammar** present perfect with *just p.16*.

places

exercise 3
go to **listening booklet** *p.11*

exercise 4
The best thing about living in a city is the nightlife.
The worst thing is the traffic.
The best thing about my flat is the location.
The worst thing is the noise.

troubleshooting adapting examples
Students in some places may not know very much about living on a farm or a boat. If that is true of your learners, substitute places that may generate more interest, e.g. living in a cave or near a volcano, living up a mountain or by the sea, living in a hot / cold climate, etc. You could supply these yourself or brainstorm alternatives as a group.

exercise 1
1 in Rio (de Janeiro) in South America
2 he worked there
3 nine months
4 ten years ago
5 yes

exercise 2
1 past simple   2 yes

exercise 3
1 Have ... spent; I've spent; Have you lived ... ?
2 past time   3 no

exercise 4
past perfect:
    Have ... lived; 've lived; when
past simple:
    ... did ... live ... ?; lived; when

exercise 5
present perfect:
    ever, all my life, never
past simple:
    yesterday, two weeks ago, in 2004

exercise 7
Have you ever worked in an airport? (last sentence)

exercise 8
1 took   4 Have you ever lived
2 has never seen   5 've wanted
3 Did you go   6 haven't been

language point the present perfect
We are restricting the focus here to the use of the present perfect for what is often referred to as 'general experience' (actions / events which have happened at some point in the past up to now), in contrast with the past simple for actions which finished at a known point in the past. This is an incomplete explanation of the difference (a past simple may be used for an action which we recognize as being completed in the past, but doesn't include a past time expression, e.g. *I saw John in the park*), but we don't want to get involved in subtle differences at this early stage. There is further consolidation of the present perfect in **unit nine** and **unit twelve**.

In some languages, there is no equivalent of a perfect form, so students have to learn both form and use. In other languages, a perfect form exists, but may or may not be used in a similar way to English.

For example, in French, you can use the present perfect to talk about general experience:

J'y suis allé (= I've been there)

But you can also use this form to talk about an action at a specific time in the past:

J'y suis allé hier

Literally translated, this would be *I've been there yesterday*: a form which is not correct in English.

35

three

read on

- Elicit one or two examples from the class for **exercise 1** before they work in small groups. The gist question in **exercise 2** is to make sure that learners grasp the very unusual circumstances of the central character in the text before they read in detail in **exercise 3**.
- **Exercise 4** moves from fact to interpretation. The absence of privacy is a fact, but how should we interpret his celebrity status? Students could discuss this in small groups, followed by a class feedback. **Exercise 5** returns to the grammar of the previous section. An alternative way of doing this exercise is to use timelines. See **ideas plus** on the right.
- The text is full of unanswered questions about Nasseri, his circumstances, his family, etc. For **exercise 6**, put learners into small groups to produce at least three questions they would like to ask him. Write a selection of their questions on the board at the end. These notes may answer some of them:

> More information about Nasseri:
> He has no family to visit him.   The airline people give him soap, etc.
> He reads a lot.   The cafe owners give him food.
> He speaks Farsi, English, and French. He keeps his books / papers in suitcases.
> He doesn't talk much, but when he does, he switches between English and French.
> *The Terminal* by Stephen Speilberg, starring Tom Hanks, is loosely based on Nasseri's story.

- The phrases in the **natural English** box in **exercises 7** and **8** are not difficult to understand, but are rarely used productively by students at this level, and they are very common.
- Do **exercise 9** with a student as an example first. Point out that students don't have to respond to a present perfect question with the short forms, *yes, I have* or *no, I haven't*: it would be natural to reply with an expression such as, *yes, several times* or *no, never*. Monitor and clarify any problems at the end.

wordbooster

30–45 mins

> This **wordbooster** is best done at this point in the unit as the vocabulary is important for the listening section that follows.

describing towns

- All the vocabulary in this **wordbooster** will be needed for the **extended speaking** activity when learners talk about their own area, so if you feel there is any additional vocabulary that they will need in their particular town, please add it to the set provided, e.g. *a sports ground or a cathedral*.
- With the pronunciation in **exercise 1**, pay special attention to collapsed syllables, e.g. omitting the /ɔː/ sound in *factory*, i.e. /ˈfæktri/ and omitting the /ə/ in *library*, i.e. /ˈlaɪbri/. For connected vocabulary practice, see **workbook**, **expand your vocabulary** places of interest *p.18*.
- **Exercise 2** is a relatively simple matching activity although see **language point** on the right for more information on the opposites of *quiet*.

distance and time

- Learners may have an instinctive feel for what is right in **exercise 1**, although there are several potential problems. See **language point** on the right.
- The **natural English** box concentrates on another language area that some learners find difficult: the facility of using numbers in compound adjectives does not happen in many other languages, so it may require a lot of practice. You could give further examples with different nouns to consolidate the concept, e.g. *a six-hour delay, a two-week course*.
- For **exercise 5**, remind learners to use language from **exercise 1** and the **natural English** box. You could provide an example to illustrate: *It's not far to the centre of town – about a ten-minute walk*.

places

exercise 1 possible answers
have a meal; read a book; have a shower / swim (depending on the facilities); browse in the shops; leave the airport (via Customs) to go shopping / sightseeing

exercise 2
a man who lives in an airport

exercise 3
1 false	3 true	5 true
2 false	4 false	6 false

exercise 4 possible answers
<u>good things</u>: he's made friends with people from all over the world; people give him presents; the airport authorities have made his life comfortable
<u>bad things</u>: he has no privacy; airports are very noisy; he doesn't have a real bed; the lights never go out

exercise 5
1 We use the past simple because we know when these things happened.
2 We use the present perfect here because we don't know when these things happened. We only know they've happened between 1988 and now.

exercise 7
go to **listening booklet** *p.11*

---

ideas plus timelines
You could use these timelines and questions to clarify the concept. Tell the students to put these events in order on the timeline:
a Nasseri landed …
b His papers finally arrived …
c He last saw daylight …

```
x_____x_____x_____NOW
1988         1995         1999
```

Once they have done this, ask them why the past simple is used here.
When you are satisfied they have grasped the idea of past simple for finished actions at a definite point in time, draw the second timeline below and ask them to compare it with the first one. This second timeline shows the present perfect for finished actions at an indefinite point in time.

(He's made friends.) (The authorities have helped him.) (He's received presents.)

```
1988_____NOW
```

---

exercise 1
1 car park	3 park	5 library	7 doctor's surgery
2 factory	4 market	6 (night) club	8 petrol station

exercise 2
clean, polluted; safe, dangerous; quiet, noisy; ugly, attractive; relaxing, stressful

exercise 3 possible answers
factory: noisy / ugly / polluted / dangerous / stressful
park: clean / quiet / relaxing / attractive / peaceful
market: noisy / lively / attractive
library: clean / safe / quiet / peaceful
nightclub: noisy / dangerous / lively
doctor's surgery: clean / quiet / stressful
petrol station: ugly / dangerous

---

language point *quiet*
It's interesting to note that in **exercise 2**, the opposite of *quiet* is *noisy* (e.g. *a quiet / noisy place*). In other contexts, the opposite of *quiet* could be *busy* (e.g. *a quiet / busy time at work*) or *sociable* (e.g. *a quiet / sociable guy*). This demonstrates not only the range of meanings of *quiet* in English – it's a very high-frequency adjective – but also the danger of thinking that an opposite of a word in one context will necessarily be an opposite in a different context.

---

exercise 1
quite near, not far, quite a long way, a long way

exercise 2
1 quite near   2 not far   3 quite a long way   4 a long way

exercise 3
go to **listening booklet** *p.11*.

exercise 4
How <u>long</u> does it <u>take</u> to <u>get</u> there?
It's a <u>five</u>-minute <u>drive</u>.
It's a <u>ten</u>-minute <u>bus</u> ride.
It's a <u>twenty</u>-minute <u>walk</u>.

---

language point collocation
There are restrictions on the use of *far* and *long*:

We can use *far* in questions (*Is it far?*) or negatives (*It isn't far*), or even after the adverb *too* in positive statements (*It's too far to walk*). But we cannot use it in a positive statement on its own (*~~It's far~~*); instead, we have to say, *It's (quite) a long way*.

Describing distance, we say somewhere is *a long way*, but not *~~quite long~~*. Furthermore, we don't say that somewhere is *~~not long~~*; we would say, *it isn't far / it's not far*.

NB Word order is a common error here, i.e. *quite a long way*, and not *~~a quite long way~~*.

37

three

listening how to ... get around town

75–90 mins

study and practise
prepositional phrases

ask where places are using **natural English** phrases

listen to a conversation in a hotel reception, and two people meeting for the first time

talk about places in your town using **natural English** phrases

vocabulary prepositional phrases

- When the students have completed **exercise 1**, you could highlight this use of *right* (= exactly), which is very common in spoken English, and give one or two more examples, e.g. *The bank is right next to the post office.*
- Learners might need one or two additional phrases to complete **exercise 2** accurately. For example, in a large city, students might carry out activities 'quite a long way from the centre', but still not 'on the edge of town'. If this is the case, feed in necessary language, then monitor what they've written before they compare in **exercise 3**.
- We would normally recommend practising directions using a local map. In this lesson students use the map in the **student's book**, as it will be required for the listening later and students will be drawing maps of their own local area in the **extended speaking** at the end of the unit.
- We anticipate that students will be familiar with some of the target language in bold in **exercise 4**, but there are a number of potential problems with prepositional phrases. See the **language point** on the right.
- The **natural English** in **exercise 6** box incorporates several common sources of error or confusion, but also integrates language from earlier exercises and the previous **wordbooster**. In real life situations, learners need to be able to ask for directions clearly and without hesitation, so in **exercise 7** it is worth getting them to practise these dialogues until they are really confident.

listen to this

- **Exercise 1** sets the scene and context for the listening, and **exercise 2** gives learners a first chance to tune in to Dane, who is American. In this context, Dane's sentence, *I need to get to Big Sound Studios*, is obviously a question, i.e. *How do I get to Big Sound Studios?* Check the students are aware of this – point out we commonly use statements as questions when someone is clearly asking for help. For example, approaching a stranger in the street for directions, you could say: *Excuse me, I'm looking for...* . Refer students back to the map on *p.30* for **exercise 3**.
- For **exercise 4**, run through the situation again to help the students to build up a number of probable or possible questions. Successful prediction here is likely to contribute to successful listening in **exercise 5**. This is a pretty intensive listening exercise so be prepared to replay the tape a number of times.

> **Want to know more?** Go to **how to ...** help learners understand natural speech (using prediction) *p.175*.

- After **exercise 6**, go to the **listening booklet**, *p.12*. This includes an exercise on 'echoing', i.e. repeating the speaker's information to check you have understood, and an exercise on the use of *place*, which is the focus of the **natural English** box in **exercise 7**.
- At the end of this section, after students have practised the use of *place* in **exercises 8** and **9**, you could finish the lesson with a short role play based on the final conversation between Dane and Andy. See **ideas plus**.

places

exercise 1
1 in the countryside
2 on the edge of town
3 right in the centre
4 very close to the town centre
5 quite near the centre

exercise 4
1 a doctor's surgery
2 a bus station / a train station / a park
3 a post office
4 a library
5 a record store
6 a pub / a market / a cinema
7 a taxi rank

exercise 6
near
far
nearest

language point prepositional phrases

Round the corner has a literal meaning (i.e. go along here, turn left / right and there it is), but it is also commonly used with the more general meaning of *quite near*, e.g. *the hotel is round the corner* (= perhaps less than a five-minute walk).

Outside can mean not inside a building, e.g. *It's cold outside*, but it is also used to mean *not inside a building but very close to it*, e.g. *I'll meet you outside the cinema at 7 o'clock*. In spoken English this is more natural than *in front of the cinema*, which many learners will already know.

You could point out that *up* is used for 'ascending', and down for 'descending'; but on a level surface the two are often interchangeable, e.g. *They live up / down the road*.

Just here means *exactly*, i.e. the car park is exactly behind the hotel, but it is slightly different from the use of *right* (= exactly) in **exercise 1**. *Right* is more emphatic in stressing the location, and *just* often conveys the added meaning of 'convenience', e.g. *the bank is just outside the hotel* (= therefore you won't have far to walk if you want to use it).

Highlight the prepositions <u>at</u> the end and <u>on</u> the corner.

exercise 1
Dane's hotel is marked on the map, but the studio isn't.

exercise 2
need to get; got some dollars; get some coffee

exercise 3
1 the studios
2 the Euro Bank
3 Pizza House
4 the snack bar

exercise 5
1 Did you find ... ?
2 ... was everything all right ... ?
3 ... is everything ... at the hotel? Are you happy?
4 Have ... seen ... ?

exercise 6
They're going for lunch at a French restaurant.

exercise 7
1 a company / office / factory
2 a city
3 a hotel
4 a restaurant

ideas plus roleplay

Divide the class into A / B pairs (equivalent to Dane and Andy) and set up the background scene as follows.

A is English-speaking, and has just arrived in (name of your town) for the first time to meet B. The two of you met in England several months ago when B was on holiday.

A: You arrived at your hotel last night and your friend is meeting you there this morning. In pairs (with another A), decide what the journey from England was like, what the hotel has been like so far, what you did last night or early this morning, and how you are feeling. Think of one or two questions to ask student B as well, e.g. *What are we going to do today?*

B: You are going to meet your friend this morning at their hotel. With another B, prepare some questions to ask, e.g. *What was the journey like? How about the hotel? Where did you go last night?* etc. Also think about your plans for today, and ask A what they would like to do.

Act out your roleplay in A / B pairs.

39

three

extended speaking this is where I live

60–75 mins

listen to a conversation about someone's local area

draw a map of the local area

ask and answer questions about the area

talk about the good and bad things in the area

write about your own area

- It is important at the beginning of this activity to let learners read the left-hand column, or tell them what they are going to do in the lesson or put it on the board. This will enable them to get the whole picture. You should also give them time to look back at the **don't forget!** boxes which appear at the end of each section in the unit.

collect ideas

- The first two exercises lead learners into the **extended speaking** activity. At the end of **exercise 1**, collect in the students' work and redistribute around the class. For **exercise 2** to work as a guessing game, it is important that learners do not know who wrote the text in front of them so mix the texts up well before redistribution.
- **Exercises 3** and **4** provide listening practice as well as a model for the activity which the students are going to do. If you wanted to replicate this idea but in a more personalized way, see **ideas plus** on the right.
- When the students are drawing their local maps in **exercise 5**, move round to check they are doing it correctly. Make it clear that they do not have to be very well drawn. It's essential that they do not write the names of the various places, e.g. *post office* or *swimming pool*, etc. or the following communication activity won't work in **exercise 6**.

exercise 3
tennis court (2), park (1), local pub (3), Chinese restaurant (4), the chemist's (5), doctor's surgery (6)

exercise 4
Do you play?   What's it like?   Have you ever been there?   Is it expensive?   How far is it?

talk about your area

- **Exercise 6** is a communication activity and not a language drill, so remind learners about the importance of follow-up questions and give them time to think of some likely questions they can ask. At the end, conduct a class feedback on their performance before moving on to the second communication activity in **exercise 7**.

Want to know more? Go to **how to** ... use learners as a resource (task performance) *p.170*.

- For **exercise 7**, move round and help learners while they complete the table, and give them time to prepare and rehearse some of the things they want to say.
- When they are ready put them in groups for the discussion in **exercise 8**. The duration of this activity is hard to predict – some groups may start running dry after five minutes while others may keep going for 25 minutes. In such circumstances there are class management issues that need to be considered. See **troubleshooting** on the right.
- After **exercise 8**, bring the class together to compare some of their ideas in **exercise 9**; this may start a new discussion. Finish with more feedback on how the class performed in **exercise 7**.

Want to know more? Go to intermediate **teacher's book, how to** ... monitor and give feedback *p.156*.

writing

- The two models in **exercise 10** provide a framework (statement of opinion, supported by two reasons, then extra information) for a short paragraph on the 'best' or 'worst' feature of their area. As it is based on a discussion the students have just had, it would make a very suitable end to the lesson. However, if you are short of time, it could be done as homework.

places

three review student's book p.42   45 mins

Want to know more about how to use the **reviews**? Go to the **introduction** p.10.

vocabulary prepositions

- This exercise type is sometimes used in formal tests, e.g. Cambridge examinations. To make this exercise more fun, you can get students to work on it together in small groups as a race. For weaker students, you can write the missing words randomly on the board.
- After doing **exercise 1**, you could focus on pronunciation: read the complete text aloud, pausing appropriately (e.g. *Most of my friends live on the edge of town PAUSE but I live right in the centre PAUSE*.) Students can repeat and copy the rhythm and intonation, perhaps underlining the stressed words; they can then practise the text in pairs as you monitor.

exercise 1
2 right **in** the centre
3 next **to**
4 very **close** to
5 best thing **about** it
6 good shops **near** me
7 just **round** the corner
8 **at** the end of the road
9 ten minutes **on** foot

grammar present perfect and past simple

- Tell students to look at the answers in the box, and ask them some questions in the present perfect or past simple: if they can find a true answer, they shout this out. Put them in pairs to play the game for five minutes before swapping partners. Monitor and correct errors at the end.

vocabulary & natural English

- **Exercise 1** introduces some useful defining language which students need both receptively and productively e.g. if they don't know the word for *butcher's*, they can paraphrase it as *it's the place where you buy meat*.
- **Exercise 3** practices the language in the **natural English** box, and also revises vocabulary from the unit. Monitor while they are writing their definitions, and correct any errors before they work with a new partner.

exercise 1
go to **listening booklet** p.14.

exercise 2
1 boring   2 library   3 five minutes on foot

exercise 3 (definitions)
A pairs: It's the place (in town) where you can walk, sit and relax; It's the opposite of *noisy*; It's another way of saying *five minutes by bus*; It's the place where you can go dancing in the evening; It's another way of saying *a famous person*
B pairs: It's the opposite of *attractive*; It's the place where you see your doctor; It's another way of saying *close to the centre*; It's the place where you buy petrol; It's another way of saying *terrible*

natural English

- Students can work in pairs before checking back in the **student's book** for answers.

exercise 2
see **natural English** boxes in **unit three** for answers
NB For question 1, *place* is the correct answer (*city* is not correct here: it would be a *beautiful city to live in*).

go to **wordlist** p.132

---

ideas plus teacher talk

Your learners may be more motivated to listen to you talking about an area they know, than listening to someone on a cassette talking about a place they don't know. For this reason, you could replace **exercise 3** with a map you have drawn of your own local area, on which you mark a number of places with a cross. Your students then have to ask you questions to find out what the crosses represent. Encourage them to ask follow-up questions as in **exercise 6**. At the end, elicit the questions again and put them on the board. If necessary, correct and feed in further questions they could have asked.

Obviously, this will not work if you live in <u>exactly</u> the same area as your students: they will know the answers already.

troubleshooting managing communication activities

With any free-speaking activity it is a good idea to give the class some idea of how long you want them to speak. Be prepared to be flexible in this – you don't want an activity to drag on when it is losing momentum; equally you don't want to stop the activity if all the groups are clearly still engaged in it. Giving one or two time checks will help them to manage their time, and particularly a two-minute warning to bring things to a close. Make sure you have something up your sleeve for any group that finishes early while the other groups are still working, e.g. add an extra topic to the list for discussion (in this case it could be 'crime' or 'places to do sport'); or you could break up the group and mix them in with other groups; or get them to write down some of their conclusions.

test yourself!

Want to know more? Go to the **introduction** p.9 for ways of using the **test yourself!**

1 noisy, safe, quiet, ugly, relaxing, polluted, dangerous, stressful, lively, peaceful
2 near, far, long way
3 corner, next, end, corner

1 have worked
2 does it take
3 Have you ever had
4 met

1 The cinema is only **a ten-minute walk** / ten minutes **on foot**.
2 Excuse me, where's the **nearest** post office?
3 They**'ve** been to my house a couple of times.
4 The library is opposite ~~of~~ the park.

four

in unit four ...

reading shop till you drop
p.42

wordbooster
p.44

listening how to ... buy clothes
p.46

extended speaking shoe shop scene
p.48

test yourself!
p.49

review
p.49

wordlist
p.133

reading shop till you drop   90+ mins

talk about goods using **natural English** phrases

read and talk about haggling in shops

say what you can afford using **natural English** phrases

focus on *will* for spontaneous decisions and offers

practise haggling using *will*

lead-in

- You could begin by telling students to look at the picture to see how many things they can name (in their heads), and then give them the chance to ask you for any words they don't know. Write these on the board, check pronunciation and then rub them off before telling students to memorize the picture and then tell a partner. At the end, ask them to feed back to the class, and correct any errors.

- In **exercise 2**, students should arrive at the correct answers by a process of elimination. The speakers are using singular forms *this / that one* in most of the dialogue, so they can only be referring to the hat, scarf, or bag, and they mention that one of them is blue and therefore they must be referring to the scarves. If necessary, play the recording again, and point out the above for any students who don't get the right answer.

- Before doing **exericse 3**, highlight the language in the **natural English** box, using demonstration if necessary, i.e point to something near you for *this one / these* and something further away for *that one / those*.

- The /ɪ/ and /iː/ contrast in **exercise 4** is a common problem for many nationalities. You will find an extra focus in the **listening booklet** *p.15*, but it might interrupt the flow of the lesson to do it now.

- **Exercise 5** will be a quick concept check if you have demonstrated the meaning as suggested above. See the **language point** on the right. **Exercise 6** provides personalized practice. Notice that further exercises are provided in the **language reference** and **practice exercises** on *p.156*.

read on

- For the brainstorming in **exercise 1**, you could impose a time limit so that students do it as a race. At the end, students could compare in groups of six, and get a point for each correct word item that other pairs <u>didn't</u> have; in other words, to find the pair with the most unusual words. You could build this into your instructions so that students don't write down elementary level vocabulary. During the pair work, listen and monitor and correct any errors.

- There is some contextually linked vocabulary in the reading text, so you could pre-teach some of it before **exercise 2**; see **ideas plus** on the right. Bear in mind that the journalist in the article did not buy the goods in the <u>sales</u>, but went to try and buy <u>non-sale</u> goods at a <u>discount</u>. If 'the sales' are a common phenomenon where your students are studying, you may need to clarify this. **Exercise 2** is a gist reading activity which enables students to familiarise themselves with the basic theme of the article while doing a simple task. They do not need to remember what she bought or how much it cost at this stage.

- In **Exercise 3** learners read for specific information. Give them time and go over the example given to check understanding of *original, final price,* and *discount.*

- **Exercise 4** gives students a chance to discuss the topic freely and in a personalized way. You might want to give them a minute to think before they work in groups. Monitor and do feedback at the end with the class on their ideas / experiences, and any language points which arose.

- When you deal with the **natural English** box in **exercise 5** and practice in **exercise 6**, notice that learners are not being asked to talk about what they can <u>really</u> afford (which might be too personal), but to imagine they have €25. (Or, you could set an equivalent amount for the country you are in, e.g. in Yen, Pesos, etc.) You could ask students to come up with a translation equivalent for *can / can't afford*: the phrase may be expressed quite differently in their L1.

buy it

exercise 2
They are talking about the scarves (the only thing that is blue).

exercise 3
go to **listening booklet** *p.14*

exercise 5
<u>this one</u>: the scarf / bag / hat that the woman is pointing at;
<u>that one</u>: the scarf / bag / hat that the man is pointing at.
<u>these</u>: the shoes / gloves / sunglasses that the woman is pointing at;
<u>those</u>: the shoes / gloves / sunglasses that the man is pointing at

language point *Which one? this / that one; these / those;*

One is used here in place of a singular, countable noun, and it is usually used to avoid repetition. In the first dialogue below, *book* is overused; *one* would normally be substituted once or twice.

A *Can you pass me that **book**?* B *Which **book**? This **book**?* A *No, the big **book**.*

A *Can you pass me that **book**?* B *Which **one**? This **one**?* A *No, the big **book** / **one**.*

Another problem is that learners tend to use singular forms, e.g. *this one* more than plural forms, e.g. *these (ones)*, although you should point out that it is not common in spoken English to use *ones* after *these* or *those*: it sounds rather laboured. When they practise the language in **exercises 5** and **6**, monitor and correct, especially with regard to the plurals.

This is another very common example of *ellipsis* (see **unit two** *p.26*)

exercise 2
she buys four things:
   a mobile phone
   two melons
   a bunch of flowers
   a washing machine

exercise 3
2 (leather coat) Marks and Spencer;
   original price £225
   final price £225
   discount £0
3 (melons) market stall:
   original price 2 for £5
   final price 2 for £4
   discount £1
4 (flowers) another market stall:
   original price £5
   final price £4
   discount £1
5 (washing machine) another electrical shop:
   original price £399
   final price £359
   discount £40

ideas plus vocabulary
Before students read the article, you could teach a few related items, e.g. *haggle* (v), *offer* (n) / (v), *(be / get money) off*, and *discount* (n). Some of these are in the **glossary**, but will probably need to be highlighted. Choose a suitable context where people haggle in your teaching environment, and an appropriate purchase, e.g. buying a chair in a second-hand shop. Ask a confident student to be the shopkeeper, and use a table in the class as the counter. Act out a little scene with the student where you ask the price, pull a face because it's too much, and you *haggle / offer a lower price*. The student will probably join in the game, and you can end up with the table at a *discount / with some money off*. At the end, use the scene to highlight that what you did was to *haggle / offer a lower price*, because you wanted a *discount / some money off*. Put the items on the board in context for learners to copy. Tell them they will be haggling later in the lesson.

43

four

grammar *will* for spontaneous decisions and offers

- In **exercises 1** to **5**, students focus on the use of *will* for spontaneous decisions. It is very common for learners to use the present simple form here in place of *will*, so monitor carefully and check the answers to **exercise 3** thoroughly. As it is difficult for learners to hear the difference between *I* /aɪ/ and *I'll* /aɪl/ (e.g. *I take* vs. *I'll take*), they may be less likely to pick it up from listening and may not be aware of the correct form. The pronunciation focus in **exercise 2** is very important here.
- The gap fill exercise in **exercise 4** is a quick concept check which students can do individually. In **exercise 5**, they are required to produce a whole sentence in response, so it is more challenging. For more practice of *will*, see **language reference** and **practice exercises** *p.156* and **workbook**, **expand your grammar** *will* for requests and *shall* for offers *p.20*.

Want to know more? Go to **how to ...** practise grammar (staging practice activities) *p.157*.

speaking it's your turn!

- If you used the suggestion on *p.43* in **ideas plus**, you will have demonstrated what to do already for this activity. If not, demonstrate with another student now by trying to 'sell' them your jacket or watch. See **troubleshooting** on the right.
- Make sure everyone has at least two things to sell and has decided their prices before they start. During the activity, it is important to monitor and check whether students are using the key phrases *I'll give you ...*, *I'll leave it*, or *I'll take it*. Encourage students to have fun: this is not meant to be taken too seriously.

Want to know more about how to haggle? Go to **People like us too** (Macmillan) Unit 24, Shopping

wordbooster

30–45 mins

This **wordbooster** should be done at this point in the unit as students will need the vocabulary for the listening lesson that follows.

clothes

- Some of the vocabulary in **exercise 1** will be familiar, but there are likely to be some new items and certainly some pronunciation difficulties with this lexical set. Once you have checked the answers, do some controlled pronunciation practice as a class. See the **language point** on the right.
- The **natural English** box in **exercise 2** highlights the confusion between: *wear* and *carry*: you *wear* clothes, jewellery, glasses and make-up, but *carry* things in your hands, arms or on your shoulders, like a bag or umbrella. If students are still unsure after checking their answers with the recording in **exercise 3**, explain the difference. You can also refer back to the picture for further clarification and ask questions, e.g. *What is the man carrying?*
- Demonstrate the guessing game in **exercise 4** yourself with the class before they play it in pairs.

phrasal verbs (1)

- The focus here is on transitive phrasal verbs (i.e. ones that take an object) which are separable (i.e. you can separate the verb from the particle, e.g. *try it on*). There is a focus on the grammar of phrasal verbs in the **language reference** and **practice exercises** *p.157* and further work on phrasal verbs in **unit seven**.
- Some of the phrasal verbs in **exercise 1** are likely to be familiar, e.g. *turn sth on / off; put sth on / take sth off; put sth down*. This will help learners to do the exercise by a process of elimination. You could turn it into a game by enlarging and photocopying the sentences and phrasal verbs, cutting them up and giving them to pairs as a matching activity.
- The sound linking in **exercises 2** and **3** focuses on linking in natural speech between a consonant and a vowel sound (catenation). With phrasal verbs, students often fail to recognize this linking and hear them as one word.

Want to know more? Go to **how to ...** help learners understand natural speech (understanding connected speech) *p.177*

- For **exercise 4**, you can use the board and different colours to highlight the changing position of the object in the example sentences. Alternatively, use flash cards: separate cards for *take, off, your jacket, it*, and show these placed in different positions. Monitor to see if they are linking the relevant sounds. Do a class feedback at the end. For further practice of the phrasal verbs see **ideas plus** on the right.

buy it

exercise 1
1 b   2 c   3 a

exercise 3
1 the present simple (habits, routines)
2 *will* + verb (spontaneous decision)
3 *will* + verb

exercise 4
1 'll   2 –   3 –   4 'll

exercise 5 possible answers
1 I'll carry it for you.
2 I'll have a coffee, please.
3 I'll take you.
4 I'll help you.

---

troubleshooting haggling role play

If you think there is a cultural problem and your students would object to doing this activity, don't do it. However, we think that haggling is probably a familiar concept for most learners, and it can be a fun end to the lesson. It is obviously quite a skill in real life, which some people are very good at, so you might find that a few 'experts' have some skills they can pass on to others: a nice opportunity for genuine communication.

You may need to make it clear that in the role play, 'sellers' can only sell an item once to the same person, so if their customers don't like what they have been offered, they should walk away and try to sell it to someone else.

---

exercise 1
The woman: top, jacket, necklace, skirt, tights, high heels, ring, bracelet, umbrella
The young man: cap, shirt, jumper, jeans, socks, trainers
The older man: shirt, tie, suit, belt, briefcase

exercise 2
wearing, carrying, wear, wear

language point clothes vocabulary

Apart from numerous difficulties with the pronunciation of these items (see phonemic script in the **student's book** for particular problems), there are some specific issues of form / meaning:

jeans / tights are always plural in English (like *trousers*), but possibly not in other languages.

top / shirt (and *blouse* /blaʊz/): a *top* can be a shirt, a t-shirt or a blouse, and is used mainly for women's clothing. A shirt can be worn by men or women; *blouses* are only worn by women.

jumper: the words *pullover* /ˈpʊləʊvə/ and *sweater* /ˈswetə/ are largely synonymous with *jumper* in British English. *Cardigan* /ˈkɑːdɪɡən/ is similar but has buttons up the front.

Most good learners' dictionaries include illustrations of items of clothing, so direct students towards this feature for clothes and other topic pages.

---

exercises 1 and 2
1 turn it on
2 put it down
3 hang it up
4 take it off
5 try them on
6 take it back
7 put it on
8 pick them up

exercise 4
1 turn it on, turn the computer on, turn on the computer
2 put it down, put the box down, put down the box
3 hang it up, hang your coat up, hang up your coat
4 take it off, take your jacket off, take off your jacket
5 try them on, try the shoes on, try on the shoes
6 take it back, take the phone back, take back the phone
7 put it on, put your jumper on, put on your jumper
8 pick them up, pick your clothes up, pick up your clothes

ideas plus running dictation

Put students in A / B pairs, facing each other. Try to keep pairs a reasonable distance apart so that they can't hear other pairs working. Go to a quiet corner of the room, or sit just outside the classroom. The A students come to you, the B students remain seated. Quietly dictate (at natural speed) one of the sentences below to the A students, who have to remember it without writing it down. They then return to their partner and dictate the sentence to them, which they write down. The B partner then comes back to you, and shows you the sentence. If it is correct, you dictate a second sentence to B, who goes back and dictates it to A, etc. If it is wrong, the A student must come back to you to listen again then go back to B and correct the sentence. Here are some sample sentences:

Put it on the table.
Can I try them on in here?
Could you pick them up for me?
Take them back to the shop tomorrow.
Tell him to turn it off and come here.
Please take them off and put them in the cupboard.

four

listening how to ... buy clothes

75–90 mins

talk about favourite shops

focus on vocabulary related to clothes shopping and **natural English** phrases

listen to a shopping anecdote

write a story using link words

focus on grammar: *too*, *very* and *too much / many*

lead-in

- Encourage students to speak as much as possible in **exercise 2** by demonstrating an example first, e.g. get students to ask you about your favourite shop, and give expansive answers.

vocabulary shopping

- For a different way to start this section, you could look at the reference below.

Want to know more? Go to **how to** ... use the learners as a resource (location, location, location) *p.169*.

- The language in **bold** in **exercise 1** consists of useful, high-frequency items for shopping situations. A few appeared in the **wordbooster**, but others may be new, e.g. *tight, fit*. Some are lexical phrases which students will probably understand but won't produce, e.g. *over there, here you are, look good on you, I'm a (28)*. Students can compare answers and use dictionaries where appropriate. Pause the recording as necessary so that learners can check their answers in **exercise 2**. **Exercise 3** is a quick concept check.

- After working on the pronunciation in **exercise 4**, pairs could adapt the dialogue, e.g. to develop a longer conversation, or change the item of clothing (a sweater would give practice with singular forms). Let students act out the scene in pairs.

- Be careful about personalizing the language in the **natural English** box if people are sensitive about their size. For more work on shop language see **workbook**, **expand your vocabulary** commonly confused words *p.23*. For more information on clothing sizes, see **culture note** on the right.

listen to this

- You could start with the picture of Jim to set the scene, or if you prefer, ask students to talk about the last time they had to buy something special to wear (for a wedding, an interview, etc.). Where did they buy it? Was it easy to find? Do they wear the outfit a lot? Then make sure they read **exercise 1** before they listen to the **tune in** section of the recording. See **language point** on the right.

- In **exercise 2**, students predict the content of the story. Don't worry if their guesses are not correct (e.g. if they put *it was too small*) but if they are wildly wrong, you may need to help them with more logical predictions. Don't let them write while listening; otherwise, they may miss some answers.

Want to know more? Go to **how to** ... help learners understand natural speech (grading tasks) *p.176*

writing

- You may decide to set up this activity in class and ask learners to do the writing for homework, thus allowing them to work together, while you monitor and help.

Want to know more? Go to **how to** ... motivate low level learners to write *p.160*.

- For the feedback on **exercise 1**, highlight the linking words in context on the board. Students by this stage should be very familiar with the story, and they will get some oral practice in **exercise 2** as a lead-in to the writing in **exercise 3**. Monitor while they are telling the stories and correct any factual inaccuracies (if there are lots of inaccuracies, play the recording again).

- For **exercise 3**, either one person in the pair can write, or both. When they have finished, they can compare their version with the tapescript. For a more challenging activity, see **ideas plus** on the right.

grammar *too / very, too much / too many*

- Some learners confuse *too* and *very*, so we have clarified the distinction in **exercise 1** and test this in **exercise 2**. If you think your learners will have no problems, you could omit these exercises.

- **Exercise 3** brings together the language learnt so far, and includes *too much / many* + noun. Students are already familiar with *much / many* (see **language reference** and **practice exercises** *pp.157* and *158*) and most learners will have come across *too much / many* by this stage. Pairs may come up with different solutions to **exercise 3** in feedback. **Exercise 4** uses the sentences in the previous exercise to exemplify the rules so far.

- You could do **exercises 5** and **6** at this point, or later as a revision activity depending on time available and students concentration levels.

buy it

exercise 1
1 e   2 d   3 a   4 f   5 c   6 b

exercise 3
a The shop assistant asks 1 and 3.
b The customer asks 2, 4, 5, 6.
c We use *they* because trousers are plural.

exercise 5
What size **are** you?   What size do you **take**?
It**'s** / They**'re** the wrong size.   It **doesn't** fit.
They**'re** a bit long / short.

exercise 6
The jumper is the wrong size. It doesn't fit. It's a bit big.
The trousers are the wrong size. They don't fit. They're a bit short.

culture note clothing sizes
Clothing sizes vary from country to country, so if your students are studying in an English-speaking country, or are planning to go to one, it would be worth looking at this. Even within Europe, sizes are not consistent (e.g. shoe sizes in France and Italy are not identical). In Japan and Korea, shoe sizes are measured in centimetres, which seems very sensible to us! You will easily find data on the Internet: just type 'international + clothing + sizes' into a search engine to find a table which you can print out. You might even use it for practising numbers.

---

exercise 1
a job interview, a department store, a suit

exercise 3
1 it was too expensive
2 it was the wrong size
3 helpful; lots of suits to try on
4 half an hour; to buy one

exercise 4
the shop assistant

language point infinitive of purpose
Notice that in **exercise 1**, there is an example of an infinitive of purpose: *He went to a department store* **to buy** *a shirt*. We use this to say why we do something, and it is a useful structure for learners at elementary and pre-intermediate level to learn, and is one that is often misused (e.g. ~~he went for buy~~ ... / ~~for to buy~~ ... / ~~for buying~~ ... You could focus on it, and then ask students to think of different reasons for doing something or going to a particular place, e.g.

You learn English to ... (get a job / watch films / talk to friends on the net, etc.)
You go to hospital to ...   You go to the beach to ...   You go to the post office to ...

---

exercise 1
so, First, but, Then, but, and, and finally

ideas plus producing their own stories
The framework in Jim's anecdote about shopping is a very familiar one:
- he sets the scene (when and why he went to the shops)
- where he went to buy it
- what he saw / tried on
- what was right / wrong about the items
- what he did in the end

Ask students to think about an outfit they bought for a special occasion using this framework. Give them time to plan before telling their stories in pairs and feed in extra vocabulary as necessary. You can still go back to **writing exercise 1** to focus on the linking words before they write.

---

exercise 1
Picture 1 – very   Picture 2 – too

exercise 2
1 too   2 very   3 very   4 too   5 too   6 very

exercise 3 possible answers
2 jeans or trousers   5 shoes
3 a computer or a mobile phone   6 television
4 food, e.g. soup   7 suitcase / wardrobe

exercise 4
1 too + adjective: long, difficult, uncomfortable, small
2 too much + [U]: petrol, salt   3 too many + [C]: channels

exercise 5 possible answers
a (night) club: too expensive, too many people, too much noise
a pizza: too small, too many olives, too much oil
a suitcase: too heavy, too many pockets
a big city: too expensive, too many people, too much traffic
a mobile phone: too difficult to use, too many buttons
a shirt: too big, too small, too expensive
a hotel: too noisy, too much noise, too expensive, too big
a holiday: too short, too many people, too hot / cold

four

extended speaking shoe shop scene 60–75 mins

do a survey about shoes

invent a conversation in a shoe shop

write the conversation

act it out

- It is important at the beginning of this activity to let learners read the left-hand column or tell them what they are going to do in the lesson, or put it on the board. This will enable them to get the whole picture. You should also give them time to look back at the **don't forget!** boxes which occur at the end of each section in the unit.

collect ideas

- In **exercise 1**, there are a few items of vocabulary which may be new: *boots*, and *stockings*. If students work together, they may be able to share their knowledge, or use dictionaries to check these items.
- Before students do the shoe survey in **exercise 2**, make sure you elicit a couple of questions from the class, then monitor as they write to check they are on the right lines. Do the survey within groups of four or five, or it will be difficult to manage. It might help to rearrange the seating into groups, or ask the groups to stand together in different parts of the room. When they have found out everyone's answer to a question in their group, they can change groups and compare answers. Monitor the group work to check everyone is doing the right thing and collect examples of language use for feedback at the end. For an alternative topic for the survey, see **ideas plus** on the right.
- For **exercise 3**, students can tell a new partner, or they can just tell the class something interesting they found out from the survey.

> **exercise 1**
> <u>Women only</u>: tights, high heels, stockings
> <u>Men and women</u>: trainers, socks, boots, shoes

invent a conversation

- It is important to be sure that students understand the picture story, so allow time for them to discuss with a partner in **exercise 4** or ask you if there are any problems. When they start to invent the conversation in **exercise 5**, you could suggest they write in pencil, as they may want to change things later. Be available during the activity to help where necessary. Learners should have the language they need from the unit, but they may want to express particular ideas and need your assistance. Monitor the practice stage in **exercise 6** to help with pronunciation.

act out your conversation

- Pairs are quite likely to produce different dialogues, so they should be motivated to listen to each other's conversations in **exercise 7**. You could invite some students to perform in front of the class if you think they would be happy to do so. The dialogue is not meant to be very serious, so encourage a bit of fun in the acting.

listen

- Students should find the listening relatively straightforward as they will have produced a similar conversation, but they may be motivated to pick out specific language which seems more natural to them than they produced in their own versions.

buy it

four review student's book p.43   45 mins

Want to know more about how to use the **reviews**? Go to the **introduction** p.10.

vocabulary phrasal verbs

- **Exercise 1** can be done and checked very quickly, and then in **exercise 2**, students have to work at speed to write the sentences. Point out the use of the present continuous (happening now). The writing can be done alone or in pairs. At the end, elicit the sentences and write them on the board for students to correct their spelling. Monitor their oral work in **exercise 3** and correct any errors of pronunciation.

exercise 1
1 put sth down
2 turn sth on
3 try sth on
4 throw sth away
5 take sth off
6 pick sth up
7 hang sth up

exercise 2
A shop assistant is putting down a box / putting a box down.
A man is turning on a light / turning a light on.
A woman is trying on a shoe / trying a shoe on.
A woman is throwing a coke can away / throwing away a coke can.
A man is taking off a tie / taking a tie off.
A woman is picking a shoe up / picking a shoe up.
A woman is hanging up a jacket / is hanging a jacket up.

vocabulary clothes

- This is an exercise type that you can adapt to revise any topic vocabulary, e.g. food items (especially vegetables) with the letter *c*; fruit and vegetables with the letter *p*, etc.
- **Exercise 3** gives students some quick oral revision of clothes vocabulary and you can also revise *wear* and *carry*. Demonstrate this activity to the class by describing someone's clothing yourself for the students to guess.

exercise 1 possible answers
S shirt, suit, skirt
J jumper, jacket, jeans
B belt, bracelet, boots
T trousers, tie, trainers, tights

grammar too / very, too much / many

- Students will need some time to think about the information in the courses in **exercise 1** and how to use the structures. Do one or two examples together, then ask them to plan some sentences with their partner (either orally or in written form).
- **Exercise 2** gives the activity an outcome, i.e. agreeing on a course with a partner. Once the pairs have decided, you can ask them to tell the class and give their reasons.

natural English

Students could work in pairs for this exercise before checking back in the **student's book** for the answers.

exercise 2
see **natural English** boxes in **unit four** for answers

go to **wordlist** p.133

---

ideas plus adapting the survey

If, for any reason, you want to avoid the topic of shoes, you can adapt the survey to make it more broadly about fashion. Here are some possible statements:

_____ always buys the latest fashion.
_____ likes to wear casual clothes.
_____ wears jeans to work.
_____ buys new clothes every month.
_____ has never worn a suit.
_____ has the most shoes.
etc.

test yourself!

Want to know more? Go to the **introduction** p.9 for ways of using the **test yourself!**

1 shoes, socks, boots, trainers, high heels, tights, stockings
2 take, put, off / on, on
3 tie, jeans, top, shirt, suit, skirt, jumper, belt, jacket, cap

1 'll
2 off
3 size
4 that

1 There's too **much** sugar in this coffee.
2 That book is too ~~much~~ expensive.
3 These shoes are no good. **They're** too small.
4 A Is there someone at the door?
   B Yes, **I'll** answer it.

49

five

in unit five ...

life with Agrippine
p.50

listening how to
... use a study
centre
p.50

wordbooster
p.52

reading taking
exams
p.54

extended speaking
education in my
country
p.56

test yourself!
p.57

review
p.57

wordlist
p.134

life with Agrippine 30 mins

reading for fun
natural English *How do you spell ...?*

spelling

Want to know more about using **life with Agrippine**? Go to the **introduction** p.7.

- For an alternative start to the lesson, see **ideas plus** on the right.
- There are some useful items in the **glossary**, so after learners have read the cartoon in **exercise 2**, it would be worth highlighting them and providing further examples. When students listen in **exercise 4**, they can pay attention to the pronunciation of *fault* /fɒlt/ and *liar* /ˈlaɪə/.
- The language in the **natural English** box appears very straightforward, but we have found that learners often make mistakes (*I don't know to spell ...*) or express ideas unnaturally (*How is the spelling for ...?*). You may also find that learners at this level still have difficulty with the pronunciation of certain letters when spelling, e.g. 'g' and 'j' and 'w' and the confusion between 'i' and 'e'. If so, you could repeat the idea in **exercise 6** at a later date with pictures of your own.

listening how to ... use a study centre 90 mins+

focus on vocabulary items in a study centre

listen to someone describing how to use a study centre

talk about how you use (or could use) a study centre

practise asking for / giving permission using **natural English** phrases

focus on *can / can't; have to / don't have to; had to / didn't have to*

talk about study habits

vocabulary study centre

- For an alternative exploitation of the picture in **exercise 1**, see **ideas plus** on the right.
- Many schools have a study centre, although it may have a different name, e.g. library, study room, resource centre, etc. You may need to point this out. If your school has a study centre which includes different things from the one in the picture, you may also want to feed in some additional vocabulary.
- After learners have labelled the picture in **exercise 2** and worked on the pronunciation in **exercise 4**, you could get them to test each other on the spelling (to revise the **natural English** phrases on *p.44*).
- At pre-intermediate level many learners use *I have* in preference to *I've got* in spoken English (**exercise 5**). Both are correct, but students should get into the habit of using *I've got* regularly – it is exceptionally common in spoken British English, especially when talking about possessions and relationships.

listen to this

- Before doing the pairwork in **exercise 1**, you may need to prompt the learners with one or two more examples, or elicit examples from the class.
- *Can* and *can't* are used freely in the comprehension tasks as we assume learners will already be familiar with them. *Have to / don't have to* also appear in the listening but are not being tested at this point. However both of these grammar areas are focused on in the next lesson.
- Again, you may have to help learners in **exercise 4** with one or two prompts of your own before you play the recording. Elicit the questions from the class, and write them on the board: students can then listen and see which were asked.
- If your school hasn't got a study centre, you could consider an alternative to **exercise 5**. See **troubleshooting** on the right.
- When you move on to the **natural English** box in **exercise 7**, you may find it is necessary to spend more time on the replies: learners are often quite poor at being able to respond quickly to requests with natural spoken phrases. You could brainstorm other phrases for them to use, e.g. *Yeah, sure* or *No, I'm afraid you can't.* (There is a focus on *I'm afraid* later in the book in **unit ten**.)

learning

ideas plus spelling game

Select about 15 words that your students often spell incorrectly (see below for suggestions) and write them on the board, an OHT, or a large piece of card which everyone can see clearly. Give the class one minute to study the words, focusing on spelling, then take it away. Dictate the words and see how many students can spell correctly. This is an idea you can repeat with different words throughout the course.

The choice of words will depend on the nationality of the students, but here is a list of fifteen words which, in our experience, present problems for many different learners.

really	necessary	building	which	receive
tonight	answer	because	address	people
beautiful	chocolate	tomorrow	completely	accommodation

---

exercise 3
1 bookshelf
2 computer
3 file
4 video
5 cassette
6 CD
7 cassette recorder
8 headphones
9 photocopier

ideas plus guessing game

Most students should be familiar with the concept of a study centre in a language school – even if it is called something else such as a 'library' or 'resource room'. You could exploit this by getting one person to look at the picture while their partner has to guess what is in it. If the person guessing makes very general suggestions (e.g. *There are some books*), encourage their partner to elicit more specific guesses (e.g. *What kind of books? How many computers approximately?* etc).

---

exercise 2
the books (on the bookshelf)

exercise 3
1 true   3 false   5 false
2 false   4 true   6 false

exercise 4
go to **listening booklet** *p.16*

troubleshooting adapting the coursebook

We don't expect every part of the coursebook to be relevant to the teaching situation in which you work, and there will be occasions when you need to leave out an activity or adapt it. This may be one such occasion. If your school hasn't got a study centre, and your students are unlikely to have had experience of one, it may seem pointless to ask them to consider what they would like to do in one. Instead, you could switch the focus to what they do or could do outside of class to help them with their English. For example you could change the questions to:

Do you read anything in English?
Do you ever use dictionaries?
Do you use grammar books? If so, how?
Do you ever make photocopies of material in English?
Do you ever watch films or music programmes in English (there are many on satellite television)?

five

grammar *can / can't, have to / don't have to*

- The most likely problem here is the use of *have to / don't have to*. See **troubleshooting** on the right.
- After learners have completed **exercise 1**, check and consolidate their understanding with further examples. You could write one or two of your own on the board, then elicit more from the class.
- When doing **exercise 2**, make sure students are distinguishing between *have* /hæv/ and *have to* /hæftuː/, and that they are producing the long vowel in *can't* /kɑːnt/ (often a problem for Spanish and Italian speakers).
- Learners will probably agree on most answers to the statements in **exercise 3**. However, there may be some disagreements which they can discuss in **exercise 4**, and we would view this very positively: discussion is likely to increase the need to use the target structures – and as part of genuine communication. You could think of more statements relevant to your teaching situation which will provide further practice, e.g. *You have to call your teacher by their family name; You can't come to class late*, etc.
- The items in **exercise 4** are not all as straightforward as they look. For example, students may think that they have to 'listen carefully' and it is the teacher who has to 'explain grammar'. In fact, teachers also have to listen carefully to their students; and students may often explain grammar to other students. Give them time to think about these statements before discussing their answers in **exercise 5**.
- For further controlled practice of these forms you can use the **language reference** and **practice exercises** on *p.158* and *159*. As an extension, see also **workbook, expand your grammar** *have got to p.26*.

grammar *had to / didn't have to / did you have to ... ?*

- Learners should now be able to make the leap from present to past in both form and meaning. Give them a chance to complete **exercise 1** in pairs without any help. If learners are able to construct 'new' grammar from their prior knowledge, it can be very satisfying. **Exercise 2** gives students practice with the form of the positive, negative, and question forms.
- **Exercise 3** is still quite a controlled activity but it is personalized so learners can use the target structures in a meaningful way. For **exercise 4**, the focus moves to question forms as well, and you should do several examples with students round the class before putting them in pairs.

speaking *it's your turn!*

- In this final activity, there should be no pressure on them to use the target language from the lesson, but if learners use it naturally in the course of their discussion, give them positive feedback at the end.

wordbooster

30–45 mins

> This **wordbooster** is best used at this point in the unit as it leads in to the topic of the reading lesson that follows and is useful for the **extending speaking** activity.

verb + noun collocation

- It is important for learners to keep a record of common collocations in their notebooks, and when there are a number of verbs / adjectives that collocate with certain nouns, they could use spidergrams to give more visual impact. In this exercise, for example, they could have the four different verbs *pass, fail, take, revise for*, radiating out from the noun *exam*. You could show learners how they can come back and add to the spidergram. In this case, for example, explain that *do* is also used in addition to *take* (they can write *do* in the same circle as *take*). For further practice of these collocations, see **ideas plus** on the right.
- Notice there is practice of this use of the zero article in **language reference** and **practice exercises** on *p.159*.

school and university

- The **extended speaking** activity at the end of the unit gives learners a chance to discuss aspects of their education system, and they will also need some language for giving opinions and agreeing / disagreeing – covered in the next lesson. Therefore, don't get too involved in personalization of the school / university vocabulary at this **wordbooster** stage, or you will pre-empt the speaking activity later. For information on the British system see **culture note** on the right.
- The phrase *what you like* is previewed in **exercise 3**, and is then the focus of the **natural English** box in **exercise 5**. In the trialling of the material, we found that many learners weren't able to express this idea. As an extension, see **workbook, expand your vocabulary** school subjects *p.27*. After students have practised the pronunciation in **exercise 6**, do **exercise 7** as a race for fun.

Want to know more? Go to ... **how to** practise grammar (try it out) *p.157*.

learning

exercise 1
Can't means it's not possible / permitted
can borrow, can't borrow
Don't have to means it's not necessary / you don't need to
don't have to pay, have to pay

exercise 5
<u>Teachers have to</u>: correct homework, prepare lessons, study grammar (sometimes), answer students' questions, listen carefully, explain grammar, teach pronunciation.
<u>They don't have to</u>: do homework, learn vocabulary, practise pronunciation.
<u>Students have to</u>: do homework, study grammar, answer students' questions, learn vocabulary, listen carefully, practise pronunciation.
<u>They don't have to</u>: correct homework (usually) prepare lessons, explain grammar, teach pronunciation.

troubleshooting *have to / don't have to*
The most common problem with this structure is the overlap between *must* and *have to*, and the confusion in meaning between *don't have to* and *mustn't*. Largely for that reason, we have decided not to tackle *must / mustn't* at this stage, but you need to be prepared for learners who may ask you about the differences.

At this level it may be counterproductive to go into the differences between *must* and *have to*: the distinction between internal and external obligation is not an easy one in many situations. In our experience, most learners at this level already know and use *must* for obligation of any kind, so we believe it is more important to focus on *have to*, which is particularly common in spoken English, and to try to make it part of the learners' productive language.

Mustn't and *don't have to* are a different matter, as confusion between them can lead to a breakdown in communication. Therefore, you may have to explain the difference. You can do this through paraphrase:

Don't have to = it's not necessary / you don't need to
Mustn't = it's wrong or dangerous or not permitted

You will need to support this paraphrase with a number of everyday examples.

exercise 1
had to; had to   didn't have to; didn't have to   Did you have to; Did you have to

exercise 2
1 She **had** to go to the dentist yesterday.
2 Did you **have** to work on Saturday?
3 I **didn't have** to pay for the book; it was free.
4 We didn't **have** to take an exam before the course.
5 Did you have to **ask** your teacher to help you?

exercise 1
go to school   wear a uniform
leave school   miss a lesson
join a club   revise for an exam
pass or fail an exam make progress

ideas plus further practice
Students will be using many of these collocations in the **extended speaking** activity at the end of the unit, but if you want to provide quick practice now, put students in pairs to six write questions using the collocations.

examples: Have you ever failed an exam? Do you ever miss English lessons?
When did you leave school? How do you revise for an exam?

Students can then interview each other and give true answers.

exercises 1 and 2
1 <u>nu</u>rsery school   3 <u>se</u>condary school
2 <u>pri</u>mary school   4 <u>co</u>llege / uni<u>ver</u>sity

exercise 3
1 go **to** state schools   4 it depends **on** the school
2 when you **are** eleven   5 **until** they are 18
  years **old**   6 but **it** depends
3 **at** the age of five

exercise 5
go to **listening booklet** *p.18*

culture note education in the UK
Nursery schools in the UK are available for most children from the age of 3–5. Children go to primary school from 5–11, then move on to secondary school until the age of 16 (minimum) or 18. Some students leave and get a job (at either age), while others go to university (currently about 40–50%). The majority of schools are free (i.e. *state schools*), but about 10% go to *private* or *independent* fee-paying schools. Confusingly, these fee-paying schools are often known as *public* schools: a false friend for many learners.

Most universities in the UK are all state universities. Students at English and Welsh universities have to pay tuition fees but not in Scotland. The majority of students have to take out loans to pay their living expenses while they are at university.

five

reading taking exams

90 mins

talk about exams you have taken in the past

talk about exam rules using **natural English** phrases

read a text about how to do well in exams

discuss the advice in the text

write a set of instructions / advice using **natural English** phrases

lead-in

- For adults in the class, make it clear to them that an 'exam' doesn't only refer to school or university: it could be a driving test or some form of test / assessment at work or for a job (but not a job interview). **Exercise 1** is designed as a warmer, but it is one of those activities which might have a life of its own and continue for some time. Be flexible if the class are all engaged, and notice if learners are using any of the vocabulary from the first section of the previous **wordbooster**.
- **Exercise 2** forces learners to concentrate on the form of the **natural English** phrases and gives them a chance to hear the contractions. We have highlighted several errors (e.g. *for me is true*) as they were extremely common in our trialling. But you may also wish to highlight the presence of *that* and the use of *it depends*. See **language point** on the right.
- For **exercise 4** you may be able to think of additional and perhaps more relevant statements for the particular culture in which you work.
- After **exercise 5**, it might be interesting to compare ideas across the class to bring this section to a close.

read on

- As an alternative to **exercises 1** and **2** in the **student's book**, see **ideas plus** on the right for a prediction lead-in activity.
- If you follow **exercise 1** in the **student's book**, refer students to the **language reminder**, otherwise some will drift back into using the present simple when describing a picture. This serves as a speaking activity, preparation for the text, but also a check on vocabulary such as *revise for an exam*. In addition, describing what is happening in a picture is often tested in exams, so it is useful to practise.
- **Exercises 2** and **3** test understanding of the text, and you could get students to compare their answers in pairs before you check them with the class. Then move on to their reaction to the advice in **exercises 4** and **5**.

writing

- When learners have completed the **natural English** box, you could add one or two more sentence beginnings which are commonly used to give instructions, e.g. *Never* (*look, go*, etc.) and *Try to* (*spend, find*, etc.). This will give the students more scope and flexibility in **exercise 2**.
- For **exercise 2**, stress that students can choose their own topic if they wish. Direct them to the example for 'Buying clothes' before they start.
- For **exercise 3**, you could extend this by passing the papers to more than one pair. It can be approached in a fun-like way with having one minute to add an instruction to the list before passing it onto their left. If you would like to link the written work more closely to the topic of the unit, see **ideas plus** on the right.

Want to know more? Go to **how to** ... motivate lower level learners to write *p.160*.

learning

exercise 2
go to **listening booklet** *p.18*

language point *that's true* and *it / that depends*

We often use *that* to refer back to what has just been said, and it's a good idea for students to learn *that's true* as a fixed phrase in order to avoid the common error, ~~I think it's true~~. With this meaning, *that* is also stressed /ðæt/.

Students learn the verb *depend* followed by the preposition *on*, but are not always aware of the use of the phrase *it / that depends* (the two forms are usually interchangeable here) when you are unable to give a clear answer / opinion because several are possible.

---

exercise 2
The student is doing the right things in pictures 1, 2, 3, and 4.
In picture 5 he's looking at another student (wrong).
In picture 6 he's talking about the exam with other students (wrong).

exercise 3
1 c
2 e
3 d
4 a
5 f
6 b

ideas plus prediction

Tell the class that you have to do a written exam in several weeks' time. Can they give you some advice about revision, what to do on the day of the exam, and finally during the exam? Put them in pairs or small groups to make a list of suggestions and give them these phrases as a way of introducing their advice:

We think it's a good idea to …
It's not a good idea to …

You could start by eliciting one or two suggestions from the class before the pair or group work.

Conduct class feedback at the end, putting the main ideas on the board, before moving on to the reading. If the class has come up with a lot of suggestions they will probably have predicted most of the content of the text – this will make it that much easier for them to understand.

---

exercise 1
Remember to write clearly.
Don't look at the people around you.
Always make a plan before you write.
It's a good idea to finish ten minutes before the end.

ideas plus learner training

As the unit is based around education and / or learning, you could ask all the pairs to work on the topic 'improving your English'. (They could do a second set of instructions on a different topic of their choice afterwards.) You may need to start with one or two examples yourself, or elicit them from the class, e.g. *Remember to write down new vocabulary in a notebook, and always include example sentences for new words*. When they have completed their set of instructions, go round and check their work, then they can write them out again clearly and put them around the wall or on a class noticeboard; different notices from different pairs. This gives the writing more of a purpose, which is important in terms of motivation, and you can make regular reference to these instructions during the course.

five

extended speaking education 60–90 mins

read statements about school

listen to people talking about the statements with reference to England

discuss the same statements about your own country

prepare a true / false questionnaire about education for students to discuss

- It is important at the beginning of this activity to let learners read the left-hand column or tell them what they are going to do in the lesson, or put it on the board. This will enable them to get the whole picture. You should also give them time to look back at the **don't forget!** boxes which occur at the end of each section in the unit.

collect ideas

- If you feel your students have had enough of the topic of education and the grammar of modal verbs of obligation and possibility / permission, you could leave the **extended speaking** activity for now and come back to it later.

- You may find one or two of the statements in **exercise 1** are quite alien to the culture in which you teach, to the point where students don't understand them. In our trialling this happened with statement 9 – some learners couldn't grasp the idea that students might legitimately be able to stay away from school and study at home. In fact, this does happen in certain circumstances in the UK: for example, there are instances of parents removing very gifted or bullied children and teaching them at home. (In the case of gifted children, they don't believe the school is stretching them sufficiently.)

listen

- **Exercises 2** and **3** follow the pattern of some other **extended speaking** activities – the recording serves as listening practice as well as providing a model for the activity.

exercise 2
1 statements 1, 3, 6, and 8
exercise 3
2 Agree: statements 1 and 8   Disagree: statements 3 and 6

discussion

- You may think that learners from the same country will all have the same answers in **exercise 4**. This was not our experience in trialling. Students from the same country had different ideas for a variety of reasons:
  – some knew more about the system than others
  – students who went to different types of school had different experiences
  – the system had changed over the years, so it was different for different age groups
  – in some countries there were regional and age differences which lead to different experiences.

- Monitor the discussion, make notes, and conduct a class feedback before moving on to **exercise 5** when learners give their opinion on certain aspects of the system for their country.

prepare a survey

- This is a slightly more light-hearted way to end the activity. To be most successful, you need learners who can think up some 'false' yet feasible statements as well as some 'true' but unlikely ones. You may need to think of one or two good examples yourself to get them thinking along the right lines. These may or may not be challenging statements for the country where you work:

  At my university:
  you have to stand up when the lecturer comes into the room.
  you don't have to do any work during the summer holiday.
  you can smoke in most lectures.
  you can't use the university library on Sundays.

  Students can choose either schools or universities rather than write statements about both.

interview other people

- At the end of **exercise 7**, bring the class together to choose some of the most interesting statements, i.e. the ones which most people couldn't answer correctly, and go over some aspects of their performance e.g. grammar, expressions used or good ideas. For a follow-up activity, see **ideas plus** on the right.

learning

ideas plus writing

At the end of **exercise 7**, if you would like to consolidate what has been discussed in the **extended speaking** activity, you could ask students to write a paragraph about their school / university. Ask them to:

- give a brief description of the school / university
- write about the rules
- say whether they liked it or not.

Students could display their descriptions for other students to read and comment on whether they like the sound of the school / institution.

five review   student's book p.62   45 mins

Want to know more about how to use the **reviews**? Go to the **introduction** p.10.

grammar *can, can't, have to, had to*

- With all 'Find someone who …' activities, it is important that students do some preparation for it to work effectively. Planning the questions in **exercise 1** will mean that they should avoid saying things like ~~You has to get up early?~~ ~~You doesn't have to use public transport?~~ Students could write down the questions for you to check, or you can do it orally: either way, go through the questions before they mingle.

- Students have probably done this type of activity before, but if not, demonstrate it yourself by asking a few students the first question. When you find someone for whom it is true, write their name in the table. Encourage students to develop conversations about each question, e.g. *What time does the person get up? What was the school uniform like? Which three languages does the person speak?* Monitor carefully during the activity and provide feedback at the end.

natural English

- After doing **exercise 2**, you could do a sentence stress correction activity. Demonstrate this first with a student in front of the class. Student A says the incorrect sentence, e.g. *I don't know to spell 'elephant'*; you correct them by stressing the missing or incorrect word, i.e. *No, you say 'I don't know **how** to spell 'elephant'* (which the student repeats). Now say an incorrect sentence and get a student to correct you, stressing the correction. Once you have done it a few times, students can do these short dialogues with a partner.

exercise 2
see **natural English** boxes in **unit five** for answers

vocabulary collocation

- Make it clear that the words which make up each phrase in the puzzle are next to each other in the table and that they can consist of more than two words. This is a useful format for revising phrases which you could adapt for other contexts.

2 go to nursery school	5 take an exam	8 leave school
3 pass an exam	6 wear a uniform	
4 miss a lesson	7 revise for an exam	

vocabulary & natural English

- Rather like **grammar** question forms **exercise 1** on *p.8* **unit one**, this exercise is one in which the sentences are the same for both students, but different words are removed, so they can correct each other in **exercise 2**. If students come up with different answers, they might want you to adjudicate; however, most of the gaps have only one possible answer which they will learn from their partner. For student A, sentence 3 could be *left school* or *left home*. For student B, sentence 1 could be *spell* or *write*.

see **student's book** *pp.62* and *145* for answers

go to **wordlist** *p.134*

test yourself!

Want to know more? Go to the **introduction** *p.9* for ways of using the **test yourself!**

1 printer, cassette recorder, headphones, files, videos and cassettes, bookshelf / bookshelves, books, dictionaries, CDs, photocopier, etc.
2 wear a uniform, leave school, join a club, miss a lesson, pass an exam
3 nursery school, primary school, secondary school

1 what
2 had
3 idea
4 spell

1 ... but I **don't have to** work at the weekend.
2 **That's** true.
3 She's going to ~~the~~ university next year.
4 It~~'s~~ depend~~s~~.

57

six

in unit six ...

listening how to ... compare things
p.58

wordbooster
p.60

reading looking ahead
p.62

extended speaking how to ... talk about the weather
p.64

test yourself!
p.65

review
p.65

wordlist
p.135

listening how to ... compare things

practise vocabulary to talk about parts of a country

focus on superlative adjectives and describe different parts of the country

listen to people describing the north and south in Germany and England

focus on comparative adjectives

talk about different places in your country using comparatives

vocabulary parts of a country

- To make this vocabulary section more personalized, use a large map of the country you are in to teach the vocabulary in **exercise 2**. However, consider this carefully: can you illustrate all the items using your map, or will you need to adapt the vocabulary slightly? Or, use the map of Germany in the **student's book** as it links to the listening activity which follows it.

Want to know more about personalizing tasks? Go to **how to ...** use the learners as a resource *p.167*.

- If you think your learners won't know the names of the countries around Germany in **exercise 1**, give them the first letter of each as a clue, or the names in random order. This is not intended to be a geography test, but a communicative activity so giving support at this stage is fine. You could also focus on the pronunciation of the countries (see **answer key**).

- For this level, most of the items in **exercise 2** will be comprehensible, but not easily produced by learners, and not accurately pronounced either. In the feedback for **exercise 2**, you should check students' pronunciation and point out the prepositions used, e.g. *in* the centre / the mountains, *on / off* the coast, *on* the border. Proceed to **exercise 4**, or see **ideas plus** on the right. For more information and practice of articles, go to **language reference** and **practice exercises**, *p.160*. See also **workbook**, **expand your grammar** *the / (–) with places p.31*.

grammar superlative adjectives

- Most pre-intermediate learners will have met comparatives and superlatives before, but are likely to be inaccurate in using the forms (see **language point** on the right); for this reason, the approach is diagnostic. For **exercise 1**, point out the rules in the table below the questionnaire and give students time to read them. Elicit the answer to the first gap in the rules from the first six superlatives in blue. Students can complete them alone or in pairs.

- You can do **exercises 2** and **3** in pairs, or as a whole class. Monitoring the pairs, however, would give you a chance to assess how well individuals understand the rules. Check students' pronunciation of the adjectives. For more controlled practice, go to **language reference** and **practice exercises** *pp.160* and *161*.

- For **exercise 4**, practise a few questions and answers across the class before students practise in pairs. If you are working in a multilingual environment, ask students to say what they think is true about the country they are in; at the end, clarify any factual errors. Alternatively, if there are nationality groups within your class, you can group them accordingly. For an extension exercise, see also **workbook**, **expand your vocabulary** superlatives + *in / of p.30*.

listen to this

- In this listening activity, learners hear comparative forms used in context, and then go on to study them afterwards. The first speaker, Trude, is German, and has a slight German accent, but her English is accurate and extremely clear (clearer than some native speakers, in fact). **Exercise 1** gives students a chance to tune in to her voice, and to pick out vocabulary which they have just studied.

- Give students time to study the table in **exercise 2**, and check they understand *flat(ter)* i.e. the opposite of *mountainous*, and *lively* meaning *very active and energetic*. Play the recording and monitor how they are managing. If necessary, play it again but avoid focusing on comparatives at this stage. **Exercise 3** provides a parallel listening, so less guidance is provided in the task; nevertheless, students should be able to grasp the key points.

the world around us

exercise 1
(going anti-clockwise)
Holland /ˈhɒlənd/
Belgium /ˈbeldʒəm/
Luxembourg /ˈlʌksəmbɜːg/
France /frɑːns/
Switzerland /ˈswɪtsələnd/
Austria /ˈɒstrɪə/
Czech Republic /ˌtʃek rɪˈpʌblɪk/
Poland /ˈpəʊlənd/

exercise 2
B is on the north-east coast
C is in the centre
D is in the south-west
E is in the south-east
F is the capital
G is in the mountains
H is on the border
I is an island off the coast

ideas plus quiz
You could turn **exercise 4** into a quiz. Put students in small groups, and tell them to plan six questions about the geography of their country. There are two rules: firstly, the question or answer must include an item of vocabulary from **exercise 2**; secondly, they have to know the answers (i.e. the questions shouldn't be impossibly hard). It would be very useful to have a map of your country available, so that students can go and look at it for ideas, and it will be useful to settle disputes. You will need to take the map down when the quiz starts. Monitor the questions the students write, and if they duplicate another group's question, tell them to find a different one. When they are ready, each group can choose a name for their team; teams take turns to ask questions, and you can award points for correct / accurate answers, and points if the vocabulary is used in the answers or the questions.

exercise 1
the cheapest; the driest; the wettest; the most boring, the most expensive; the best

exercise 2
1 short adjective + *est*
2 most adjectives with two syllables or more take *most* + adjective.
3 short adjectives ending in 1 vowel and 1 consonant double the consonant
4 adjectives ending in *-y* change to *-iest* in the superlative

exercise 3
the most industrial, the most dangerous, the flattest, the coldest, the most cosmopolitan, the liveliest, the most agricultural

language point superlative forms
Many errors arise through L1 transfer with both comparatives and superlatives. Most are to do with form; the concept is not difficult for most learners to grasp. For superlatives, the most common errors are as follows:
- using *most* for one syllable adjectives e.g. ~~the most cheap~~
- using *more* with all adjectives, e.g. ~~the more beautiful~~ / ~~the more big~~
- irregular adjective forms, e.g. ~~the baddest~~ / ~~the most bad~~
- preposition error, e.g. *the most beautiful city of the world*

It is therefore important to highlight the rules and give learners practice. For further practice, go to the **language reference** and **practice exercises** *p.159*.

exercise 1
industrial   international   agricultural

exercise 2
the south: more agricultural, smaller cities, hotter in the summer, colder in the winter, more dramatic countryside, more relaxed people
the north: wetter, flatter, livelier people

exercise 4
weather: the north is wetter and cooler
the people: are much friendlier in the north
the cost of living: cheaper in the north

59

six

grammar comparative adjectives

- With **exercise 1** you could simply point out the similarity of rules for superlatives and comparatives. Alternatively, tell students to shut their books, write the five adjectives (i.e. *long*, etc.) on the board, ask students to come and write the comparative forms. Highlight the use of *than* with comparatives, e.g. *Today's hotter **than** yesterday*. This is a common cause of error for learners, e.g. *hotter from / that yesterday* (Greek). Comparatives are necessary for the **extended speaking** at the end of the unit and they were a common source of error in our trialling data.

- **Exercise 2** could be done as a race to liven the pace of the lesson; or split the class in half and give them half the list each to do. Do a class feedback, then some controlled practice, e.g. putting students in pairs to test each other. Alternatively, see **ideas plus** on the right.

- It would help class management in **exercise 3** to divide the class and tell one half to focus on one pair of pictures, and the other half on the other pictures. Before they begin, remind them of *than* and its pronunciation in the weak form /ðən/, and practise with the examples given.

- **Exercise 4** introduces an information gap: the sentences to describe the pictures are fairly predictable, so some guesses should be accurate. Students will have worked on accuracy in **exercise 3**, and now they produce examples more spontaneously, which provides slightly more challenge. See also **language reference** and **practice exercises** *pp.161* and *162* for a review of comparatives and superlatives.

Want to know more? Go to **how to** ... practise grammar *p.153*.

speaking it's your turn!

- With a monolingual class, there should be no problem for students to think of two different cities to compare in **exercise 1**. In a multilingual class, you have a choice: students can either compare the city they are in with somewhere else in the country, or they can work with a partner who knows the same two cities (anywhere in the world).

- Make sure students understand the vocabulary in **exercise 2**, especially *environment* and *the cost of living* which may be new. Give them time to think, as this will help the pair work to get off to a good start. **Exercise 3** can be done orally, but you could ask them to make notes or write out their ideas at the end. See **ideas plus** on the right.

- **Exercise 3** may take some time and should provide useful freer practice of comparatives. Monitor carefully, making notes of examples of good language use and errors (particularly of comparatives). At the end, do class feedback on some of their ideas, and go over the language points you noted down.

wordbooster

30–45 mins

> This **wordbooster** can be used either at this point in the unit or before the **extended speaking** activity.

weather conditions

- When you do these **wordbooster** activities, it is important <u>not</u> to ask students to produce a weather report for further practice, as this is exactly what they will do in the **extended speaking** activity at the end of the unit. You could however ask students what kind of weather they like / dislike most.

- We included this exercise on weather conditions because, in our trialling, learners made a lot of mistakes with syntax so it is worth spending a bit of time on it. See **language point** on the right.

climate and temperature

- We learnt from the student data that there were a number of lexical items included here in **exercise 1** that were needed for the **extended speaking** at the end of the unit and some of them caused pronunciation problems. We have highlighted these with phonemic script. Learners could use dictionaries to check the meaning of any new words, or you could pre-teach a few, e.g. *thunder, rise / fall, showers*. See **ideas plus** on the right.

- *A bit* is a very common item in spoken English, and *a bit of* is usually followed by an uncountable noun, like *snow* or *rain*. Students should be able to complete the gaps in **exercise 2** by a process of elimination. This phrase will be very useful generally, but is certainly needed in the **extended speaking** activity at the end of the unit.

the world around us

exercise 2
more attractive, busier, noisier, better, younger, more expensive, more interesting, more boring, smarter, thinner, friendlier, more beautiful, more peaceful, worse, faster, easier, more crowded, more dangerous, more modern, bigger, more serious, more comfortable

exercise 3 possible answers
picture 1   Bill is older, smarter, more serious than Joe
picture 2   Joe is thinner, more attractive, younger, friendlier, more interesting than Bill
picture 3   Villages are more boring, more attractive, friendlier, more beautiful, more peaceful than cities
picture 4   Cities are busier, noisier, more expensive, more crowded, more dangerous, more interesting, bigger than villages

ideas plus adjective games

To focus on comparative forms, tell everyone to take a piece of paper and tear it into five pieces. They write the following on the different pieces in large letters:

| + ER | + IER | MORE |

| CONSONANT + ER | IRREGULAR |

Everyone has three lives. You shout out adjectives from the exercise, e.g. *easy*, and students have to hold up the appropriate card. If they get it wrong, they lose a life. Keep the pace really quick to make it fun, but don't lose sight of the practice aim.

For output practice, students work in two or more teams. A student from team A holds up a card, e.g. *+ ER*: the opposing team have to call out as many appropriate adjectives as possible.

ideas plus boasting posters

You could include a writing activity here as a vehicle for practising both comparative and superlative forms. Students in pairs or small groups should prepare a poster to present to the class, saying what is good about their town compared with another town. It can be quite simple, like this:
Choose Rio!
X (e.g. Rio) is better than Y (e.g. São Paulo), because ...
- *the people are friendlier and more relaxed*
- *the restaurants are better*
- *it's got the best carnival in the world*
- *the city is more beautiful, etc.*
So come to Rio now!
Provide some large sheets of paper, and monitor and help with vocabulary. At the end, each group can present / display their poster for a class vote.

exercise 1
go to **listening booklet** p.20

language point will

During the trialling, instead of *it will be* + adjective, or *it will* + verb, we had examples of ~~tonight will be cloud; tomorrow will sunny / will be shining / will be rain; tonight snow~~. They also rarely used *There will be ...* + noun (*snow*), so this is something you could highlight. You could write these patterns on the board for them to record with the examples. Emphasize the pronunciation of *it'll* /ɪtəl/ and *there'll* /ðeəl/ in **exercise 2** and monitor this in **exercise 3**.

exercise 1
1 showers   4 fall   7 degrees
2 dry   5 thunder   8 icy
3 temperature 6 heavy   9 rise

exercise 2
cloudy
rain
colder
time

exercise 3
1 It's **quite** nice today.
2 It's a bit hot**ter** than yesterday.
3 There's going to be a bit of **sunshine / sun** later.

ideas plus revision

Later (perhaps just before the **extended speaking** activity) you could do a revision 'gap-fill dictation'. Plan 6–8 sentences in which you can gap the last word (an item from the **wordbooster**), like this:

Tonight, there's / 're going to be a lot of _____ .

Tomorrow, the temperature will probably_____ .

There's going to be heavy _____ .

Dictate your sentences, and make a noise like a whistle or clap to illustrate a gap for students to complete. (These sentences also contain contractions and weak forms, which will be useful for listening). Students then complete the gaps with as many suitable words as possible. They can take turns to write a complete sentence on the board, and you can correct spelling and vocabulary. You can adapt this exercise to practise other grammar and lexis.

six

reading looking ahead

90+ mins

- **guess** what things might be using **natural English** phrases
- **read** children's predictions for the future
- **focus** on **natural English** phrases used in questions
- **focus** on *will, be going to, might* for predictions
- **make** predictions about the future and discuss them
- **listen** to people making predictions

lead-in

- *Might* is introduced in the **natural English** box in **exercise 2** to express possibility, and then recycled later in the grammar focus of the lesson. You can introduce this using the illustration in the book, as suggested. For an alternative presentation, see **ideas plus** on the right. You can check understanding *of might* with concept questions, e.g. Are you sure / certain it's a cat? (no) 100% or 50% certain? (50%) Is it possible that it's a cat? (Yes) Is it possible it is something different? (Yes). Highlight the form of *might* (i.e. *might* + verb) and point out the phrase *I've no idea*, as it is very common indeed.
- Monitor student practice in **exercises 3** and **4**, then conduct feedback, eliciting examples of the **natural English** phrases. Don't say what the pictures actually represent, as this is the reading task in **read on**, **exercise 2**.

read on

- To introduce the article, you could ask learners one of the questions the children were asked (A–D in **bold** in the article), and then direct them to **exercise 1**, which focuses on the gist of the text. Students will probably need to work alone on **exercise 2** as it requires concentration, but they can compare answers afterwards. The **glossary** explains some unknown items, but not all, e.g. *see-through*. We don't think learners need to understand every word, although if they show interest, you could explain to them.
- **Exercise 3** gives students a chance to react to the children's answers, and also provides some recycling of superlative forms. After doing **exercise 4**, you could see if there is a consensus of their favourite answers.
- **Exercise 5** focuses on the frequently asked question *What sort / kind of ...?*: one which learners need for everyday use at this level. **Exercise 6** helps with the pronunciation of the weak form /əv/ before they do the personalization in **exercise 7**. For a follow-up activity, see **ideas plus** on the right.

grammar *will, be going to, might* for prediction

- The approach in this grammar presentation is a bit different: the rules are spelt out, and students show their understanding of the rule by completing an example for each one (see the **language point** on the right for common problems). You can work through **exercise 1** as a class, allowing time for students to stop and ask if they have queries, and you can ask them to practise saying the completed sentences for pronunciation (especially *'ll* /əl/ and *won't* /wəʊnt/). If necessary, go to the **language reference** and **practice exercises** *p.162* at this point, and come back to **exercises 3** and **4** afterwards.
- You can use **exercise 3** for pronunciation practice of the contracted forms by asking students to read aloud the full sentences.
- One possibility for **exercise 4** is to put students in groups of three after they've done the matching. Each student has to memorize two of the sentences from the matching exercise. Everyone then shuts their books, and student A says their first sentence to B and C, who say whether they agree with the idea or not, and give reasons. Adult learners should appreciate the linguistic and intellectual challenge of this activity.

speaking it's your turn!

- This is the students' opportunity for free practice, and they will need time to think and prepare their answers. While they are planning in **exercise 1**, make it clear you are available to help and answer queries.
- You could do the listening activity in **exercises 3** and **4** before the speaking activity in **exercises 1** and **2** if you feel your students need the linguistic / content support. **Exercise 5** is intended as a round-up to this section and can be done as a whole class, if you prefer.

the world around us

exercise 2
In isolation, or as a full form it is pronounced might /maɪt/

In combination, or as a weak form, the 't' is dropped, e.g. It might/maɪ/ be a cat.

ideas plus presentation
You can use realia to present the language in the **natural English** box if you prefer. Find a number of objects which students can name in English, e.g. *cup, ruler, rubber, keys, box of matches, diary, video cassette, bar of chocolate*, etc. Either wrap each one in paper (newspaper will do) or put each one in a (different) paper bag. Avoid anything that is obvious when wrapped, as there would be no reason to say, *it might be a …* .Put the objects where everyone can see them, and ask the class what they think they are. Students may say something like *Perhaps / maybe / it's possible that it's …*.' : if so, that's the moment to introduce *it might be …* . You can also use the objects as prompts for practice of the language in the **natural English** box. And of course, reveal the answers at the end.

exercise 1
b children's ideas about the future

exercise 2
1 Sheikha (Canary islands)
2 Lucy (go to the moon)
3 Chloe (circular house)
4 Ellie (house with roof terrace)
5 Katie (house on wheels)
6 Katie (gymnast)
7 George (eat rock)

exercise 5
go to **listening booklet** *p.20*

ideas plus following up a text
You can use the questions in the text as a freer speaking activity at this point, i.e. after **exercise 7**. Ask students (or pairs) to choose one question from the article (different questions each) which they are going to ask as many different people as possible, and note their answers. You can also include other questions, for instance, *What kind of clothes will people wear? What will people do in their free time?* Give time for the mingling, and monitor their language. Notice whether they use *will* or *might*, as this will help with the grammar focus which follows. Ask students to tell the class some of the most interesting answers at the end. This would also be a good point to jump to listening activity **6.6** if you wish.

exercise 1
1 will live, 're going to live   4 'll probably stay
2 won't pass   5 might come
3 'll be

exercise 3
1 I think Milan will ~~to~~ win the game tomorrow.
2 correct
3 He'll **probably finish** soon.
4 I **don't** think they**'ll** like the film; it's very sad.
5 correct

exercise 4
1 c   2 a   3 d   4 b   5 e

language point future forms
Future forms undoubtedly cause problems for many learners. Some languages use a present form for the future, sometimes with a future time marker; others have a future form, but not equivalent to all uses of *will / be going to*. It's good to be able to tell students that in these examples (<u>general</u> predictions in the positive – which are beliefs and opinions) both *will* and *be going to* are correct. For your own information, they are <u>not</u> interchangeable. If predictions are based on evidence in front of us or if an event is starting to happen, only *be going to* is used, e.g. *Look! Henry's going to score!* (He's the only person near the goal and he has the ball.) We don't think learners at this level need to be burdened with this information, but it is here in case someone asks.

Highlight the pronunciation of *won't* /wəʊnt/ – not to be confused with *want* /wɒnt/.

Students often ask about *shall*, but it is mainly used in suggestions and offers, e.g. *Shall we go now? Shall I carry that for you?*

exercise 3
Where do you think people will go on holiday?
Where do you think people will live?
What kind of hairstyles will people have in the future?

exercise 4
1 people will stay at home (because it will be dangerous / polluted)
2 houses will have a lot of glass (because people want light)
3 the population will get bigger (and so people will live in smaller houses closer together)
4 men and women will have the same hairstyles

63

six

extended speaking a weather forecast 75–90 mins

talk about recent weather

listen to a weather forecast

plan a weather forecast in pairs, then write it

practise the forecast, then **present** it to another pair

- It is important at the beginning of this activity to let learners read the left-hand column or tell them what they are going to do in the lesson, or put it on the board. This will enable them to get the whole picture. You should also give them time to look back at the **don't forget!** boxes which occur at the end of each section in the unit.

collect ideas

- The activity as a whole may look quite challenging, but in the trialling we found that pre-intermediate learners coped surprisingly well and put great effort into producing very good weather reports. The presentation stage at the end was often excellent, especially where students had had time to prepare carefully and rehearse, and some of them relished playing the role of TV presenters. This is an integrated skills activity: learners are listening, speaking, and writing for a specific goal.

Want to know more? Go to **how to** ... motivate learners to write (multi-skills approach) *p.162*.

- Before the lesson, try to get large sheets of paper, OHTs, or flipcharts for students to draw their maps on. For a multilingual class, you need to decide what kind of report students should produce. If you have several students of the same nationality, they could produce weather reports about their own country, but for some classes / groups, it might be more straightforward to do a forecast for the country they are studying in – in which case, you may need to provide a map for them.
- **Exercise 1** introduces the topic and can be done quite quickly. **Exercise 3**, provides a model for learners when they come to write their own weather reports. Alternatively, see the **ideas plus** box on the right.

exercise 3
1 the south   2 the south   3 the west   4 the north   5 the north-east

plan a weather forecast

- It would be wise to demonstrate briefly what to do for **exercise 4** on the board, and then give the students time to prepare their maps in pairs. Make sure they discuss what the weather is going to be like before they start drawing / marking symbols (or they'll be back for more paper!).
- If students use some language from the tapescript when preparing the forecast in **exercises 4** and **5**, that is no bad thing. They may select some very natural and useful phrases which will help their report sound more fluent. However, you should discourage lifting whole paragraphs.
- It can be difficult to estimate when to proceed to another stage in an activity like this, i.e. when to move onto **exercise 6**. If everyone is proceeding at a different pace, you might decide to give instructions to pairs as and when they are ready to move on (this is only practical with a small class). It is crucial to monitor the pairs attentively while they are planning in **exercises 4** and **5** to see how far they have got, and to help if necessary.

write the forecast

- If students have made notes, this would be helpful, but it is not essential for **exercise 6**. It may be better if they write the forecast together, but both students should write, then they will each have a record of what they have done. This is your opportunity to monitor and help them polish their efforts.
- We don't often include new language in the **extended speaking** activity, but the language in the **natural English** box is very relevant, and can be fed in easily once they are starting to read through and edit their reports.

present your weather forecast

- While students are rehearsing in **exercises 8** and **9**, they will probably need help with reading aloud. Get them to divide sentences into sense groups i.e. pausing after meaningful chunks (you will probably need to help with this), and encourage them to read to a listener – if they work in pairs, can they actually follow what their partner is saying? Help, too, by correcting specific pronunciation problems. For a final rehearsal, they should practise the forecast using the map, referring to the different regions. This will bring the forecast to life and help them to communicate the message.
- If your students have managed to do these reports and presented them well in **exercise 10**, they deserve a lot of praise: be very encouraging at the end, and where necessary, give feedback on any common errors. Comment too on specific examples of good language use.

the world around us

six review student's book p.63   45 mins

Want to know more about how to use the reviews? Go to the introduction p.10.

grammar will / won't, be going to

- This activity needs to be done either at the beginning of this lesson or the next one, for obvious reasons.
- Notice that in **exercise 1**, students can use either *will* or *be going to*, as they will be making general predictions not based on present evidence. Monitor as they write and correct any errors. Then carry on with the lesson, leaving five minutes at the end to go back to **exercise 2**.

grammar comparatives and superlatives

- You can make this a competition between small groups rather than pairs if you prefer. Students can concentrate on one set of pictures after another, or they can brainstorm them all at the same time. Make it clear that you will help them with vocabulary if they need it, and they must include a comparative or superlative form in their answers.

> **exercise 1** possible answers
> The rabbit is the smallest / quietest; the tiger is the most dangerous, etc.
> The car is quicker / more dangerous than the bicycle; The bicycle is cheaper than the car; the plane is the fastest / most comfortable, etc.
> X is the most beautiful / the richest / the smartest / the most intelligent / the best singer / actress; or X is more attractive than Y, etc.

natural English

- In addition to revising the **natural English** phrases from this unit, this exercise gives students some practice in paraphrasing, a useful communication skill.

> **exercise 2**
> see **natural English** boxes in **unit six** for answers

vocabulary weather

- For **exercise 1**, put pairs of A students together to work on their clues, and the same with B students. They should have some idea whether their answers are right by counting the letters. If they can't answer a clue, they should leave it for their B partner to guess in **exercise 2**.
- Rearrange students into A / B pairs for **exercise 2**. They read the clues which they have completed, but <u>not</u> their answers, to see if their partner can get the clue. They can take it in turns to read their clue for their partner to answer. At the end, they should look at the clues they couldn't solve, and see if they can work out the word in dark green squares as this might help with any missing answers. Go over any problems at the end.

1 weather	4 rain	7 forecast	10 snow
2 lightning	5 dry	8 rise	11 degrees
3 cloudy	6 shower	9 wet	12 temperature
the vertical word is 'thunderstorm'			

go to **wordlist** p.135

> **ideas plus** video listening
> As an alternative to **exercise 3**, you could use a short authentic weather report from an English-speaking TV station (e.g. Sky News). It would have the advantage of being real and topical, so very motivating, and the visual element would be very helpful. At the same time, you would need to keep your guidance questions very simple, and reassure learners that they do not need to understand everything. The video would not necessarily follow the same framework that is provided in the **extended speaking** activity, so you would have to accept that it would be a looser model. Nevertheless, students could refer to tapescript **6.7** in the **listening booklet** p.22 for ideas.

test yourself!

Want to know more? Go to the introduction p.9 for ways of using the test yourself!

> 1 sun / sunshine, wind, fog, snow, cloud, thunder, lightning, storm, showers
> 2 kind; it might be; about 50 / 50 or so; I've no idea
> 3 better / the best; more crowded / the most crowded; happier / the happiest; wetter / the wettest; more dangerous / the most dangerous; flatter / the flattest; more boring / the most boring

> 1 worse
> 2 coast
> 3 There
> 4 will

> 1 The ~~most~~ friendliest people live in the south.
> 2 I'm sure our team **won't** win the match tomorrow.
> 3 It might ~~to~~ rain tomorrow.
> 4 ... it's going to be a bit ~~of~~ cloudy later.

seven

in unit seven ...

listening how to ... tell a story
p.66

wordbooster
p.68

reading we had a terrible time
p.70

extended speaking tell a picture story
p.72

test yourself!
p.73

review
p.73

wordlist
p.136

---

listen to a true story about a marriage proposal

talk about marriage proposals

focus on the use of *anyway* in storytelling

talk about plans for social activities using the phrases with *go*

write a story about a great day / weekend linking it with **natural English** phrases and language from the lesson

---

listening how to ... tell a story   90+ mins

lead-in

- This is a simple warmer activity as a lead-in to the listening, so keep it brief.

listen to this

- The recording in **exercise 2** is a true story. You mustn't tell the students that it is a marriage proposal, otherwise it will spoil the story, but after they have listened, they might be interested to compare what happens in their own country with the UK. See the **culture note** on the right.

- The story is told naturally and spontaneously, and the illustrations in **exercise 1** are there to give learners support: they set the scene for the story, and the **glossary** introduces students to some key vocabulary. Give the pairs time to build up a clear idea of what is happening in the pictures. After doing **exercise 1**, conduct an open class feedback so that everyone starts with the same information before they listen to the beginning of the story in **exercise 2**.

- Encourage learners to come up with several different possible storylines in **exercise 3**: the closer they get to predicting what happens, the easier it will be for them to understand when they listen. Again, conduct a class feedback and put a few of their ideas on the board, but don't confirm or reject anything at this stage.

- After the listening in **exercises 4** and **5**, it is inevitable that students will think up questions in **exercise 6** that aren't answered in **exercise 7**. If you are good at thinking on your feet, you could invent some answers or ask the class what they think they would be. (A likely question is the cost: in fact, it cost £600.)

- It is very difficult to provide meaningful controlled practice of *anyway* (**natural English** box), but learners will have an opportunity to use it in the final activity in this lesson, and again in the **extended speaking** activity at the end of the unit. At this stage, it is important that they see how it is used, and comparisons with their first language in **exercise 9** may be interesting as well as serving as a useful concept check (assuming you have a good knowledge of the students' mother tongue).

- As a follow-up discussion, you could put students in groups to think of interesting places or ways to propose to people. Students could put their ideas on the board, and then vote on the best idea.

vocabulary phrases with *go*

- These are frequent patterns with the verb *go* in **exercise 1**. We have included some common nouns for each one, but with a good class you could ask them to add one more common example to each type, e.g. *go for a drink, go for a swim* (used as well as *go swimming*); *go riding, go sailing; go and find (a restaurant), go and have (a pizza); go to a club, a match*, etc. See the **language point** on the right.

- Monitor while your students fill in the statements in the questionnaire for **exercise 2** to make sure they are correct. They then do **exercise 3** as a mingling activity, i.e. moving freely round the class talking to different students, while you monitor again. At the end, conduct class feedback on both the outcome of the questionnaire and the language used.

stories

exercise 4
Tyler asked Janet to marry him.

exercise 5
1 get in the helicopter
2 the sea
3 Please, marry me.
4 Yes
5 a bottle of champagne
6 picnic
7 two weeks

culture note marriage proposals, weddings and honeymoons

In the UK it is traditional for men to propose to women (by saying, 'Will you marry me?'), although it is now acceptable for women to propose, too. These *marriage proposals* may be casual or dramatic (there are examples of surprise proposals taking place on television in front of millions of TV viewers), and it is normal for a delay of months or even a year between the proposal and the time when the couple *get married (the wedding)*. The man used to have to ask the woman's father for permission to marry her, but this custom has fallen into disuse.

In the next lesson there is a reading text about a disastrous *honeymoon*. Don't talk about honeymoons in class now or you will spoil it, but afterwards you may want to point out to your students that couples traditionally *go on their honeymoon* (a holiday) immediately after the wedding ceremony and reception. Is it the same in the culture where you teach?

exercise 1
go for: a run, a walk, a picnic, a meal in a restaurant
go: sightseeing, shopping, skiing, swimming
go and: see a film, watch a match, see a friend, buy something
go to: a wedding, a party, a disco, a meeting

language point verb + noun combinations

Where other languages often express an idea using a verb, English often has a preference for a verb + noun combination, e.g. *I had a wash* (NOT ~~I washed~~), *Let's have a drink* (NOT ~~Let's drink something~~). Other examples are: *go for a walk, have a look, give someone a push*, etc. It's worth making learners aware of this feature of English, and it is important that they keep a record of these common expressions when they meet them.

67

seven

writing

- The potential problem with asking learners to recall an experience from the past is that one or two of them will say they can't think of anything. See **troubleshooting** on the right.
- The table for **exercise 1** is designed to help learners with the construction of their story and provide them with a basic framework. You could relate this back to the story in the listening to reinforce and exemplify the structure: what would Tyler answer to these questions? If their story doesn't involve three different activities, it doesn't matter as long as they have enough to say.
- The link words and phrases in the **natural English** box in **exercise 2** shouldn't present problems but you will need to highlight and practise the pronunciation of *afterwards*. Point out that in this context, they can use either word in each pair: they mean the same thing. You may also find that learners become aware of the need for other link words in their stories; feed these in where appropriate in **exercises 3** or **4**.
- It may be more convenient to set the writing activity in **exercise 5** for homework, but if learners do it in class, it gives you valuable time for individual attention.

wordbooster

30–45 mins

This **wordbooster** is best done at this point in the unit as some of the phrasal verbs appear in the reading lesson that follows.

irregular verbs

- If you feel your learners need more general practice of irregular verbs, see **ideas plus** on the right.
- Some of the verbs in this **wordbooster** will be needed in the **extended speaking** activity at the end of the unit, and students will need to know the past tenses (NB This is why the regular verb *bark* has been included). Do **exercises 1** and **2** in pairs and encourage the use of dictionaries: they should be able to match the verbs and pictures and fill in the table easily. Once they have completed it and had a quick practice saying the verbs, they could test each other on the various forms, e.g. One student says the verb and the other student supplies the past simple. **Exercise 3** provides further consolidation at sentence level.
- This is a useful point at which to remind them about the irregular verb list on *p.175*.

phrasal verbs (2)

- The reason for this specific choice of phrasal verbs is that learners will meet and use most of them again in the reading text in the next lesson, and they can also use some of them in the **extended speaking** activity at the end of the unit.
- The contexts provided by the sentences will help learners to establish the meaning in **exercise 1**, but you will probably have to reinforce this with more examples when you go over the answers (before **test your partner**). See the **language point** on the right.
- **Exercise 2** highlights another key feature of phrasal verbs, namely that the meaning is usually (but not always) different from the root verb. Good example sentences are an important way to help learners to remember the meaning of these 'non-literal' verbs, the restrictions on meaning, and the grammar of individual phrasal verbs. See **language reference** and **practice exercises** *p.163* for further practice.

stories

exercise 2
go to **listening booklet** *p.24*

troubleshooting recalling past experiences

If you have any learners who cannot recall a great day they have had recently, you could try one of these strategies:

- warn them a day in advance that they are going to do this activity, i.e. give them time to think of something
- defer this writing stage of the lesson until the following lesson, and ask them to think of their story for homework (but not write it)
- if they can't think up a true story, they can invent one
- if they can't think of a 'great day', they can describe a 'terrible day'
- let them work with a partner and learn his / her story. Let them write their partner's story.
- if all else fails, tell them to build a story around the pictures provided in the **student's book.**

exercise 1
a fall over   f catch
b hurt   g hit
c bark   h run after
d bite   i throw
e steal   j break

exercise 2
go to **irregular verb list** *p.174*

ideas plus past tense bingo

On a blank piece of paper, each student should make a square containing sixteen segments (4 x 4). In each square they write the infinitive of an irregular verb (they can use the irregular verb list on *p.174*). You then dictate past tenses of irregular verbs (tick them off or make a list). When students hear one of their verbs, they cross it off on their square. When a student has two complete lines of the square crossed off (horizontally or vertically), they shout 'bingo'. You can check their paper by asking them to say the verbs in the past form.

You can repeat this simple game as many times as you like. Once students have learnt how to play it, they can do it in groups of four with one student as the questionmaster using the irregular verb list; or students can write the past simple and the questionmaster calls out the infinitive form.

exercise 1
1 ran away   4 turn up   7 stood up
2 fell over   5 broke down   8 take off
3 lie down   6 set off

exercise 2
Phrasal verbs which are similar in meaning to the main verb: lie down, fall over, run away, stand up

language point phrasal verbs

You can often paraphrase the meaning of a phrasal verb with a more formal verb, e.g. *make up a story* = *invent a story*. At a receptive level this may be quite adequate for students, but for accurate productive use, learners often need more information with regard to meaning. In the case of *set off* for example, they need to know that it usually refers to a significant journey, and not one that is either short, or one you make every day. With *turn up*, it is often used in the negative when someone fails to arrive for work / a meeting / a date, etc., or when someone arrives unexpectedly. It is not commonly used in a more casual way (*I always turn up for work at 7.30* sounds rather odd). How much information you give learners is up to you, but it's wise to be prepared for questions which may require you to refine the meaning.

It is also important to remind learners that most phrasal verbs have more than one meaning, so they shouldn't assume when they meet a familiar verb that they will know the meaning in that particular context, e.g. *breakdown* can mean to stop working as in *My car broke down* or it can refer to someone who is very upset and starts crying uncontrollably, e.g. *She broke down in tears when she heard the news.*

seven

reading we had a terrible time

75–90 mins

focus on the **natural English** phrase *have a good / terrible time*, etc.

read a story about a disastrous honeymoon

talk about your idea of a perfect honeymoon

focus on common uses of *get* in the **natural English** box

focus on the use of the past simple and continuous

act out simple situations using the past simple and continuous

lead-in

- It's worth spending time on this very common expression in English, i.e. *have a good / bad time*. Students at this level rarely seem to know it, and if they do, they don't seem to use it. If they can make it a part of their productive vocabulary, they will find lots of opportunities to use it, and it will help them to sound more natural. See also the **language point** on the right. After they have listened to the expressions in **exercise 2**, **exercise 3** gives them some controlled oral practice whilst focusing on the main stresses.

read on

- For **exercise 1**, see **ideas plus** on the right. Get learners to focus on underlining the things that went wrong in **exercise 2**, so they won't be distracted by the new vocabulary in the text, which they can return to in **exercise 3**. It is a useful reading strategy if learners can extract the main points from a text without getting too concerned with new vocabulary at an early stage – this not only slows down their reading, but they may also lose the thread of the text.

- For a quick bit of revision before they do **exercise 3**, you could ask them to underline all the phrasal verbs in the story which they studied in the **wordbooster**, on *p.67*. It can be a very useful strategy for learners to deduce the meaning of an unknown word from context. However, it's important to remember that not all words are guessable, so explain to your learners that sometimes you can guess (e.g. *several* in *line 8* must be a quantity) and sometimes you can't (e.g *at least* in *line 15* would be quite hard to guess).

- **Exercise 4** is obviously an opportunity for a light-hearted response, but if you think some learners might make suggestions which will upset other members of the class, you could omit it. Instead, you could ask the class if they know of any similar holiday disasters (not just on honeymoon).

- *Get* is one of the most common verbs in spoken English, and comes with the obvious difficulty of having many different meanings. After **exercise 5**, they could write down at least three more sentences for each meaning, perhaps about themselves, e.g. *I got to school at 8.45 this morning; I didn't get any letters today*, etc. **Exercise 6** consolidates of the uses of *get*.

grammar past simple and past continuous

- **Exercise 1** refreshes students memory about the story and recycles quite a lot of new vocabulary.

- Learners could answer the first three questions in **exercise 2** individually or in pairs before you check their answers; question 4 would work well if you write the sentence on the board with the timeline and then ask the three concept questions. You could ask for a show of hands for each answer to see how many are confident of the answers. If necessary, repeat the procedure with another sentence, e.g. *When I was crossing the bridge, a boy fell off his bike in front of me*. See also the **language point** on the right.

- If you get students to write down their sentences in **exercise 3**, it will give them time to think about the structure without being forced to produce anything orally, and give time for you to monitor their answers. You can then focus on the weak form of was /wəz/ and intensive oral practice in **exercise 4**.

- **Exercise 5** allows a little more learner creativity, and the final activity (**speaking it's your turn!**) is really designed to provide a light-hearted way to end the lesson while still consolidating the target structures from the lesson. You can use the **language reference** and **practice exercises** on *p.163* and *164* for homework or as revision and consolidation in the next lesson. For more work on these tenses see also **workbook, expand your grammar** past continuous with *while p.38*. To extend students' knowledge of useful verbs for this kind of story, see also **workbook, expand your vocabulary** synonyms *p.36*.

speaking it's your turn!

- If you want to make this a little more competitive, see **ideas plus** on the right.

- Introduce this activity by preparing a mime yourself which members of the class have to guess, or prepare one in advance with a willing student to perform in front of the class. This is obviously an activity that can provide lots of laughter and can fulfil an important function in helping to build a good atmosphere in the class.

stories

exercise 2
go to **listening booklet** *p.24*

language point fixed phrases
A number of common phrases follow a similar pattern, i.e. *Have a* + adjective + noun, which we use when we are saying goodbye or finishing a conversation. Here are three, which you could teach your students as fixed phrases:
Have a good journey! (e.g. when someone is about to start on a sizeable journey)
Have a good / lovely weekend! (e.g. when you say goodbye on a Friday afternoon)
Have a great holiday! (e.g. when someone is about to go on holiday)

exercise 2
things that went wrong:
the taxi to the airport didn't turn up
the pilot was sick and they had to wait two hours
the bus to the hotel broke down
there was a fire alarm at the airport (two-hour delay waiting for the bus)
a taxi drove into the back of their bus
John fell over and broke his shoulder
somebody smashed their car window
thieves stole everything from their home

exercise 5
arrive: Can you get here by 7.00p.m.? I got to work half an hour late.
receive: I didn't get the information until today. Did you get my e-mail?

exercise 6
1 arrive: they got there just in time (line 11); got to the hotel (line 23);
  receive: got a phone call (line 29).
2 got married (line 2); get on a plane / bus (lines 12 and 17)

ideas plus predicting content
This is a good example of a headline and accompanying photo which provide a number of clues about the content of the article. Elicit as much as you can from the class and point out the value of doing this in future when a text is accompanied by pictures: it can help them predict the content.
Predicting content can lighten the reading load for students: as some of the ideas, lexis and structures will have already come up in the predictive phase, they should be less distracted and freer to read more fluently.

exercise 1
1e 2b 3a 4f 5c 6g 7d

exercise 2
1 was leaving (c), were waiting (f) 2 was / were + *-ing* 3 past simple
4 'Leaving the car park' is longer; 'the accident' is the main action; we use the past continuous for the longer event, and the past simple for the main action.

exercise 3
1 I hit my head when I was washing the car.
2 Chris got here when I was having lunch.
3 I was sitting in the garden when my sister arrived.
4 The car broke down when I was driving to work.
5 It started raining when I was waiting for the bus.
6 I was working in the garden when I heard a noise.

exercise 5 possible answers
1 ... I was having a shower.   4 ... I was shopping.
2 ... I dropped my money.   5 ... they saw the accident.
3 ... I was playing football.   6 ... she was watching TV.

language point past continuous
We use the past continuous to describe something in progress at a particular past time, and it is often used with the past simple – the past simple referring to an action or event which happens while the past continuous action is in progress (often referred to as the 'interrupted' past continuous), e.g. *I was having lunch when the phone rang*. Almost all the examples in this lesson are of this type.
We also commonly use the past continuous to give more background information e.g. *When I got up, the sun was shining; When I left the building, crowds of people were running down the street*. In these cases, the past simple events clearly don't interrupt the actions in progress; they happen alongside the events in progress.

ideas plus introducing a competitive element
When pairs act out their sentences, you could award the watching pair one point for correctly guessing what happened and one point for saying it correctly and the same for guessing what they were doing, i.e. 4 points in total for each sentence.
A likely scenario here is that if a pair is unable to identify an action, they will blame the other pair for being very bad at miming. This will probably lead to some good-natured argument and you may be called upon to judge whether the fault is with the mime or not. But it should be good fun if your class get on well.

seven

extended speaking stop thief!

60–75 mins

talk about picnics and tell the beginning of the story

use natural English phrases to ask how to say things

prepare the story with a partner and decide the ending

tell the story to a new partner

listen to an English speaker telling the story

- It is important at the beginning of this activity to let learners read the left-hand column, or tell them what they are going to do in the lesson or put it on the board. This will enable them to get the whole picture. You should also give them time to look back at the **don't forget!** boxes which appear at the end of each section in the unit.

collect ideas

- During the trialling of this activity we found, rather to our surprise, that learners had quite a lot to say about picnics: it seemed to be a particularly common activity in Japan where people often go on picnics in large numbers in the spring to enjoy the cherry blossom on the trees, and was also popular with Chinese students. It may or may not prompt much discussion in the culture where you teach.
- After discussing **exercises 1** and **2**, students can look at the pictures and start constructing their narrative in **exercise 3**. The feedback stage in **exercise 4** is vital: it gives you an opportunity to check that learners have got the idea and that they understand the degree of detail they need to provide. You could ask pairs to shout out their beginnings and write some of the best examples on the board.
- The questions in the **natural English** box in **exercise 5** are a reminder for learners who want to ask you about any items of vocabulary in the story. Almost everything they need has been taught in the unit, except *brick* which is in the **natural English** box; but they may have forgotten items taught earlier such as *bite, smash,* or *bark*.

invent the story

- A very useful strategy in storytelling is the use of direct speech to make it more dramatic. You could tell learners this before they do **exercise 6** and give them examples:

  I came in the room and said to Giles, 'What are you doing here?'. He said, 'Nothing. Go away'.

  There are one or two places in the narrative where students can use direct speech to good effect.
- In order to construct a clear, coherent story which they can tell fluently, learners need to be prepared to practise the story at least two or three times. It is not enough for them to talk through it once and imagine they will be able to tell it clearly, accurately, and confidently. Make that very clear to them. We found in trialling that each time students went through the narrative, they recalled the events more fluently and were able to improve on their last effort – particularly if they had also had help from the teacher in the meantime. If you want to see how learners improved in the trialling of this activity, follow up this reference:

Want to know more? Go to **how to** ... use learners as a resource (task repetition) p.172.

- When the pairs decide on their ending in **exercise 7**, monitor carefully and be available to help with vocabulary items they may need, e.g. in trialling, several pairs wanted the word *arrest*.

tell the story

- Before **exercise 8**, it is a good idea for the pairs to have one complete rehearsal of telling their story. When they are ready, put them in new pairs and monitor carefully. At the end, give feedback on their performance and ask them how they felt about it. For example, did they feel they were able to tell the whole story clearly and without hesitation? If so, were they pleased with their performance?

listen

- Although the story is being told by a native speaker at normal speed, learners should be able to follow it quite easily as it is so familiar.

exercise 9
The boys ran away, but they didn't steal anything. Tom caught one of them because he fell over. The police arrived and they arrested the boy he'd caught and they caught the other boy the next day.

writing

- Use the **writing** as suggested, or see **ideas plus** on the right.

> **ideas plus** students recording themselves
>
> As this is essentially a spoken narrative, you could suggest to your students that they try this experiment for which they will need a tape recorder. First of all, they record themselves telling their story. They can then play it back and record it again if they are not happy with their first effort. When they are satisfied with what they have done, they transcribe their spoken narrative and, if necessary, correct any errors in their spoken effort. This is a time-consuming activity, but we have found that some learners find it very rewarding and learn a great deal from it.

test yourself!

> **Want to know more?** Go to the **introduction** *p.9* for ways of using the **test yourself!**

1. stole, bit, threw, caught, fell, hurt, went
2. go: sightseeing, shopping, swimming, skiing
   go for a: walk, run, meal in a restaurant, picnic
3. off, down, down, up

1. have
2. got
3. after
4. called

1. When I looked outside, it **was raining**.
2. He **arrived** at my house when I was having lunch.
3. How **do** you say 'zimmer' in English?
4. Shall we go **to** a night club this evening?

stories

seven review student's book *p.82*   45 mins

> **Want to know more** about how to use the **reviews**? Go to the **introduction** *p.10*.

vocabulary phrasal verbs

- If you use each phrase once only, there are really only six logical sentences in this activity, so students should arrive at the same answers.

> **exercise 1**
> The plane takes off at six o'clock tomorrow; The car broke down on the motorway; Please lie down on the sofa; The thieves ran away with the money; The boss didn't turn up for the meeting; The child stood up to ask a question.

grammar past continuous

- For **exercise 1**, if you prefer to provide some oral practice first, put students in pairs and give them two minutes to describe everything they can see (they will do this in the present simple or present continuous). Doing this will make the memory task in **exercise 2** easier, though.

> **exercise 2**
> 1 Yes, the waitress and the man standing behind the bar.
> 2 One man was wearing a red shirt, a cap and jeans, the other man was wearing a T-shirt and jeans.
> 3 No.
> 4 She was sitting and talking to her husband.
> 5 Three: a boy and girl were playing with a ball, and a woman was running.
> 6 Nando's.
> 7 Yes, a man was reading a newspaper. Someone was working behind the bar.
> 8 It was lying down, beside the table.

vocabulary past simple

- This type of maze is fun to do, and you can make your own to revise different things. e.g. a 'chain' of uncountable nouns, or verbs followed by *-ing* form or infinitive, or topic vocabulary. Show them how to move from one square to another in different directions before they begin. Do the irregular verb chain first in **exercise 1** and check the answers.
- The second chain in **exercise 2** will need a little demonstration: highlight the pronunciation of the past form of wait (waited /waɪtɪd/, and then set them off to find the rest of the chain. At the end, ask them why these verbs are pronounced /ɪd/ in the past simple form (the verbs end in /d/ or /t/ or a vowel sound).

> **exercise 1**
> irregular verbs: bite (bit), hurt (hurt), break (broke), catch (caught), fall (fell), steal (stole), hit (hit), go (went)
>
> **exercise 2**
> /ɪd/ endings: wait, need, carry, want, decide, start, shout, post, paint, rest

natural English

- During the feedback on **exercise 1**, ask students to explain any differences in meaning between the a / b sentences.

> **exercise 2**
> see **natural English** boxes in **unit seven** for answers

go to wordlist *p.136*

73

eight

in unit eight ...

life with
Agrippine
p.74

reading free time
p.74

wordbooster
p.76

listening how to
... make
arrangements
p.78

extended speaking
plan a night out
p.80

test yourself!
p.81

review
p.81

wordlist
p.137

life with Agrippine

30 mins

reading for fun
natural English suggestions

holidays

Want to know more about using **life with Agrippine?** Go to the **introduction** *p.7*.

- The present continuous for future arrangements is used several times in this cartoon, e.g. ... *is anyone coming to dinner this evening?* If students haven't come across this before, don't worry; it shouldn't cause problems of understanding and is dealt with thoroughly in the **how to** ... lesson on *p.78*.
- The main issue with the **natural English** language here is the diversity of verb form, i.e. *could* + verb, and *what / how about* + *-ing* form and **exercises 4** and **5** aim to highlight this. Notice too that there are several responses which are rather indirect ways of refusing a suggestion: both *Hmm, maybe,* and *I don't like (burgers) very much* are less confrontational in English than *No, I don't want to*.
- You could turn **exercise 8** into a game: students keep making suggestions until they run out of ideas. As a follow-up, see **ideas plus** on the right.

reading free time

90+ mins

talk about hobbies in their countries using **natural English** phrases

read a text about free time in either Ecuador or Hong Kong, and **talk** to a partner about it

focus on be *going to*, *might*, *would like to*

listen to people talking about plans

talk about your own plans for this week / weekend

lead-in

- Start off **exercise 1** by asking students to look at the pictures on *pp.74* and *75* for ideas, and elicit one activity popular with younger people and one with older people. Set a time limit of two minutes to encourage students to work quickly, and let them use dictionaries, or feed in vocabulary yourself. For more information about the **natural English** box, see the **language point** on the right.
- In **exercise 3**, don't worry if learners only use the **natural English** phrases once or twice; that would be entirely natural. After **exercise 4**, you could ask learners to write their top five on the board to compare with other groups.
- There is a note to go to the **language reference** and **practice exercises** *p.165* after **exercise 4**. This is an important use of the zero article, which is a problem for many nationalities. The use of the zero article in time expressions comes up again in the **wordbooster** on *p.77*. For more activities and actions, see **workbook**, **expand your vocabulary** expressions with *have p.41*.

read on

- The listening activity in **lead-in** should have prepared students for the reading texts. For **exercise 1**, divide the class in half: As and Bs to read different texts. If you divide them down the middle, A students will be able to answer the questions in **exercise 3** with another A sitting near them, as will B students. If your learners are from Ecuador or Hong Kong, give them the choice. See the **culture point** on the right for similar information on free time in the UK.
- **Exercise 2** gives students a chance to check new words, but if there aren't many, pass on to **exercise 3**. (Please refer back to **unit seven**, **exercise 3** *p.00* for guidance on deducing meaning from context.) Try to check the answers to this exercise with pairs as you monitor the class.
- **Exercise 4** gives them the opportunity to activate the details they picked out in **exercise 3**, and express their opinions. At the end, allow a short time for students to read the text they didn't read in **exercise 1**.
- As a follow-up, focus on one of the texts, highlighting the way it is organized, and picking out useful phrases. Students then write about their own country.

free time

exercise 4
go to **listening booklet**, *p.25*

exercise 5
could + verb
how about / what about + *-ing*

exercise 7
... we could go shopping.
... how about going abroad this summer?
You could go and stay with a Spanish family ...

ideas plus acting out a dialogue

Students will be very familiar with the cartoon by the end of this cycle, and this particular cartoon lends itself well to acting out in pairs, as Agrippine and her mother speak roughly the same amount. You could start by replaying the recording and letting students repeat some of it, copying the intonation. Then they work in pairs, reading the dialogue. Encourage them to take on the roles, i.e. sensible, reasonable mother and difficult teenage daughter. If there are males in the class, they could be father or son. Pairs could act for each other, or choose one or two pairs to act it for the class.

---

exercise 2
go to **listening booklet**, *p.25*

language point *it's popular / common*

These vocabulary items in the **natural English** box are a source of error for many learners and are sometimes false friends.

popular means something that a lot of people like: a popular hobby, place, person.

common means that something happens frequently, e.g. a common problem or illness, or exists in quantity, e.g. *Smith is a common name*.

Learners often use the words *typical, usual,* or *normal* in place of *popular / common*.

typical means someone or something which is close to what most people imagine they are like, e.g. a typical restaurant (if different people describe a typical restaurant, they tend to say similar things).

normal means 'what you would expect', e.g. a normal day is one where nothing unusual happens.

---

exercise 1
The Ecuador text mentions family parties, volleyball, jogging, window shopping, dancing, going to the cinema
The Hong Kong text mentions window shopping, going to the cinema, dancing, going to restaurants, going to the beach, basketball.

exercise 3
Ecuador text:
1 family celebrations
2 football and volleyball
3 people can't afford to buy things
4 American and Latin American films
5 walking in the parks, jogging, cycling
6 football and volleyball

Hong Kong text:
1 shopping
2 basketball, also tennis and swimming
3 women go to the boutiques, and men to the computer centres
4 Jackie Chan films
5 shopping
6 horseracing

culture note free time in the UK

In winter, football and rugby are the most popular team sports, while in summer it is cricket. Swimming in heated swimming pools is popular as the sea is cold even in summer. Tennis (either watching or playing) is quite popular with both men and women these days, as is going to the gym. Older people enjoy golf and bowls. Many people spend time working on their homes (DIY) and gardens. TV is very popular and a common topic of conversation: in recent years, reality TV shows have become very successful. Younger people go to clubs and bars at the weekend, but for many, going out to restaurants is extremely popular, as you can try food of almost every cuisine in the world.

eight

grammar *be going to, might, would like to*

- Wordpools (i.e. the activity in **exercise 1**) are a very useful device in the classroom. You can use them very effectively as a way of introducing different grammar points, usually where at least some of the language point is familiar, e.g. conditional sentences. For **exercise 1**, tell learners they need to include all the words in the wordpool in their sentences. (You can, if you prefer, photocopy the words, and cut them up – enough sets for students to rearrange them in pairs or small groups.) Monitor while they are writing, and if necessary, give them the first couple of words of a sentence to start them off.

- After **exercise 2**, you could write three of their sentences on the board. You might find it useful at some point to focus on the forms, e.g. *would like to* + verb. **Exercises 3** and **4** both check the concept of these different forms.

- **Exercise 5** is a pair work substitution drill; you may have already done this exercise type in **unit three, exercise 6** *p.27*. Start the drill off with one student, saying the prompt words yourself and getting the other student to say the changed sentences. Don't go on too far, or you will give them too many of the answers. Monitor to make sure they are doing the drill accurately. **Exercise 6** checks whether they have completed the drill correctly. Notice there is more practice of these forms in the **language reference** and **practice exercises** on *p.165*.

Want to know more? Go to ... **how to** ... practise grammar (substitution drills) *p.156*

- **Exercises 7** and **8** provide some contextualized listening practice of the grammar point, and referring back to the completed table for **exercise 9** will provide learners with prompts to generate examples of the forms taught. If you like, ask students to write the sentences down, and you can monitor and correct their written work.

- The **natural English** box in **exercise 10** helps students to sound more natural in **speaking it's your turn!** by discouraging the use of *go* after *going to*. It's worth spending a few minutes raising awareness of this as students often confuse 'intention' for 'arrangement' in this instance.

speaking it's your turn!

- This is a chance for students to personalize the language, and you will need to decide whether they talk about the coming week or weekend (or both). See the **troubleshooting** box on the right.

- As usual, it is wise to demonstrate communication activities. Prepare some sentences about your own plans, then demonstrate with a student using the questions in **exercise 2** and your plans. Students will probably have to communicate with a lot of people before they find two people with similar plans. Monitor as they write down their ideas and help with vocabulary where necessary. Make sure they are using the structures taught.

wordbooster

20–30 mins

> This **wordbooster** is best done at this point in the unit as the time phrases are useful for the language points in the following lesson.

time phrases

- Show students what to do in **exercise 1** with the first example and point out that 'today' is Thursday 7th in the diary, then they can work alone. See the **language point** on the right. If students work in pairs for **exercise 2**, you will need to monitor carefully and correct pronunciation errors. You may prefer to do class feedback so that you can check answers and pronunciation of the phrases.

- **Exercise 3** is a further check on these phrases, especially the difference between *this* (week) and *next* (week). In the **test your partner** activity, students will be getting some useful practice of dates (i.e. *Wednesday the 6th*, NOT *Wednesday 6*) as well as pronunciation, in particular the /θ/ sound. You may still find at this level that some learners are mispronouncing days of the week, especially vowels, e.g. /ˈmʌndaɪ/, /ˈwensdaɪ/.

- The **natural English** box in **exercise 4** highlights a common collocation: *all* + time expression. In **exercise 5**, check that students are not saying *all the day / week*, etc. **Exercises 6** and **7** provide some communicative practice using this language. You could set the **language reference** and **practice exercises** on *p.166* for homework.

Want to know more? Go to ... **Natural Grammar**, Scott Thornbury OUP 2004 *pp.4* and *5*

free time

exercise 1

I'd like to	see a film	next week
I'm going to	have my hair cut	this evening
I might	stay in	at the weekend

exercise 3
1 c   2 a   3 b

exercise 4
1 I'd like to   3 I might   5 I'm going to
2 I'm going to   4 I might

exercise 6
Last sentence: We might see a film next week.

exercise 7
T: meet friends, go shopping, have her hair cut, rent a video, go away for the day
L: meet friends, go to the park, go shopping, go swimming, invite friends for lunch, stay in

exercise 8
<u>meet friends</u>: T / going to / Friday evening; L / might / Sunday evening
<u>go to the park</u>: L / would like to / Sunday morning
<u>go shopping</u>: T / would like to / Saturday morning; L / going to / Saturday morning
<u>have her hair cut</u>: T / might / Saturday morning
<u>rent a video</u>: T / might / Saturday evening
<u>go swimming</u>: L / might / Sunday morning
<u>go away for the day</u>: T / would like to / Sunday
<u>invite friends for lunch</u>: L / going to / Saturday
<u>stay in</u>: L / would like to / Saturday evening

---

troubleshooting class management

Once students have made a note of their plans in **exercise 1**, make sure that they don't show their papers to other learners in the mingling activity in **exercise 2**, otherwise very little will be said. This way you will create an information exchange, and their notes will be useful for two reasons: to focus their thoughts, and to enable them to memorize what they wrote so that they won't be too reliant on the written word. This activity is useful for you to check with individuals whether they are using the forms correctly and appropriately.

---

exercise 1
1 three days ago
2 the day before yesterday
3 last night
4 tonight
5 all tomorrow afternoon
6 tomorrow evening
7 the day after tomorrow
8 this Sunday
9 next Monday
10 all day Tuesday
11 in ten days' time

exercise 3
1 4th – 10th   4 18 – 24th
2 9th – 10th   5 16th – 17th
3 11th – 17th   6 9th

language point time phrases

Here are some typical problems students have with the time phrases in **exercise 1**:
- use of the definite article in place of zero article, e.g. *I'm going away* ~~the~~ *next Monday.* (Although occasionally the article is required if more than one Monday is mentioned.)
- *I'm going out* ~~this night~~ instead of *tonight*
- *I saw him* ~~last evening~~ instead of *last night*; and *yesterday* ~~night~~ instead of *yesterday evening*
- *I'm leaving* ~~after ten days~~ instead of *in ten days' (time)*
- the form *the day / week after tomorrow* and *the day / week before last* are likely to be new for learners.
- confusion between *ago* and *before*: *I met her two weeks ago* vs. *I met her two weeks before,* i.e. before a previously mentioned past time, e.g. *two weeks before the wedding*

You might like to consider contrasting these forms with the students' L1, particularly in monolingual situations: they might find it useful to keep a record of the translations and possible errors.

eight

listening how to ... make arrangements

75–90 mins

talk about arrangements using new **vocabulary**

invite people, and **accept or refuse** invitations using **natural English** phrases

listen to phone conversations about invitations and arrangements

practise making arrangements using **natural English** phrases

focus on the present continuous for future

role play invitations and arrangements

write an e-mail inviting someone

vocabulary verb + noun collocation

- Learners will probably be able to complete most of the words if they work together in **exercise 1**, but they will also need you to draw attention to the collocations. See **language point** on the right.
- In **exercise 3**, students get the opportunity to personalize the language they have learnt. It's important they don't treat it as a drill: encourage them to turn each sentence into a mini-discussion – you can demonstrate with a student in front of the class beforehand. Monitor the group work and give feedback on language, then ask learners to report on anything interesting or amusing from their discussion.

inviting

- Students sometimes make invitations using the verb *invite* (e.g. *I invite you to*...). Point out this is not natural in English, and listen out for this error elsewhere in the unit.
- For another way to exploit **exercise 3**, see **ideas plus** on the right.

listen to this

- In tapescript **8.7**, the present continuous for future is previewed but, as in the **Agrippine** cartoon at the beginning of this unit, learners should understand the concept because the context and time references indicate that it is about the future. **Exercise 1** focuses on useful greetings language. See also the **listening booklet**, *p.27* for activity on the speakers' tone.
- If students can predict suitable ideas in **exercises 2** and **4**, they will listen with more interest to see if they were right. You can do these as a class or in pairs and write their suggestions on the board.
- The language in the **natural English** box includes high-frequency examples of *shall*: most learners only need to use *shall* for suggestions and arrangements. Focus on the weak form /ʃəl/ and provide practice.

grammar present continuous for future

- **Exercise 2** can be done as a whole class. You might like to refer students back to the **Agrippine** cartoon on *p.73* and ask them to find examples where the present continuous is used to talk about future arrangements. For more information, go to the **language point** on the right.
- **Exercise 4** is a simple controlled practice drill; in **exercise 5**, the present continuous is contextualized and the function used is in 'excuses', which is quite a common use of the present continuous in English. This exercise also revises invitations and polite refusals from the **natural English** box on *p.78*. Practise the first few dialogues as a whole class before pair work. See also the **language reference** and **practice exercises** *p.166*.

speaking it's your turn!

- Discourage the use of the verbs in the prompts in their dialogue in the flow chart, e.g. *invite*: *I invite you to ...*; *accept*: *I accept* as this will sound unnatural. For a more controlled activity, see **troubleshooting** on the right.
- At the end, you could ask learners to act out their conversation for the class or another pair. The writing in **exercise 3** can be done in class or for homework. As an extension (or possibly after the writing stage), see **workbook**, **expand your grammar** present simple for events on a timetable *p.43*.

writing

- The e-mail brings together much of the language taught in the lesson and provides a model for students' own writing. For **exercise 2**, put students in pairs. Then tell each pair which other pair they are writing to, so that when they have finished, pairs can easily swap e-mails. If you have used computers as suggested in the **ideas plus**, this activity will seem more realistic. Monitor and help where necessary.

Want to know more? Go to **how to ...** motivate learners to write *p.160*

free time

exercise 1
1 accept invitations
2 make an appointment
3 make arrangements
4 invite friends
5 refuse an invitation
6 book a table
7 make a booking
8 make plans

language point collocations

The main problem here is with the collocations. In some cases, students may not know which prepositions to use, e.g. *make arrangements **for** sth, accept an invitation **to** sth*, and in others they may not be the most obvious way learners express the concepts, e.g. *make plans for sth NOT do a plan*. Make sure they make a note of these collocations in their notebooks.

ideas plus invitations

You can turn this activity into a game and at the same time revise *be going to* and *have to*. Learners can extend the conversation and give an excuse each time, e.g. *I'd love to, but I can't – **I'm going to** my sister's / **I have to** stay at home and work*. Tell students to keep doing the dialogues, changing the invitations and excuses each time – at least six each – and see how long they can carry on.

exercise 1
Hello Nadia; It's Jon; I'm fine, how about you? It was really nice to see you.

exercise 3
1 Jon
2 Nadia
3 Jon and Nadia
4 go to the cinema
5 outside the cinema at 8.30

exercise 4
Nadia rings her old boyfriend, Monty, to tell him she can't go out with him on Thursday. She says she has to work, but in fact she's going out with Jon (as found out in recording **8.7**).

exercise 1
'm having dinner   'm seeing

exercise 2
1 the future
2 yes
3 present continuous
4 be (am / is / are) + -ing
5 yes, because there is a definite time for each

exercises 3 and 4
2 She's going shopping with her friend tomorrow afternoon.
3 He's going to a meeting next Tuesday.
4 He's playing tennis this afternoon.
5 She's having dinner with friends this evening.
6 He's having a drink with his girlfriend tonight.

language point present continuous for future

When we talk about ways of expressing the future, it is very easy to get involved in minute differences which only confuse and frustrate students. The present continuous for future and *be going to* are quite often used interchangeably; as are *will* and *be going to* in the context of general prediction. The differences between future forms need to be addressed, but at this stage, don't be too concerned if students don't see the finer detail: like many aspects of language, understanding develops gradually over a long period.

troubleshooting dialogue building

If your class needs more support start by doing this as a dialogue building activity with the whole class: i.e. elicit what A and B would say in the first exchange, practise it, then elicit the second two exchanges, practise them, and so on. Or, write the dialogue on the board, then erase a word / chunk from each line, and ask students to practise in pairs. Then rub out a bit more, and they practise again, etc. until they can do it with no prompts at all.

exercise 1
1e 2i 3b 4d 5h 6a 7g 8f 9c

ideas plus using computers

For **exercise 1**, if your class has access to computers in your teaching situation, you could copy the e-mail onto their terminals and they can re-arrange the dialogue. A low-tech suggestion is to photocopy it and cut it up for pairs to re-arrange.

79

eight

extended speaking plan a night out   60–75 mins

talk about your last evening out

discuss what to do on a group night out

plan the night out in detail

tell a partner about your group's plans

- It is important at the beginning of this activity to let learners read the left-hand column or tell them what they are going to do in the lesson, or put it on the board. This will enable them to get the whole picture. You should also give them time to look back at the **don't forget!** boxes which occur at the end of each section in the unit.

collect ideas

- This **extended speaking** activity will work best if students are genuinely motivated: see **ideas plus** on the right.
- **Exercises 1** and **2** provide a way in to the topic, and give students some personalized speaking practice. Keep this fairly light and brief but elicit some ideas in feedback as they might be useful for the rest of the lesson.
- When you are going through the instructions for **exercise 3**, you might want to feed in one or two suggestions for local activities to set them thinking. (Bear in mind if you do this that students will have to make adjustments to some of the questions in **exercise 5**).
- At this point, you have a choice in class management terms: you can either put students into groups according to how they are sitting, or you could ask for a show of hands: who wants to go to a bar / restaurant, etc. who prefers the barbecue, who has another idea. At this point, students with your assistance can re-arrange themselves in groups according to the activity they prefer. Allow time for this stage; if the groups are well formed, it will add to the chances of success of the activity. Try to keep groups to a maximum of four or five: anything larger will mean that some students won't contribute and it may well be harder for them to reach agreement.

Want to know more? Go to **how to** … do pair and group work *p.146*

plan a night out

- Once students are seated in their relevant groups, you may want to appoint a leader for each group (or ask for volunteers). They must keep this stage focused, move the planning along, and they should also try to make sure that everyone in their small group gets a chance to contribute and express their opinion. You will probably need to tell the leaders this beforehand.
- For **exercise 5**, allow students a few moments to read through the questions by themselves and think of what they are going to say. For this exercise, suggest that they don't write until they have finished speaking. Allow plenty of time for this stage: it is the main part of the lesson, and should generate plenty of talk. Monitor throughout **exercise 5**. You may need to help with ideas, or encourage students to plan in more detail, but you also need to be collecting examples of good language use and learner errors for feedback at the end.
- For **exercise 6**, encourage all the students to make notes: the groups can go over their finalized plans, with everyone writing notes as they go. Students might need their notes when they talk to other students in **exercise 7**.

talk about your plans

- Notice that in **exercise 7**, it is natural to use the present continuous for future arrangements; equally, learners can use *be going to*. Monitor to see how well they use the language and express their ideas.
- When they have exchanged opinions on the other groups' ideas in **exercise 8**, you could have a class vote: which is the best evening out?
- At the end, provide feedback on their language use: write some examples of good language and errors on the board, which learners have to correct where necessary. Be sure to praise groups for achieving their communicative goals.

free time

eight review student's book p.83   45 mins

Want to know more about how to use **reviews**? Go to the **introduction** p.10.

grammar present continuous for future

- You may need to check that students understand *everybody*, *somebody*, and *nobody* before you begin. (See **workbook**, **expand your grammar** p.48). You could also put some sentences on the board about your class, e.g. *Everybody in this class* has got a course book; *somebody in this class* is wearing a blue jacket; *nobody in the class* has blonde hair, etc. Students have to say if they are true or false. (*Everybody* = all the people in the class; remember it takes a singular verb; *somebody* = one person in the class and *nobody* = no people).

- Before students work in groups, do a couple of examples from the questionnaire in front of the class. Divide them into groups of three or four for the activity, and monitor while they are doing it. At the end, each group could tell the class two or three true sentences.

natural English

- After you have established the pairs, point out that these situations represent an ongoing conversation. It is a good idea if the students read the whole flow chart to get a sense of the conversation before working through the individual stages.

- You could ask the students to memorize their conversations and act them out at the end for other groups.

> A Would you like to come / go for a drink this evening? or Do you want to ...?
> B I'd love to, but I can't. I have to ...
> A Would you like to come / go for a drink tomorrow? or Do you want to ...? or How about tomorrow? (to avoid repetition)
> B Yes, (great). I'd love to.
> A We could go to the Piano Bar. or How / What about going to the Piano Bar?
> B Yes, good idea / lovely.
> A When shall we meet?
> B Why don't we meet at 7.00? / How about 7.00?
> A Yes, fine.

grammar be going to, might, would like to

- This activity revises the grammar point, but also provides personalized practice and encourages learners to think and talk about their use of English outside the classroom. This might be a very good opportunity to have an open-class discussion about things they can do in English in the learning environment. For example, as they approach intermediate level, they may feel more confident about watching films in English (with subtitles), and to make use of the Internet in particular, where they can work on areas of interest and at their own pace.

- Encourage students to think carefully about their answers to **exercises 1** and **2**, perhaps even setting it for homework; you could then do the discussion in **exercise 3** in the following lesson. Illustrate what to do in **exercise 3** by demonstrating a couple of questions with a student in front of the class. Let the activity develop into a real communication task, and monitor / provide feedback on the content and their language use at the end.

go to wordlist p.137

---

ideas plus motivating learners

The most effective way to really make this activity come to life is to make it genuine, i.e. the students really do plan an evening out together, and the class (or as many as possible) then go out, possibly with you. If there is a type of social activity or venue in your teaching situation which is relevant and not suggested in the **student's book**, you could suggest it yourself.

Another way to motivate students is to bring in some authentic materials: leaflets or advertisements of restaurants, clubs, events, etc. or a listings magazine. In English-speaking countries this is not difficult to find and in non-English speaking countries, there are often tourist leaflets in English or even a local news sheet obtainable from tourist information offices, or listings in ex-pat magazines. You could use these first with some authentic reading tasks, so that students will be familiar with them.

test yourself!

Want to know more? Go to the **introduction** p.9 for ways of using the **test yourself!**

1 last week, month, year; this morning, afternoon, evening, week, month, year; next week, month, year; the day after tomorrow; in ten days' time; the week after next; all day Tuesday
2 make; accept / refuse; make; book; make; make
3 How about ... ? We could ... Why don't we ... ?

1 shall; don't
2 having
3 might
4 going

1 What **are** you **doing** this evening?
2 I was in town all ~~the~~ day yesterday.
3 A How about go**ing** for a walk?
   B **I'd** love to, but I'm a bit busy.
4 What **would** you like to do this evening?

81

nine

in unit nine ...

listening life changes
p.82

wordbooster
p.84

reading how to ... give opinions
p.86

extended speaking from home to home
p.88

test yourself!
p.89

review
p.89

wordlist
p.138

listening life changes

talk about changes in your life using **natural English** language

focus on the present perfect with *for* and *since*

listen to people talking about changes in their lives

focus on the use of *long* in questions

discuss attitudes to change

90+ mins

lead-in

- For an alternative start to the lesson, see **ideas plus** on the right.
- Before asking learners to talk about changes in their lives in **exercise 1**, you could give an example from your own life; this will provide very motivating listening practice as students are usually curious about their teacher and this helps to develop their relationship with you.
- The grammar focus of the unit is the use of the present perfect with *for* and *since* for unfinished activities / states. The **natural English** box in **exercise 3** presents the use of *still*, which occurs frequently in this context of describing things that continue from the past into the present. Some learners find it very difficult to use *still* productively, so the practice in **exercises 5** and **6** may be essential. Make it clear that the prompts in **exercise 5** are there to give them ideas, but that they should put down anything which is true for them.

grammar present perfect with *for* and *since*

- This use of the present perfect is difficult for many learners. See the **language point** on the right.
- As the learners are already familiar with the form of the present perfect, having studied it in **unit three**, the focus here is on the new concept, i.e. present perfect for unfinished past. There is quite a long sequence of activities, but we suggest that you work through all of them carefully if this is a difficult concept for your learners. We have also suggested that learners work in pairs on a number of the activities: this gives you a chance to move round and monitor the learners on a more individual basis, and assess for yourself which students might be having problems.
- The use of *still* in **exercise 3** is partly for useful recycling of the language taught in the **natural English** box on *p.84*; but it may help to reinforce the concept that learners need to grasp here, i.e. of something from the past that has not changed and continues to be true into the present.
- For **exercise 4** if necessary, clarify the meaning of *how long* (= how much time). When students have completed it, you could check the answers by asking one student to read out a question and another to read out the correct answer. Make sure they are producing the question forms accurately as some learners easily slip into these errors: highlight and practise the weak forms /əv/ and /əz/ in the question forms, i.e. *How long have /əv/ they had Bobbi? How long has /əz/ Natalia know Roberto?* Then consolidate the rules in **exercise 5**.
- You can use the time line from **exercise 2** to reinforce the meaning of *for* and *since* in **exercise 6**, or draw a similar time line on the board. Students don't usually find it difficult to understand *for* vs. *since* but they need practice, as they often make mistakes.
- Monitor **exercises 7** and **8** carefully to make sure students are producing correct sentences. Then demonstrate **exercise 9** yourself with a strong student (get them to ask you some questions), so that you can show them that they don't need to repeat the whole of the present perfect form in their answers; it would, in fact, sound unnatural to do so.

changes

exercise 3
go to **listening booklet** *p.28*

ideas plus changing the classroom

As the focus of the unit is 'change', this game is very appropriate. Send half the class out of the room and ask the remaining students to make various changes, e.g. swap places, put something on a wall, move a piece of furniture, etc. Make sure everyone is aware of all the changes. When the rest return to the classroom, give them two minutes to write down all the changes they notice. They can then work with a partner who stayed in the classroom and tell them what they have noticed. They could, in fact, be using the present perfect here, e.g. *Someone has moved the teacher's table, Maria has taken off her shoes*, etc. You will need to highlight this if you want learners to use the present perfect. (It is also possible to use the present / past simple tense, e.g. *The table is near the door now; it was in front of the board before.*)

exercise 2
B They got married.   E Roberto got a job.
C They got a dog.   F They bought a flat.
D They moved to Rome.

exercise 3
| 1 true | 3 true | 5 true |
| 2 false | 4 true | 6 true |

exercise 4
| 1 e | 3 b | 5 d |
| 2 f | 4 c | 6 a |

exercise 5
present perfect
past
present

exercise 6
for three months; since last year; for two years; for a long time; since last July; for six months; since he was a child; since 1995

exercise 7 possible answers
Roberto has known Natalia for four years.
They've been married for three years.
They've had a dog for two years.
They've lived in Rome for six months.
Robert's worked at Gucci for five months.
They've had a flat since last month / for a month.

language point present perfect with *for* and *since*

For many learners, this use of the present perfect (unfinished past) is translated into their own language by the present simple tense, and the concept therefore may be difficult to grasp. It is particularly difficult in the negative form i.e. the idea that something has continued not to happen or 'negative duration' (e.g. *He hasn't worked at the bank for two years*), so at this level we are concentrating on the positive form and question forms, especially with *how long*.

You will need to clarify the difference between *for* and *since*, which are commonly confused. (e.g. *I am here since three months*). There is further information in the **language reference** and **practice exercises** on *p167*, which you could use in the lesson.

We would suggest putting the timeline from the **student's book** in **exercise 2** on the board. Get everyone's attention focused on this, and add further examples based on your students' own lives as a way to consolidate the meaning,
e.g. *Martha has had a driving licence for nine months.*
   Ahmed has been here since September.
   Carina has known her best friend for ages.

nine

listen to this

- Students should work in pairs after listening in **exercise 1**, to check they agree.
- Monitor the students' answers while they listen to the recording for **exercises 2** and **3**. Don't go on to **exercises 4** and **5** until you are happy they have completed the previous exercises satisfactorily.
- This use of *long* (= a long time) in the **natural English** box in **exercise 6** is a common feature in spoken English but few students are aware of it. After they have practised the questions and replies in **exercise 7**, you could extend the practice by getting learners to think up their own questions using *long* to ask others.

speaking it's your turn!

- This is a free speaking activity to end the lesson. Give the learners several minutes to think about the questions, and also rehearse some of their ideas in their head, before starting the discussion.
- The reason for the final question in **exercise 2** (*Who doesn't like change in your group?*) is to create a purpose or outcome to the discussion, and may lead on to more discussion about the desirability of 'change' in general. This will very much depend on the age and attitudes of your group.

Want to know more? Go to **how to ...** do pair and group work (setting up) *p.150*

wordbooster   30–45 mins

> This **wordbooster** can be used at this point in the unit or just before the **extended speaking** activity.

homes

- This is a potentially confusing lexical area in **exercise 1**, and if learners are using bilingual dictionaries, they may come up with different translations for the various items. See the **language point** on the right.
- **Exercise 2** is listening practice, but more importantly it provides a pronunciation model: students often have problems with the pronunciation of items such as *garage, balcony,* and *toilet*, and general difficulty with word stress on compound nouns e.g. dining room /ˈdaɪnɪŋ ruːm/.
- Students should be familiar with the language in the **natural English** box in **exercise 4**, but many learners at this level need a lot of practice with *have got* before it becomes part of their productive language. The pronunciation of there's /ðeəz/ and they're /ðeə/ can also be problematic. **Exercises 5, 6** and **7** practise all of these areas.
- For **exercise 7**, answers will probably depend on the country where you teach: learners might notice the absence of a *utility room* (for laundry), *swimming pool, playroom,* or *cellar* (an area below floor level without windows, usually for storage). You may have to introduce several new items. If you don't think your students will be able to think of many answers here, do the activity with the whole class. For more work on vocabulary connected with homes, see **workbook, expand your vocabulary**, *p.47*.
- Learners will have an opportunity to personalize the vocabulary and talk about their own homes in the **extended speaking** activity at the end of the unit, so please avoid doing it at this point. However, if you would like to follow up the theme and explore some of the cultural issues connected with homes, see the reference below.

Want to know more? Go to **People like us** (Macmillan), unit 3, Home Comforts

adjectives describing homes

- The most interesting item here is probably *ordinary*. This is a very high-frequency lexical item but students rarely use it or even understand it at this level. The main difficulty is that it can have a neutral meaning, i.e. *normal, average, without any unusual features*; but sometimes it has a negative connotation, i.e. *rather boring and lacking in interest*. However, it is an item that learners should be aware of at this level.
- For **exercise 3**, talk through the example and make it clear that they don't have to restrict their comments to the house itself: encourage them to consider the surroundings as well, e.g. the garden, the location. If necessary, give them a couple of minutes to think before putting them in pairs or small groups.
- As a follow-up to the lesson, see **ideas plus** on the right.

changes

exercise 1
1 1 Julia: picture 2
   2 Sonia: picture 3
2 nearly four months; four months

exercise 2
She says sentences 1, 2, and 4

exercise 3
She says sentences 2, 3, and 5

exercise 5
go to **listening booklet** *p.28*

exercise 6
go to **listening booklet** *p.28*

---

exercise 1
1 hall   8 garden
2 toilet   9 landing
3 stairs   10 bedroom
4 living room   11 bathroom
5 dining room   12 balcony
6 kitchen   13 garage
7 patio

exercise 3
the stress is on the first syllable for all the words except for *ground floor* and *first floor* where the main stress is on <u>floor</u>.

exercise 4
go to **listening booklet** *p.28*

exercise 7 possible answers
it hasn't got a games room, a cellar, a swimming pool, a utility room, an attic room, a conservatory

language point overlapping meaning

There are a number of easily confused items here because of cultural differences and overlapping meaning.

In British English, the *hall* is the area inside the front door of a house that leads to other rooms; in American English this is often called a *lobby*. A *landing* only refers to an area at the top of a flight of stairs, that may also lead to other rooms (but not used at ground floor level).

In a public building such as a hotel or hospital, the area leading to other rooms is usually called a *corridor*, but we might still say *entrance hall* or *foyer* for the area immediately inside the front door.

Living room is one option here for the main family room, but British speakers also use *sitting room, lounge,* and *drawing room* (more formal).

A *balcony* is an outside area usually at an upper-floor level (coming out from the wall of the building). If it is a very large area, or it is at ground level, the same area is usually called a *terrace*. A *patio* is also at ground level, but usually refers to a flat area at the back of the house where people can sit; it is not normally enclosed in any way like a *terrace*, which often has a low wall around it.

Garden is British English; in American English it is called a *(back) yard*.

---

exercise 1
clean / dirty
spacious / small
ugly / beautiful
light / dark
modern / traditional
unusual / ordinary
tidy / untidy

ideas plus house websites

If your class has access to the Internet, you could direct them to some websites for estate agents, e.g. in the UK, **www.rightmove.co.uk**. Look at it yourself first to see how to navigate the site, and then show students how to use it. Let them work in pairs to find a property to rent or buy in an area of the UK and a price of their choosing. They can then print off the details and tell others about the house and why they chose it. They can also use it as a vocabulary resource. Alternatively, you could devise tasks, e.g. Find a house to rent with two bedrooms and a garden for £500 a month.

Want to know more about using the Internet? Go to the **natural English** website at www.oup.com/elt/naturalenglish and select 'internet lesson plans'.

nine

reading how to ... give opinions

75–90 mins

talk about household chores you did as a child

focus on the use of *should / shouldn't*

read and discuss an article about attitudes to married women in the 1950s

focus on the use of *thing(s)*

talk about what married men should / shouldn't do

lead-in

- You could expand the vocabulary exploitation in the **lead in**. See the **ideas plus** on the right.
- When you go over the answers to **exercise 1**, highlight the difference between *do the washing* (= washing clothes) and *do the washing up* (= washing dishes). You could also point out that you can also say, *make your bed* as well as *make the bed*. For **exercise 2**, you could provide an outcome for this discussion, i.e. Who is the laziest in your group?

grammar *should / shouldn't*

- When you go over the answers to **exercise 1**, you could paraphrase the difference between *should* and *have to*, but we think it is advisable to keep it fairly brief and simple at this stage, e.g. just say *should* is 'in my opinion, it is the best thing to do', but it is not as strong as *have to*. As a quick concept check, ask learners to complete these sentences with *should* or *have to* (or adapt them to your learning context):

    Young men_____ do military service. (answer: *have to*)

    Young people_____ help older people on buses and trains. (answer: *should*)

    In **exercise 3**, point out that they are expressing their opinion here, so there are no 'right' or 'wrong' answers. Monitor the pair work in **exercise 3** carefully to check they are using the target language and also make a note of any interesting opinions. You could then focus on these in a class feedback at the end. For **exercise 4** be prepared to help them with their sentences before they show them to another pair.

- Although this is the end of the section on *should / shouldn't*, learners will actually be getting a lot more exposure and practice of the language in the next part of the lesson.

read on

- You could start **exercise 1** by giving one example yourself, and then eliciting another from one of your students. Then put the class into pairs to think of four more. Before doing **exercise 2**, make sure your students realize the article was written in the 1950s. See the **culture note** on the right.
- **Exercise 2** is a *scanning* exercise, i.e. learners are reading the text for specific information rather than reading every word carefully. This is to encourage fairly quick reading and to discourage getting too concerned with the meaning of individual words. However, you can tell learners they will have an opportunity to focus on new vocabulary later.
- In **exercise 4**, give learners time to complete the task individually, then put them in pairs to compare. Tell them that they have to be able to point to the correct part of the text to justify their answers. You can move round and monitor at this point to assess how well they have understood.
- We have defined some new items in the **glossary**; **exercise 5** is an opportunity to focus on three more items of their choice. You may need to give them some help here. If you want more guidance on the use of dictionaries in class, see the reference below:

Want to know more? Go to **how to ...** use dictionaries with learners, upper intermediate **teacher's book** *p.174*

- **Exercises 6** and **7** give students an opportunity for a personal response to the text. After this, it is worth spending some time on the **natural English** box in **exercise 8**: learners will sound more natural if they can use the word *thing(s)* to refer to objects, facts and actions, and they can also use it in place of many words they may not know. It is one of the highest-frequency nouns in spoken English and should be part of their productive language. Direct them back to the text in **exercise 9** for more examples.

writing

- This final activity continues the theme of the lesson, but reverses it. If your class are predominantly young and single, you could focus on 'boyfriends' rather than 'husbands'. In this case, ask the class to think of four things that boyfriends should / shouldn't do to keep their girlfriends happy. It might be more fun to divide up the sexes so that boys are working together and girls are working together; when they have finished they can compare what they have written and see if they would be willing to follow any of the advice and / or rate each one.

changes

exercise 1
1 do the washing up
2 do the washing
3 make the bed
4 do the cooking
5 tidy up your room
6 clean your shoes

ideas plus phrases with *do*

If you have a strong group you could introduce a few more phrases with *do*, e.g. *do the housework / the cleaning, do my / the ironing, do the shopping*.

A class survey would then be possible: students have to find out who does all these tasks at home, and which student does the most work in their own home. Alternatively, give students some sentence heads to complete, and discuss like this:

The worst job is (doing the ironing) because ...   *I quite like ... because ...*
The easiest job is ... because ...   *I never ... because ...*

exercise 1
a sentences 1 and 3
b sentences 2 and 4
c *should / shouldn't* + verb

exercise 3 suggested answers
5 should
6 shouldn't
7 should
8 should
9 shouldn't
10 shouldn't

ideas plus mumble drills

After you have clarified the meaning, practise the pronunciation in **exercise 2**. You could do this as a mumble drill: in other words, students practise saying the sentences to themselves over and over, and you walk round and listen / correct where necessary. Mumble drills provide a lot of repetitive practice that students can do at their own pace and gives you the opportunity to tune in to individuals. For further practice of *should / shouldn't* + verb, go to **language reference** and **practice exercises**, *p.167*.

exercise 2
<u>Before her husband gets home, a good wife should</u>:
get dinner ready, get ready herself, do all the washing and cleaning, light a fire during the winter, tidy up the children's things and get them ready.

<u>When he gets home, a good wife should</u>:
make sure the children are quiet, greet him with a warm smile, listen to him, make him comfortable, give him a drink, speak in a low, pleasant voice.

<u>She shouldn't</u>:
complain if he comes home late, tell him about her problems, ask him questions about the things he does, or disagree with him.

exercise 4
1 no
2 yes
3 no
4 yes
5 no
6 no

exercise 9
children's things = objects (line 13)
lots of important things = facts (line 19)
the things he does = actions (line 24)

culture note the role of women in marriage

This article is <u>not</u> a joke. It is a simplified version of an authentic text, which appeared in a magazine (largely aimed at women) in the 1950s. At that time, the ideas expressed in the article would have been considered reasonable by a very significant percentage of the population. To most people in Britain now, such views appear funny or ridiculous. For one thing, the majority of married women go out to work; for another, very few people (men included) believe that women should adopt a servile or submissive role in the marriage.

Would the same be true for the culture in which you teach, either in the 1950s, or now in the 21st century?

ideas plus role play

To activate the language in this lesson and you could ask students to role play 'getting it off your chest'. They prepare a role in pairs: either mother and son, or father and daughter, or husband and wife. The pairs prepare grievances, e.g. wives' complaints: *you should ... play with the children, help me with the cleaning*, etc; husbands' complaints: *your cooking is terrible, you're always bad-tempered*, etc. Let them then rehearse their role play, with counter-arguments, e.g. *I haven't got time, it's your job*, etc. When they are ready, they can act it for another pair.

87

nine

extended speaking from home to home

60–75 mins

listen to someone talking about homes they've lived in

prepare an interview with a partner about their past and present homes

interview a new partner

report back to the first partner

discuss attitudes to living at home at different ages

write about your own home

- It is important at the beginning of this activity to let learners read the left-hand column, or tell them what they are going to do in the lesson or put it on the board. This will enable them to get the whole picture. You should also give them time to look back at the **don't forget!** boxes which appear at the end of each section in the unit.

collect ideas

- If some of your students have lived in the same home all their lives, they will have less to talk about than others in the class. See **troubleshooting** on the right.
- **Exercise 1** is designed as a warmer activity, so keep the discussion quite brief. The listening task in **exercise 2** is quite straightforward, so if learners complete it easily, you could see how much of **exercise 3** they can complete from memory. Then play the recording again so they can complete and / or check their answers. Alternatively, see **ideas plus** on the right.

exercise 1 possible answers
a new job; the flat is too noisy; they want to be in a different area; they want to be nearer the children's school.

exercise 2
four

exercise 3
1 the country   2 a house   3 got a new job   4 a flat   5 four years   6 thinks

exercise 4
How many,   What,   Why,   Where,   How long,   How long

prepare an interview

- Monitor the students while they complete **exercise 4**, and then **exercise 5**. You may need to feed in and correct their questions in **exercise 5** before they move on.
- The interview in **exercise 6** is a rehearsal for the students, and for you to see how well they can perform when thinking about language and content. Give feedback at the end of the rehearsal so they can incorporate your suggestions in the next phase, e.g. they may be giving short answers, and not taking the opportunity to speak at length. In this case setting a goal of about ten minutes may help.

interview

- If some interesting stories have emerged, ask the people involved to tell the whole class at the end.

discussion

- The time you devote to this freer discussion in **exercises 9** and **10** will probably depend on the age and circumstances of your learners. You can adapt the statements to make them more relevant for your particular group, e.g. *Students should all go to university in their home town and live at home.* Either way, give learners thinking time before the discussion, and bring it to a close before they start losing momentum.

Want to know more? Go to **how to ...** do pair and group work (winding down) *p.151*

writing

- **Exercise 11** focuses on a difficult aspect of the writing skill: try to do it in class so that learners can work together and compare and you can go over the answers with them. An alternative to **exercise 12** is to get learners to write a short text about their partner. They can then show it to them in the next lesson and the pairs can correct any factual or language mistakes.

exercise 11
Five months ago I came to England to learn English. I'm living in a flat with four other students. The ground floor of the building is a shop, and we live on the first and second floors. The first floor has got three bedrooms, a bathroom, and a kitchen. The second floor only has one bedroom. I'm sharing it with another Chinese student. The flat hasn't got a garden, but it's warm and clean. It's near Westminster College and I can walk or cycle to college. I like it very much.

changes

nine review
student's book p.100 — 45 mins

Want to know more about how to use the **reviews**? Go to the **introduction**, p.10.

vocabulary homes + *there's ...* / *it's got ...*

- Put students in A / B pairs, facing each other, so that they cannot see each other's **student's book**. Start the activity as a class, and ask an A student to describe one thing they can see, e.g. *My house has got a hall and there are some stairs on the left*. Ask the Bs in the class if their picture is the same — you should be able to elicit that B's stairs are on the right. Ask them to take turns to describe their pictures, and find 7 more differences and write them down as they go. You can also highlight *there's ... / it's got ...* before they start.
- Monitor and make a note of errors for feedback at the end when you can bring the class together and ask them to call out the differences.

Student A's house	Student B's house
the hall and stairs are on the left	they're on the right
the kitchen is at the front of the house	it's at the back
has got a patio at the back	it's at the side
hasn't got a tennis court	there's a tennis court on the right
there's a garage on the right	there is no garage
there's a bathroom (with shower)	there's a separate shower room
the bathroom is at the front upstairs	it's at the back
has got two bedrooms	has got three bedrooms
hasn't got a balcony	has got a balcony on the right

grammar present perfect

- By this stage of the course, your students should be able to share knowledge they have about classmates. However, if need be they can invent sentences which may or may not be true. Using the gap fill sentences, elicit one or two examples, before the class begins working in pairs. Monitor and help with language (especially the present perfect). You may wish to draw a time line on the board showing that they are talking about unfinished actions / situations from the past until now.
- If students have only a few sentences, that's fine. Ask pairs to call out their sentences; whoever it is about should then say if it is true or not.

vocabulary adjectives describing homes

- This activity can be done as a homework activity, or if done in class, you could give students a couple of minutes to work alone, then compare with a partner. If you have an overhead projector, you could make a copy of the grid and circle the answers — this would make feedback easier. At the end, practise the pronunciation of the words.

<u>Horizontal</u>: modern, ugly, dark, tidy, ordinary, untidy, light
<u>Vertical</u>: traditional, clean, unusual, cold, warm, small, beautiful

natural English

- This is an exercise type you can easily produce yourself to revise other **natural English** phrases, or for grammar / vocabulary revision (particularly where vocabulary consists of two- or three-word phrases).

See **natural English** boxes in **unit nine** for answers.

go to **wordlist** p.138

---

troubleshooting class management

At the beginning of the activity, ask for a show of hands to find out who has lived in the same home all their lives. Then, as far as possible, pair up those students with someone who has lived in at least two different places; this should ensure that the interview doesn't run out of material very quickly.

If you find that a majority of your learners have not lived in more than one home, then shift the focus of the activity so that they spend more time on talking about their current home, and also more time on the discussion in **exercises 9** and **10**.

ideas plus live listening

You could omit the recording and do it yourself as a 'live' listening, i.e. you tell the class about the different homes you have lived in, what they were like, and why you moved each time. At the end, ask them questions and get them to write down their answers. They can compare with a partner, and if there is anything they haven't understood, you can tell that part of your story again.

test yourself!

Want to know more? Go to the **introduction** p.9 for ways of using the **test yourself!**

1. been, had, known, studied, spent
2. untidy, dirty, small, ugly, dark, ordinary
3. patio, hall, garage, balcony, study, ground floor

1. long
2. since
3. still
4. thing

1. I've **lived** here for six years.
2. You should ~~to~~ look before you cross that busy road.
3. We **still have** a house near the beach.
4. It **has** ('s) got three bedrooms.

89

ten

in unit ten ...

reading
sleepwalking
p.90

wordbooster
p.92

listening how to ... make an appointment
p.94

extended speaking
nightmare!
p.96

test yourself!
p.97

review
p.97

wordlist
p.139

reading sleepwalking

90+ mins

talk about a sleep questionnaire using new vocabulary

read an article about sleepwalking

talk about yourself using *-ed* / *-ing* adjectives and **natural English** focus on *really*

write a dream story using link phrases

vocabulary sleep

- Students will need the vocabulary in **exercise 1** in different stages of this lesson, as well as in the **extended speaking** at the end of the unit. You can teach the items through mime if you prefer. As there are several issues with this vocabulary, see the **language point** on the right.

- In **exercise 2**, students should think through what they want to say in English, and ask you for any vocabulary they need. This will enable them to speak with more confidence in **exercise 3**.

read on

- **Exercise 1** includes sentences from the text and the aim is to encourage learners to predict the endings: this will help to motivate them to read with interest, and not get too concerned with unknown vocabulary. Don't go over the answers until after **exercise 2**, as students will be able to find them for themselves in the article.

- **Exercises 3** and **4** are designed to encourage more detailed reading. Check students' answers to **exercise 3** before you go on to the next exercise. See **troubleshooting** on the right.

- **Exercise 5** allows students to interpret and react to the story. This could develop into a discussion. Alternatively, you might want to ask students to think about any similar experiences they or members of their family have had (though not necessarily so extreme). Sleepwalking is quite common in children, so it is quite possible they will know of similar incidents.

grammar *-ed* / *-ing* adjectives

- As a lead-in to the grammar, ask students to scan the article again and circle these words: *relaxed, terrified, worrying, surprised*.

- In **exercise 1**, notice that students are tested on the lexical meaning of the *-ed* / *-ing* adjectives, and then, in **exercise 2**, they look at the grammar of these words. You could present the difference yourself after **exercise 1** by miming these sentences: *This book is boring / I'm bored (by the book)*.

- For **exercise 2**, tell students to look back at the sentences in **exercise 1** for examples. Comparison with their mother tongue may be useful.

- The sentences in **exercise 3** provide controlled practice which then becomes personalized speaking in **exercise 4**. Go over the answers to **exercise 3** and check pronunciation, especially *interesting* /ˈɪntrestɪŋ/, and the pronunciation of *-ed* in *embarrassed* /ɪmˈbærəst/ (not /ɪmˈbærəsed/ and *frightened* /ˈfraɪtnd/. Notice the use of *get* + adjective in this exercise, e.g. *get excited / worried*. We often use this to mean 'become or start feeling sth'.

- *Really* + adjective in the **natural English** box in **exercise 5** is extremely common in English; notice that there are more examples in grammar **exercise 1**. After doing **exercise 6**, to provide more practice, go back to **exercise 1** and ask students to substitute *really* for *very* and *very* for *really* in the sentences and say them aloud. For an extension to this lesson, see **ideas plus** on the right.

how do you feel?

exercise 1
wake up: <u>stop</u> sleeping
dream: <u>think</u> and feel things when you are asleep
have a nightmare: think and feel <u>bad</u> things when you are asleep
wake sb up: make sb <u>stop</u> sleeping
talk in your sleep: <u>talk</u> when you are asleep
sleepwalk: <u>walk</u> when you are asleep

language point sleep vocabulary
- *asleep* and *awake* are adjectives, but they can't be used before a noun: *the baby's asleep*, but not *an asleep baby*. Students often say *she's sleeping* when it would be more natural to say *she's asleep*, i.e. *asleep* describes a state, *sleep* (v) an activity. You can't *feel asleep* but you can *feel tired / sleepy*.
- *fall asleep* is a collocation which is not common in other languages, and may be translated by a reflexive verb in some, e.g. dormirse (Spanish), s'endormir (French). *Get / go to sleep* means *to succeed in sleeping*, and is often used in the negative *I couldn't get to sleep last night*.
- *dream* can be a noun or verb. As a verb, it is irregular *dreamt* (past simple), *dreamt* (past participle) /dremt/. The phrases *have a dream / a nightmare / a sleep / a rest* are also common.

exercise 3
1 her sleeping husband
2 a gun
3 climbed on a chair
4 poured the drink
5 climbed on a table
6 the fridge
7 a balcony
8 rats
9 the washing machine

exercise 4
<u>Andrew Jones</u> climbed on a chair, then stepped off a balcony.
<u>Martine Hopcroft</u> walked through the house with a gun in her hand and once hit her husband.
<u>Alina Lato</u> climbed on a table because she had a nightmare about rats.
<u>Sara Molina</u> took a drink from the fridge and poured it over her sleeping husband.

troubleshooting reducing the level of challenge
Exercise 4 is quite challenging, but we feel achievable for many learners. However, you may wish to make the exercise slightly easier. If so, write some questions on the board, like these for students to answer in pairs:
Who...
turned on the washing machine?   fell a long way but wasn't hurt?
walked through the house with a gun? got on a table because of a bad dream?
woke her husband up with orange juice? took something cold out of the fridge?

In this way, learners will only have to produce names instead of full sentences.

exercise 1
1 interesting   4 exciting   7 surprised
2 boring   5 frightened   8 embarrassed
3 relaxing   6 worried

exercise 2
-ing; boring, interesting
-ed; bored, excited

exercise 3
1 interesting   4 frightened
2 embarrassed   5 boring
3 relaxing   6 worried

exercise 5
a book
going to the dentist
a dog

ideas plus surveys
To revise -ed / -ing adjectives in a later lesson, you could ask students in pairs to produce their own questions based on the ones in **exercise 3**. Write some skeleton questions on the board, e.g.
  Do you get excited / exciting when ...
  Which is more bored / boring: X or Y?
  Do you get worried / worrying when ... ?
  Do you feel frightened / frightening if ... ?

Ask students in pairs to think of suitable endings, and choose the correct form (i.e. -ed or -ing). Then give them two more adjective pairs to think up their own questions. Check their questions are correct, then ask them to interview other students.

You can use questionnaires and surveys like the ones in this lesson on different topics to practise different grammar / vocabulary: health, leisure activities, driving, reading, local transport, etc. They can be a great way to revise grammar or vocabulary, and giving learners control over the questions will make the survey culturally relevant and motivating. You could refer students to the **language reference** and **practice exercises** *p.168* for further practice of the -ed / -ing adjectives.

ten

writing

- This writing activity is a piece of collaborative writing: one pair produces some prompts which another pair uses to produce a dream story, and vice versa. (The fact that it is a dream and not a realistic story means that they will be able to incorporate a wide range of prompts.) Each pair should be motivated to read the dream story produced from their prompts.
- You could start by copying the prompts in **exercise 1** onto the board, and asking students to add a few more examples to each category, to demonstrate the idea. Then get each pair to produce their own prompts. Finally, let them read the dream story and do the task in **exercise 2**.
- For **exercise 3**, redistribute the prompts randomly between the pairs. Monitor as students write their stories together and suggest improvements. If you prefer, students can write the stories without the language constraints suggested in **exercise 2**.
- After the students have done **exercise 4**, they can read out the best ones to the class. A little rehearsal, which you can monitor, would be wise in this case. For an extension activity, see **ideas plus** on the right.

Want to know more? Go to **how to** ... motivate learners to write (collaboration) *p.162*

wordbooster

30–45 mins

aches and pains

> This **wordbooster** is best done at this point in the unit as the vocabulary leads in to the topic of the following lesson.

- The vocabulary in this **wordbooster** includes words with overlapping meaning. For more information, see the **language point** on the right.
- To some extent, students may be completing the sentences in **exercise 1** and matching them with the pictures at the same time: this would be perfectly acceptable. Once they have compared with a partner, you will need to go over the answers and provide pronunciation practice. These items are often mispronounced so it is worth spending a bit of time on them: *headache* /ˈhedeɪk/, *stomach ache* /ˈstʌməkeɪk/, *toothache* /tuːθeɪk/, *hurt* /hɜːt/. Highlight the phrase *I don't feel very well*: this is not one that learners readily use, and is very natural. Point out to your students that we use *my / your*, etc. when referring to parts of our bodies, e.g. *I've got a pain in my foot*. NOT *in the foot*. If your group found the vocabulary easy, you can always feed in some more items by using the **workbook**, **expand your vocabulary** health *p.51*. See also **language reference** and **practice exercises** *p.168* for a focus on the use of the indefinite article here.
- **Exercise 2** introduces ways of asking and sympathizing about health. Practising these short dialogues in pairs in **exercise 3** will help with fluency: monitor students' pronunciation. When they practise similar conversations they can get up and do this as a mingling activity; encourage students to come up with their own suggestions, e.g. *Why don't you ... go to bed / to the doctor's / get some aspirins, You should / shouldn't*, etc. For more work on structures for giving advice, see **workbook**, **expand your grammar** *had ('d) better* + verb *p.53*.

Want to know more? Go to **Oxford Advanced Learner's Dictionary** Topic Pages *Health*

how do you feel?

exercise 2
past continuous to introduce the activity: *was watching*
An *-ed / -ing* adjective: *surprised*
A short dialogue: *She said 'I want that! ... and leave me alone!'*
An example of *really*: *I was really surprised!*

ideas plus drawing dreams
Depending on the artistic talents of your students, as dreams are so visual, you could ask them to draw a scene from their dream to describe to a partner – this can help to make the description of the dream more detailed and colourful. Use similar prompts, i.e. an activity, a place, a feeling, something strange / unusual, an unexpected person, etc. The final version can be displayed with the visual representation on the wall. If students seem to enjoy writing and talking about their dreams you could repeat it another time. This would give them confidence using the structures taught here as well as good past tense revision and practice.

exercise 1
a 4 pain / hurts
b 7 ache
c 8 pain / hurts
d 2 feel
e 6 ache
f 5 ache
g 3 pain / hurts
h 1 feel

exercise 2
go to **listening booklet** *p.31*

language point overlapping meaning
Ache (v) suggests something that continues for a longer time; *pain* (n) is generally shorter, sharper and more focused. You can demonstrate *pain* through mime, e.g. a sharp pain in your arm.

Hurt (v) in **exercise 1** means *feel painful*: e.g. *My leg hurts*. We also use *hurt* to mean *cause pain to sb or yourself*, e.g. *I hurt myself jumping off the wall. She hurt her sister while playing.* At this level, we feel it is best to limit the meaning to *feel painful*, otherwise it becomes quite complex.

I feel sick in British English means that you want to vomit; in US English, it means *I feel ill / generally unwell*.

NB A limited number of ailments can be expressed using the suffix *-ache*: *a headache, (a) toothache, stomach ache, backache, earache*. You cannot say ~~legache / armache / footache / noseache~~, etc. Notice that in British English, only *headache* is countable (although *toothache* can be used with the indefinite article e.g. *I've got a toothache*).

93

ten

listening how to ... make an appointment 75–90 mins

study verb patterns in a questionnaire

learn phrases in a sequence

listen to people making appointments by phone

practise accepting and refusing suggestions using **natural English** phrases

role play making an appointment including **natural English** phrases

grammar verb patterns

- Before **exercise 1**, you could do a short warmer about appointments. See **ideas plus**, on the right.
- The verb patterns which the students will focus on in this lesson are all included in **exercise 1**. Let students read the questions and ask you if there are any words they aren't sure about, e.g. *surgery, advice, appointment*. When they are comparing answers in **exercise 2**, ask them to say why, and give an example yourself. Monitor and see how accurately they are using the verb patterns at this stage.
- For **exercise 3**, you could make flashcards of the verbs and ask students to stick them in the correct column in the table on the board. They can then copy it. For extra practice, include a **test your partner** activity here: student A says a verb, student B says which pattern follows it, e.g. A *Speak?* B *Speak to somebody*, etc. For further practice, refer students to the **language reference** and **practice exercises** on *p.169*.
- Monitor what students write in **exercise 4** and correct errors before they mingle in **exercise 5**.

making an appointment

- The stages for making an appointment in **exercise 1** include revision of useful lexical phrases, e.g. *look up a number, you don't feel very well, the doctor's busy*. You could point out to students at the end that there are three verbs used with *appointment*: *ask for / make / give sb an appointment*. This language will be needed for the **extended speaking** activity at the end of the unit. When students compare answers, ask them to read out their sentences to each other rather than just pointing; this will provide more oral practice. For extra practice, see **ideas plus** on the right.
- **Exercise 2** is a quick vocabulary check. Another way to do this would be as a dictation: students shut their course books, and you dictate the text, clapping or making a bleep noise for the missing words. At the end, they complete the text and compare it with the one in **exercise 2**.

listen to this

- This listening activity leads up to a role play at the end of the lesson in **speaking it's your turn!** If you do the **student's book** and the **listening booklet** exercises thoroughly students will be well prepared for this communication activity. Notice that in recording **10.4**, the receptionists both summarize the information about the appointment at the end: there is an exercise focusing on this in the **listening booklet** on *p.32*.
- **Exercise 1** asks students to listen for detail while tuning in to the speakers' voices. Make sure that they have written *I'd like*, not *I like*. The first conversation in **exercise 2** is a little easier than the second. In both cases, students are asked to pick out key information but don't worry if they misspell the clients' surnames. For information on the **natural English** box in **exercise 4**, see the **language point** on the right.
- **Exercise 6** is an information gap activity to practise the language from the **natural English** box. Divide the class into A / B pairs; they should individually add one more activity of their own to their diary. With a good student, demonstrate to the class how the conversation can go by taking A and B roles.

speaking it's your turn!

- The role play in this section can either be done first as a writing activity, and then rehearsed and acted, or can be done orally from the start. Before you begin, read the **troubleshooting** box on the right.
- Monitor while students are working together on **exercise 1** and suggest corrections where necessary.
- We included this **natural English** box in **exercise 2** on fillers because, during the trialling of this activity, we found that students' dialogues were a little awkward, and these phrases helped them sound more natural. Check that students are putting them in appropriate places; they only need a few.
- To simulate the phone conversation in **exercise 3**, sit students back to back, or with one learner talking over their partner's shoulder. If you do this, you will find that noise levels increase, but it's more realistic and more fun. At the end, provide feedback on their role plays.

how do you feel?

ideas plus discussion warmer
Write these professions on the board: *doctor / vet / lawyer / hairdresser / dentist / optician*. Check students understand them, then write up these questions for them to discuss in small groups:
- If you want to see these people, do you have to make an appointment?
- Have you made an appointment recently? Who with? Was it easy?
- Do you have to make appointments with other people? Who?

exercise 3
verb + sb / sth:
    ask sb (for sth)
    phone / ring sb
    text sb
    e-mail sb
    tell sb
    thank sb (for sth)
verb + to + sb / sth:
    speak to sb (about sth)
    talk to sb
    write to sb

exercise 1
a 4 you ring the surgery
b 9 you note down the time of your appointment
c 3 you look up the phone number
d 1 you don't feel very well
e 5 you speak to the receptionist
f 7 the doctor's busy this morning
g 8 the receptionist gives you an appointment this afternoon
h 2 you decide to make an appointment to see a doctor
i 6 you ask for an appointment this morning

exercise 2
1 well
2 make
3 looked up
4 surgery
5 receptionist
6 asked
7 busy
8 gave

ideas plus memorizing sequences
To help memorize the phrases in **exercise 1**, you could do a memory test. Tell students they have two minutes to learn the sequence in the correct order. At the end, they work in pairs: A says the sentences with their book shut, B checks to see if they are correct. They should listen out for inaccuracies with prepositions and articles.

Memorizing sequences like this is a useful way of helping students to practise chunks of language, e.g. writing an e-mail (you turn on your computer, open the e-mail program, open a new e-mail page, type the name / e-mail address of the person you're writing to, fill in the subject box, type your e-mail, press 'send').

exercise 1
go to **listening booklet** *p.32*

exercise 2
1 appointment with: Dr Harper
  day: tomorrow
  time: 3.30
  caller's name: Peter Phillips
2 appointment with: Sandy
  day: Saturday
  time: 10.30
  caller's name: Rosie Webber

exercise 3
1 The traffic is terrible and he can't get there for 3.30.
2 4.30.

exercise 4
go to **listening booklet** *p.32*

language point *I'm afraid (that)...*
When you are going through the **natural English** box in **exercise 4**, point out the useful apology *I'm afraid I can't*. Explain that *I'm afraid* /əˈfreɪd/ means *I'm sorry* here, and it is very common in spoken English for giving bad news, or politely telling someone something they might be upset or angry about, e.g. *I'm afraid I'm going to be late for the meeting / I can't help you / I've broken a glass*. Students sometimes make the mistake of saying *I'm afraid but ...*, confusing it with *I'm sorry but ...*

troubleshooting levels of formality
In the chart, notice that verbs such as *greet, suggest, offer, agree* are part of the instructions, and not normally used in 'performance', i.e. we don't say *I offer you an appointment at 10.00*. If learners did this, their English would sound stilted and formal. To avoid this, you could quickly work through the chart with the class, asking for some suggestions about what to say in each case, but don't do it in too much detail, or the pairs will have little to do when they come to devise their conversation.

95

ten

extended speaking nightmare!

60–75 mins

talk about dentists

practise telling a picture story and invent the end of the story

tell the story to a new partner

listen to someone telling the story

write the story

- It is important at the beginning of this activity to let learners read the left-hand column or tell them what they are going to do in the lesson, or put it on the board. This will enable them to get the whole picture. You should also give them time to look back at the **don't forget!** boxes which occur at the end of each section in the unit.

collect ideas

- Most people have something to say about going to the dentist: bad experiences, amusing anecdotes, or just the sense of fear it can induce. You could tell a simple anecdote of your own on this topic, at the beginning of the class. For the brief talking points in **exercise 1**, monitor the pair work, and at the end, invite a couple of students to share their experiences.

prepare a story

- During the trialling of this narrating activity, we were aware that, at this level, it was important to break it into stages: first, help learners with vocabulary as in **exercise 2**, then gradually describe what happens in the pictures in **exercise 3**, and then go back to retell the story, including link phrases, which makes the story more coherent in **exercise 4**. See also **ideas plus** on the right for alternative staging.

- Check students' pronunciation of the lexical items in **exercise 2**. They may also want to check back through the lessons in this unit for vocabulary such as *have a nightmare, wake up*, and *ring the doctor*.

- It is important that students tell the story in the context provided in the example in **exercise 3**, i.e. she's on holiday in the Bahamas. However, they could tell the story in the first person if you prefer. While they are working their way through the picture story, monitor the pair work and try to ensure that both learners are practising. If the pairs are contributing unequally, intervene and suggest that they take turns to describe a picture each. It is also worth thinking about which pairs should work together. If two students are very extrovert and chatty, it might be wise to put them together; at least they won't dominate quiet learners. Be available to help anyone with language they require.

- In **exercise 4** and beyond, students will re-tell their stories. See **troubleshooting** on the right.

- For **exercise 5** suggest they complete the story in not more than two or three sentences. Remember that they are going to hear one example of an ending in the listening in **exercise 7**.

- If students create their own endings, the re-telling of the story in **exercise 6** will be purposeful: students don't know how each story will finish, so there will be a real reason for listening.

exercise 2
turn round – picture 7   run away – picture 8   moustache – picture 3   needle – picture 3   beard – picture 3
NB In picture 8, she isn't *actually* running away, but will *probably* run away.

tell the story

- You might prefer to do this in groups of three or four, all of whom devised a different ending. During this activity, monitor and make notes for feedback at the end. Ensure that you have positive comments as well as error correction in your feedback.

listen

- If you want to exploit the recording in **exercise 7** more fully, there are some useful features of spoken English, some of which are relevant to story-telling. For example, the speaker uses direct rather than indirect speech to make the story more vivid; he also links parts of the story using *anyway* (see **unit seven** p.65), and checks that the woman is listening, e.g. *yeah; right; you know*. You could ask learners to listen again and follow the tapescript.

writing

- If writing is a priority for your learners, you may prefer to devote classroom time to **exercise 8**. This would have the advantage that you could monitor your learners and make suggestions as they write, thus giving them individual attention. If you have facilities for word processing, this would be a very suitable activity; or the writing could even be done collaboratively in pairs.

Want to know more? Go to **how to** ... motivate low level learners to write *p.160*

how do you feel?

ten review student's book p.101   45 mins

Want to know more about how to use the reviews? Go to the introduction p.10.

natural English

- This review activity is a continuation of the one they did in **how to ...** make an appointment on *p.96*. We suggest you give students an opportunity to look back at the **natural English** boxes in **unit ten** to remind them of some useful language. Divide the class in half and put As into pairs to prepare their roles together; ditto Bs.
- During the preparation in **exercise 1**, allow students to make notes but discourage them from writing full sentences.
- For the role play in **exercise 2**, pair up A and B students, and put them back to back. Let them do the role play a couple of times until it sounds natural. For the second role play in **exercise 3**, students should prepare alone. During the whole of **exercises 2** and **3**, monitor and make notes for feedback at the end. You could ask one or two pairs to act out their conversation and / or write out the conversation for homework.

grammar verb patterns

- This is an exercise which becomes a personalized speaking activity. Go over the answers after **exercise 1**. At this point you could check students' pronunciation of the questions (focus on *do you* /dʒuː/).
- Tell students to ask you questions 1–7 in **exercise 2**, and answer them as fully as possible. If you do so, this will encourage students to talk more when they ask the questions again with different partners.

exercise 1
1. How often do you phone your parents?
2. Do you often ask people for advice?
3. Do you send postcards when you are on holiday?
4. How often do you write to friends?
5. Do you often talk to strangers on trains?
6. Have you e-mailed anyone today?
7. How do you thank people for birthday presents?
8. Has the teacher spoken to you in this lesson?

vocabulary sleep and -ed / -ing adjectives

- Ask students to look back at the *sleep* vocabulary and *-ed / -ing* adjectives in **unit ten** before they begin **exercise 1**. If students spend some time describing the picture in **exercise 1**, it will help them with **exercise 2**. They could work together when answering the true / false questions in **exercise 2** if you prefer. In the feedback at the end, suggest where some of the vocabulary might be used, e.g. *fall asleep, feel sick,* etc.

exercise 2
1. False. The man is having a nightmare.
2. False. The young boy feels sick.
3. True
4. True
5. True
6. True
7. False. The woman looks very relaxed.
8. True

go to **wordlist** *p.139*

---

ideas plus lesson staging
If you feel your learners would benefit from a listening model before they tell their stories (perhaps for a class which is not very confident) you could play recording **10.6** after **exercise 2**, but make sure that they have looked through the picture story carefully first. Only play the part of the recording as far as '... *it was the dentist from her nightmare*', otherwise, the students may just use the ending on the recording.

troubleshooting re-telling stories
During the trialling of different story-telling activities in the course, we found that students benefited considerably from re-telling the stories, with a little input from the teacher. As a result, they became more fluent, confident and got considerable speaking practice. For example, when you are listening to them, note down words or phrases that will improve their stories, or perhaps encourage them to incorporate direct speech to make their stories more dramatic: the dentist might say, 'please come back and sit down', when the girl runs out of his surgery. To read more about this, see the reference below.

Want to know more? Go to how to ... use learners as a resource (task repetition) *p.172*

test yourself!

Want to know more? Go to the introduction *p.9* for ways of using the test yourself!

1. headache, toothache, backache
2. surprised / surprising; bored / boring; frightened / frightening; excited / exciting; worried / worrying; relaxed / relaxing; embarrassed / embarrassing
3. write to sb, phone sb, speak to sb, tell sb, ask sb

1. fall
2. pain
3. make
4. feel

1. I enjoyed the film; it was really excit**ing**.
2. A What about meeting at 6.00?
   B I'm afraid ~~but~~ I can't.
3. I had a dream **about** my sister.
4. I was very surpris**ed** when I saw him.

97

eleven

in unit eleven ...

life with
Agrippine
p.98

reading how to ...
describe office life
p.98

wordbooster
p.100

listening can my
girlfriend come
too?
p.102

extended speaking
24.com
p.104

test yourself!
p.105

review
p.105

wordlist
p.140

life with Agrippine   30 mins

reading for fun

natural English leaving out words

concert

Want to know more about using **life with Agrippine**? Go to the **introduction** *p.7*.

- Learners meet the expression *had better* in this cartoon. There is a short paraphrase and example in the **glossary**, but the structure has been introduced in **unit ten** of the **workbook**, *p.53*. If you haven't used the **workbook** exercise, you could use it before or after the cartoon. See **language point** on the right.

- If you have been to a concert recently, you could introduce the topic by telling the class about it. After the students have read the cartoon and answered the questions in **exercise 2**, you could introduce the **natural English** box. The omission of words in this way is called *ellipsis*, and it is a very common feature, especially in spoken English.

Want to know more? Go to **Practical English Usage** by Michael Swan *section 177–182*

- The practice in **exercise 6** is designed to make learners more aware of *ellipsis* but we would not expect them to incorporate many examples of it in their own spoken English. If you are very familiar with your learners' mother tongue, you could ask them if such a feature exists in their language. For more work on *ellipsis*, see **workbook**, **expand your grammar** ellipsis *p.55*.

reading how to ... describe office life   90+ mins

talk about offices

read a text about office rules

discuss office rules using **natural English** phrases

focus on vocabulary of work and working conditions

focus on the use of *work* in a **natural English** box

interview a partner about an office

lead-in

- You could start by asking the students to describe the office in the picture (without giving opinions at this stage). You may need to teach the phrase *open-plan office*.

- After students have talked to a partner about the office in **exercise 2**, you could personalize the discussion. See **ideas plus** on the right.

read on

- For an alternative exploitation of the article, see **ideas plus** on the right.

- Please note that **exercise 1** is only based on the introduction to the text (the first paragraph), so don't let learners read beyond that at the moment.

- After learners have completed the comprehension task in **exercise 2**, we think it is worth drawing their attention to the **glossary**. For adult learners in particular, there are some very useful items here, and after clarifying the meaning you could set up a short **test your partner** activity to practise pronunciation and consolidate meaning. This is also a natural introduction to **exercise 3**, which invites students to guess the meaning of selected phrases from the article.

- **Exercise 4** offers an opportunity for further personalization, but even learners who don't work in an office should be able to express an opinion and a preference for one of the companies.

- The language in the **natural English** box in **exercise 5** may not be new, but it is a source of error for many learners, so the intensive practice in **exercise 6** is probably necessary. As well as providing a further opportunity to practise language from the **natural English** box, **exercise 7** also recycles *should / shouldn't* from **unit nine**. This is important as learners will need *should / shouldn't* in the **extended speaking** activity at the end of the unit.

98

do you get on?

exercise 2
1 worried   2 not to be

exercise 4
Are you ready?
I don't know.

exercise 6
2 Are you
3 Did you
4 Would you
5 Do you
6 I'll

language point had better + verb

Had better is used when we want to give people advice.

*It's going to rain – **you'd better** take an umbrella.* (= I think you should take an umbrella.)

*The train leaves in 15 minutes, so **we'd better** go now.*

The form is almost always contracted, as in the examples above. There is no negative form, and students at this level are unlikely to need the question form.

Had better is often interchangeable with *should*, as in the examples given. However, there is a difference. *Had better* refers to advice for a specific situation in the immediate future, whereas *should* is used for advice in general situations at any time. For example:

People should take regular exercise. NOT *People had better take* ...

Students should try to practise English every day. NOT *Students had better try* ...

Learners at this level may hear *had better* in spoken English, so it is useful receptively, but it is probably safer and simpler for them to use *should*, as it is used more widely.

ideas plus personalization

You may like to follow up with a few questions: How many of your students work in an office? What are they like? What do they think of them? etc. With an adult group, this topic might generate a lot of genuine communication, and there is an obvious link with the **extended speaking** activity they will do at the end of the unit. Avoid talking about working conditions, though, because they will discuss these in **speaking it's your turn!** at the end of this lesson.

exercise 1
b

exercise 2
1 bank
2 department store
3 mobile phone company
4 computer software company
5 mobile phone company

exercise 3
in your own time = in your free time, not when you are working
hours on end = a long time
in moderation = only a little
in a relationship = going out with each other, i.e. seeing each other as boyfriend and girfriend

exercise 5
go to **listening booklet** *p.34*

ideas plus prediction

Tell the students to close their books. Then write the five questions from the article on the board (*At work, can you wear jeans? Can you e-mail your friends?* etc). Put learners in groups to discuss these questions and decide what they think the answers would be if it were large companies in their country. Remember this is not their opinion, but the answers they think large companies will give. Then they can open their books and read the article to see how their answers compare.

This is a more natural and probably more meaningful task, but it is also more open and less focused, and probably more difficult for you to assess your learners' comprehension of the article.

99

eleven

vocabulary work and working conditions

- The exercise type used in **exercise 1** is a useful way of presenting and practising vocabulary. See **ideas plus** on the right.
- After **exercise 2** you may need to explain or clarify some of the new vocabulary in **bold**, although the potential confusion between *job* and *work* is highlighted in the **natural English** box coming up in **exercise 4**.
- As a noun, *work* is often confused with *job*, resulting in the common error *I haven't got a work*. For **exercise 4**, you could also point out a number of common collocations with this meaning of *work*, which students should learn as fixed phrases. Here are some:

  I get to work (at 8 o'clock)   *She's at work (now)*
  After work (I often go for a drink)   *He's out of work at the moment (= without a job)*

speaking it's your turn!

- If no-one in the class works in an office, it doesn't really matter – this is an easy activity for learners to invent plausible answers. However, if you have people who work in offices, it would be more genuinely communicative if they took the B roles.
- For **exercise 1**, put the As together in one half of the room to prepare their questions, and Bs in the other half of the room (or a separate room if you have that luxury). We have suggested As prepare their questions with a partner, but as the Bs are working individually at this point, you may prefer to have the whole class working individually.
- When students come together in **exercise 2** to do the interview, the activity will recycle quite a lot of vocabulary and grammar from the lesson. When you give the class feedback at the end, make sure to praise good examples of language use from the lesson. You could also suggest that students go through the material on *pp.104–107* and note down all the *work* vocabulary which has come up in the lesson.

wordbooster

30–45 mins

> This **wordbooster** is best done at this point in the unit as some of the vocabulary appears in the listening in the following lesson

office jobs

- The jobs here include those that learners will need in the **extended speaking** activity at the end of the unit, but if you have a number of students who work in offices, you could extend the activity by eliciting more from the students or jumbling a few others yourself, e.g. *marketing manager, finance manager, clerk, supervisor,* etc. Notice that *personnel managers* are sometimes called *human resources managers*. For more work-related vocabulary, see also **workbook, expand your vocabulary** computers *p.56*.

relationships

- Some learners may be unaware of the different uses of the word *relationship*. See the **language point** on the right.
- An important feature of the target vocabulary here is that they are either fixed phrases, e.g. *fall in love*, or words that commonly combine with other words, e.g. *have + an argument* and *good + at + noun or -ing*. Make sure learners are aware of this and write them down as phrases in their notebooks.
- An interesting point about *good at* is that we often say, for example, *I'm **not very** good at (maths)*; but when we leave out the adverb, *I'm **no** good at maths* is more natural than *I'm not good at maths*.

100

do you get on?

exercise 1
1 boss; work; break; salary
2 job; hours; share; get

exercise 2
go to **listening booklet** *p.34*

exercise 4
1 c   2 a   3 b

ideas plus paraphrase

Using paraphrase or partial synonymy can be a useful way of introducing new vocabulary, i.e. using known vocabulary as a guide to the meaning of new vocabulary. It also reflects a common feature of conversation: instead of repeating a word or phrase someone has just used, we often repeat the idea but through a different word / phrase with the same meaning. For example:

A *It was **boring**, wasn't it?*
B *Yes, very **dull**.*

This means that you can practise the new vocabulary in a very natural way.

exercise 1
3 How many people work there?
4 Where is it, exactly? / Where exactly do you work?
5 How / What time do you get to work?
6 What are the working hours?
7 How long are the breaks?
8 Do you share an office with other people?
9 Do you get on well with them?
10 Do you like your job? Why / Why not?

ideas plus interviews

If you are teaching in a place where there are support staff who speak English – for example, a school or college with secretarial and administrative staff – it could be very motivating for learners to interview them using Student A's questions. Alternatively, you may be able to arrange for students to interview English-speaking workers in offices nearby. You could start with a class role play in which you act the part of a worker (e.g. a secretary to a bank manager), and the students interview you; encourage them to ask follow-up questions. They could conduct the interviews with 'real' workers in pairs, record the conversations or make notes, and then come back to class to exchange information with other pairs. They could also write a summary of the information they obtained.

exercises 1 and 3
2 acc<u>ou</u>ntant   4 recep<u>ti</u>onist   6 s<u>a</u>les m<u>a</u>nager
3 s<u>e</u>cretary   5 personn<u>e</u>l m<u>a</u>nager

exercise 1
2 h   3 e   4 c   5 b   6 g   7 a   8 i   9 f

language point meanings of *relationship*

The combination of 'romance' and 'office work' in this unit brings together the two different meanings of *relationship*:

a between colleagues, friends, and relatives,
   e.g. *I have a good relationship with my boss.*
b a romantic relationship, e.g. *She had a relationship with a Frenchman.*

101

eleven

listening can my girfriend come too?

75–90 mins

talk about possible holiday problems

listen to a family discussing holiday arrangements

discuss the solution to their problem

focus on conditional sentences with *will / might*

talk about possible problems using **natural English** phrases

write a holiday postcard

lead-in

- Much of the lesson is based round the family in the picture in **exercise 1**. It is, therefore, very important that they are familar with the different characters and their names. See **ideas plus** on the right.
- The first question in **exercise 1** previews the first conditional, but don't discuss it at this stage; let students see and work with it as they will probably have a good passive understanding of what it means.

listen to this

- **Exercise 1** is an opportunity to tune in to the different characters and voices, and **exercise 2** checks how well they can hear short sentences when there are contractions and words are strung together. If you want to know more about teaching features of connected speech, follow up the reference below:

Want to know more? Go to **how to ...** help learners understand natural speech (understanding connected speech) *p.177*

- When they listen to the full recording, **exercise 3** tests their understanding of some of the key points, while **exercise 4** returns to the problems of being able to hear chunks of connected speech. If your learners find one exercise more difficult than the other, this may indicate the need, in future, to focus a little more on either gist understanding, or more detailed understanding.
- When you have completed **exercise 6**, the group can react to the family's solution and discuss it in **exercise 7**. See **ideas plus** on the right.
- While you listen to students' discussions in **exercise 7**, notice whether any learners incorporate (or try to incorporate) first conditional sentences. If so, you may want to refer back to it during the next section.

grammar conditional sentences with *will / might*

- Conditional sentences present certain problems of form and meaning, especially for northern Europeans. See the **language point** on the right. Learners will need first conditional sentences throughout the **extended speaking** activity at the end of the unit, so it is important that this section prepares them thoroughly.
- When they are doing **exercises 2** and **3**, move round and monitor their answers so you can see if any students are having particular difficulty with either the form or concept.
- Students could talk to a partner for **exercise 4**. The aim of this exercise is to reinforce the use of the present tense in the *if* clause and the possibility of reversing the clause order. Point out the lack of a comma when the *if* clause comes second.
- **Exercise 5** is not particularly difficult, but conditional sentences are often quite long and most learners benefit from an opportunity to work on their rhythm and fluency without having to worry too much about the content of what they they are saying. Start by practising them as a class, then let them practise quite intensively in pairs – two or three times if necessary. **Exercise 6** provides further practice of concept.
- The structure *what if* in the **natural English** box in **exercise 7** is not usually taught at this level. However, it is quite a high frequency structure and good monolingual dictionaries normally include it as a phrase. It also has the advantage that it allows learners to simplify and use a shortened conditional structure (*What if it rains?* = *What will we do if it rains?*). Students practise this in **exercises 9** and **10**.

writing

- Check the answers to **exercise 1**, then let them work on their postcards from Mark to Anna in **exercise 2**. If you are able to bring in some blank postcards, it would make the activity seem more realistic and purposeful; if not, get them to draw a rectangle of a suitable size in their notebooks to represent a postcard.
- Move round and offer help where needed in **exercise 2**. Correct any significant mistakes but don't be too fussy, otherwise learners may feel inhibited about writing anything. If the results are amusing, it will make **exercise 3** more enjoyable. For further practice, see **ideas plus** on the right.

do you get on?

ideas plus exploiting a picture

For **exercise 1**, you could start by exploiting the picture. Ask the class to describe the people they can see. Get them to read the short text below the picture and then tell them to cover the text and write down the names of each member of the family. When they have done this, they can think about the questions.

exercise 1
1 Dan   2 Mark   3 Sarah

exercise 2
It'll be nice for Mark; I get on really well with her. (Mark says: It will be great fun.)

exercise 3
Conversation 1: yes   Conversation 2: they'll be able to spend more time together
Conversation 3: she would like a friend to come with her.

exercise 4
1 Mark   2 Dan   3 Christine   4 Dan   5 Christine   6 Sarah

exercise 6
The villa: they'll get a bigger villa.
Anna: can come with them for the first week.
The money: Anna's father will have to pay the air fare.
Sarah: can have a friend with her for the second week.

ideas plus revising *should*

Before the discussion in **exercise 7**, you could put several sentence beginnings on the board to help students to introduce their opinions:
I (don't) think it's a good idea to (take ...)
I (don't) think Anna should ...
This would enable you to revise *should* again, which will be useful for the **extended speaking** activity at the end of the unit.

exercise 1
If they get a bigger villa, it'll be more expensive.
If Anna's father pays for the flight, Dan will be happy.
If Mark is with Anna all the time, Sarah might be lonely.
If her friend comes for a week, Sarah won't be lonely.

exercise 2
1 the future   2 sure   3 possible

exercise 3
if + present tense, *will* + verb   *won't* + verb   *might* + verb

exercise 4
1 no (If they ~~will~~ get ...)   2 yes (NB but without the comma)

exercise 6
sentences 2, 6 and 7 are logical.
1 If you go to Brazil in the summer, it'll be **hot**.
3 If we go to Spain in July, there **will** be **a lot of people** on the beach.
4 If we stay at the best hotel in Buenos Aires, it'll be **expensive**.
5 If you go to Switzerland in July, there **won't** be **any** snow.
8 If you book your flight on the Internet, it **will / might** be cheaper.

exercise 7
go to **listening booklet** *p.36*

exercise 9 possible answers
2 What if you're late?   4 What if the bank is closed?
3 What if it rains?   5 What if there's no snow?

language point conditional sentences with *will / might*

German speakers often confuse *if* and *when* (*if* in German is *wenn*), and this can be a difficult error to spot sometimes as the sentence *When I go there, I will tell him* is grammatically correct, but may not communicate the message the speaker intends (*If I go there, I will tell him*).

Negative transfer from L1 may also produce this type of error from Russian or German speakers:
If I will see him, I will tell him.

Portuguese speakers may have a similar problem, but in reverse:
If I see him, I tell him.

Many learners find it difficult to hear the contracted form *'ll*, and some find it difficult to hear the difference between the negative *won't* /wəʊnt/ and the verb *want* /wɒnt/.

For further practice of conditionals with *will / might*, refer students to the **language reference** and **practice exercises** on *p.169*.

exercise 1 possible answers
1 mum and dad / there!
2 lovely / great
3 nice / fantastic
4 wonderful / gorgeous
5 a swimming pool / a tennis court
6 at the beach / by the pool
7 shopping / sightseeing / for a drive
8 Saturday / Sunday, etc.

ideas plus reading aloud

Reading aloud used to be a common classroom activity but went out of fashion on the grounds that it was unnatural: we normally read silently. Though generally true, postcards are exceptions. Because they aren't enclosed in envelopes they are perhaps seen as public and it is quite common to read them out. For example:
Oh, it's a postcard from Jim. He's in Morocco. He says he's having a great time ...

Put each person with a new partner to read their postcards aloud. Monitor and give feedback on their pronunciation. Then repeat the activity with a new partner.

eleven

extended speaking 24.com

60–75 mins

learn about the different people in a company, partly through a recording

discuss a series of problems these people have and agree on your advice / solutions

present advice / solutions to the rest of the class.

- It is important at the beginning of this activity to let learners read the left-hand column, or tell them what they are going to do in the lesson or put it on the board. This will enable them to get the whole picture. You should also give them time to look back at the **don't forget!** boxes which appear at the end of each section in the unit.

collect ideas

- Give students plenty of time to look at the pictures of the 24.com employees. Making predictions about the characters in **exercise 1** will motivate learners to listen to the recording in **exercise 2** to find out whether they were right. Allow the students to work in small groups / share ideas before feedback.
- For **exercise 2** see the **language point** on the right.
- As the students are going on to discuss a series of problems that the employees have in **exercise 5**, you needn't make too much of **exercise 4**; the aim here is to arouse interest.

> **exercise 2**
> Justin: boss
> Carol: accountant
> Clancy: Justin's secretary, lovely, sweet, hardworking
> Sadie: receptionist, worked with Jaz in his last company
> Jaz: sales manager, started at 24dotcom a month ago
> Mattias: computer programmer, a nice guy, in love with Clancy

discuss problems

- As the activity is set in a company context, it should appeal to adults with work experience. However, the problems the students are going to discuss are about personal relationships, and no work or office experience is necessary to contribute to the discussion.
- There are three problems to discuss in all in **exercises 5** and **6**. We think it would be wise for you to read them beforehand to make sure they are all suitable for the age and culture of the students you teach. If any are not suitable, omit them and possibly substitute some of your own.
- Don't let the students discuss all three problems at once, otherwise it will become chaotic and some issues may not be addressed as fully as they deserve. Direct the students to the first problem and make it very clear at the beginning that they must:
  - discuss the problem in as much detail as they can.
  - reach a decision they can all agree on.
  - write down their advice.
- During the discussion in **exercises 5** and **6**, monitor the groups. At the end of the first problem, you have a choice. You can let them go on to the second problem (and then the third) before conducting a class feedback; or you can give the class some feedback after they have discussed each one. The second approach could disrupt the flow of the discussion, but may be warranted if there is a significant language or content problem that you feel can easily be rectified for the subsequent discussion.
- If you want to build in an extra group feedback stage before **exercise 7**, it will be necessary for each person in the group to write down their advice. If not, it can be left to a spokesperson for the group to tell the class at the end.

do you get on?

eleven review student's book p.120   45 mins

Want to know more about how to use the **reviews**? Go to the **introduction**, p.10.

grammar conditional sentences with *will / might*

- Start by highlighting the tenses in the questions in **exercise 1**. Students will be focusing on conditional sentences with *would* in **unit twelve**, so it's important they have a firm grasp of the first conditional by the time they finish **unit eleven**. Point out that in their answers, they can write *will*, *'ll*, *might*, or *won't*. Monitor while they are writing and help / correct errors. Make a note of your own answers to a few questions before the next exercise.

- As a way of setting up **exercise 2**, bring the class together and put one of the questions on the board. Get a student to ask you that question. Answer it, then throw the same question back at the student by saying *How about you?* (See **natural English** box **unit one**, *p.14*.) If they have a similar answer, put a tick or the student's name next to your answer on the board. Show them that the aim is to find as many people with similar answers, so they will need to ask quite a few people.

- Monitor the activity, noting language points for feedback at the end. Do feedback on language and content and get some students to tell the class which answers were similar to other students'.

natural English

- This **natural English** revision focuses on *ellipsis*, i.e. words which can be omitted. Avoid asking students to 'cross out' the words, because they are not wrong – it is just that they can be left out. Go over the answers at the end, and then use the dialogues for pair practice: get students to rehearse them until they can say them without looking.

See **natural English** boxes in **unit eleven** for answers.

vocabulary work and relationships

- This vocabulary section is in two parts: a game, and phrase completion. The game in **exercise 1** is one that you could adapt to any sets of paired synonyms you want to revise with this level or higher levels. Put students in A / B pairs, and let them study their set of words. Go over the rules of the game, stressing the five-second rule: their partner could perhaps count to five, or time them. Monitor the game and listen to students' pronunciation, and correct any errors at the end. (*From nine to five* is an idiom meaning 'work a full day': in your students' culture, though, the working hours themselves may be different.)

- For **exercise 2**, see how much students can do for themselves, then let them refer back to the unit to help them with their answers.

exercise 1
be the boss / run a company; have a lot of work / be busy; lazy / not wanting to work; from nine to five / working hours; stop going out with each other / split up; have a good relationship / get on well; argument / angry discussion; frightened / afraid; client / customer; earn a lot / get a good salary; lose your job / get the sack; upset / angry or unhappy

exercise 2
| 1 love | 3 work | 5 split | 7 upset |
| 2 break | 4 share | 6 good | 8 stairs |

go to wordlist *p.140*

---

language point intonation
One feature of the recording in **exercise 2** which you could highlight is the predictable intonation pattern of the speaker when presenting a list. The speaker's voice rises as he announces each of the characters in the company, but then falls when he says 'Mattias', which is an indication that this is the last name in the list. You could play the recording and ask learners to focus on the intonation, and then get them to copy it in pairs.

test yourself!

Want to know more? Go to the **introduction** *p.9* for ways of using the **test yourself!**

1 in, of, at, of
2 receptionist, accountant, sales manager, secretary
3 on well, salary, boss, busy

1 won't
2 if
3 with; It

1 He hasn't got a **job** at the moment.
2 Sorry, I **don't** agree with you.
3 If you**'re** late, I'll wait for you.
4 I usually get a train to ~~the~~ work.

twelve

in unit twelve ...

listening how to ... talk about the past
p.106

wordbooster
p.108

reading friends reunited
p.110

extended speaking
school reunion
p.112

test yourself!
p.113

review
p.113

wordlist
p.141

listening how to ... describe the past   90+ mins

talk about activities using new vocabulary and **natural English** phrases

listen to people talking about making friends abroad

focus on *used to* + verb

talk about your past using *used to* + verb

vocabulary activities

- **Exercise 1** focuses on noun + verb collocation. For more information, see the **language point** on the right. Students will probably know the words for most of the activities in the illustrations, but give help where necessary.

- You can use recording **12.1** to check answers and for pronunciation practice in **exercise 2**, or you can provide your own model for oral practice. You could set up a quick **test you partner** activity whereby Student A says an activity or sport and Student B says '*play, go to the, go*' etc.

- At this point, the class could brainstorm other collocations. Write *play, have, go to* and *go + -ing* in a table on the board, and ask students to suggest other activities (especially ones that they do) for each column, e.g. *play tennis / chess / volleyball / the guitar; have a meal / party; go to the cinema / theatre / races; go climbing / surfing*.

- In the **natural English** box in **exercise 3**, notice that *neither* can be pronounced /ˈnaɪðə/ or /ˈniːðə/. It is also possible to say *so do I / neither do I* in place of *me too / me neither*, but for this level, the latter form is a little simpler. You will need to stress that *me too / me neither* both show agreement with the speaker.

- For **exercise 4**, if you did the vocabulary expansion suggested above, students could also ask talk about these activities. Monitor and correct errors, particularly with collocations, and *me neither* being used to agree, not disagree.

listen to this

- Start with an example of your own for **exercise 1**, highlight the language in the example (i.e. *I'd like to*), then ask students to get up and mingle. Their aim is to find someone with similar destinations and reasons.

- Set the scene for the listening in **exercise 2** by focusing on the photos of Liz and Chris and play tapescript **12.3**. The task here focuses on the main points for each conversation.

- Students do not have to write anything in **exercise 3**, which avoids distraction. Before you start the recording, make sure they are looking at the pictures on *p.112*. **Exercise 4** can also be done orally. Notice that *used to* + verb is used naturally by both speakers throughout. You don't need to deal with it here as it is taught in the next part of this lesson, and learners should be able to understand the recording without knowing this form.

- After students have completed **exercise 5**, see **ideas plus** on the right.

- Some learners living in an English-speaking country may have a particular interest in discussing **exercises 6** and **7**. You might spend some time on this, encouraging peer suggestions and giving your own ideas for ways in which they can make friends (e.g. evening classes, joining a sports club, through other students). Students studying at home can refer to specific places / activities in their town, or think about their foreign friends. If you are a temporary resident in the learners' country, this activity could set up a very real dialogue between you.

we'll meet again

exercise 1
1 beach
2 clubbing
3 skiing
4 clarinet
5 baseball
6 barbecue
7 cards
8 horseriding

language point activities vocabulary

Go clubbing i.e. going to clubs in the evening to dance and drink, is a more up-to-date term than *go to discos*. People who go clubbing regularly are called *clubbers* (usually under 30s).

Play is used for sports (e.g. football, squash), or games (e.g. cards, chess) and for musical instruments (e.g. the piano, the flute). In some languages, a different verb is used for playing games / sports, and playing an instrument e.g. Portuguese *jogar* = *play* (a game) / *tocar* = *play* (an instrument). Notice too that with most musical instruments, we use the definite article, i.e. play **the** saxophone.

Go is often used with *-ing* forms, e.g. *go fishing / shopping*, etc. but also in the phrase *go for a walk / swim / ride*. Students studied these in **unit seven** (phrases with *go*). The forms are not always interchangeable: *I'm going walking* suggests a walking holiday; *I'm going for a walk* suggests walking for a limited time, and straightaway. Notice the example in Chris's interview in recording **12.3**.

exercise 2
1 Chris   2 Liz   3 Liz   4 Chris

exercise 3
go to the beach, play baseball, have a barbecue

exercise 4
He met people through work, went to salsa bars, went walking, joined a sports club, met neighbours

exercise 5
activities in vocabulary **exercise 1**: play the clarinet, go skiing, go horseriding.
other things: met people through work, including her students, shared a flat with an ex-student, joined a jazz band

ideas plus listening with the tapescript

Once students have listened to a recording a few times without the tapescript, most of them find it extremely useful to listen again with the tapescript. This allows them to focus on specific points within the recording which they had not understood. Reading the transcript while listening to the recording also illustrates the discrepancy between the way many English words are written down, and the way they are spoken. They can listen and underline particular phrases / words which they had not understood while listening, and can then ask you to replay those specific phrases. At this point, you can clear up any misunderstandings to do with features of connected speech; for example, phrases where sounds are linked to other sounds, or are elided, or where there are weak forms or contractions which tend to make comprehension more difficult for learners. At the same time, students will also be able to *scan* the tapescript for new lexis or lexical chunks. The exercises in the **listening booklet** focus on such features throughout.

twelve

grammar *used to* + verb

- You could start this section by referring to the **listening booklet** and highlighting some examples of *used to* + verb from listening **12.3** and **12.4** in the previous section. Then go on to **exercise 1**. If you prefer, write the first two (positive) sentences on the board, and use questions 1–4 to check understanding and form. Then add the negative example from the third speech bubble and check understanding and form. (*Never used to* + verb is in fact more common in spoken English than *didn't use to*, and is also easier for learners to use.) Practise pronunciation by drilling these sentences. See the **language point** on the right for typical learners' problems.

- **Exercise 2** checks the concept of *used to*. If students aren't able to correct certain errors, you may need to clarify them. You could also do pronunciation practice as a class before students work in pairs in **exercise 3** to build their confidence. At the same time, you can highlight the pronunciation issues in the **language point** box on the right.

- Students will already have done this type of substitution drill in **exercise 4** in **units three** and **eight**. **Exercise 6** requires students to produce sentences based on the listening activity. You could suggest that they look at the **listening booklet** *p.38* to check their answers and look for more examples. If students require further practice, refer them to the **language reference** and **practice exercises** on *p.170*.

speaking it's your turn!

- This activity gives students the chance to talk about themselves and use *used to* + verb and *me too / me neither*. It shouldn't be a drill, but if students only use the forms a few times, don't worry – it's also an opportunity for freer speaking. For a different approach, see **ideas plus** on the right.

- You could demonstrate **exercise 1** by selecting sentences that are true for yourself and also giving examples of extra ideas. Monitor while students work alone and help with vocabulary.

- Again, you could show what to do in the activity by replicating the dialogue in **exercise 2** with a student. It can then be done in pairs or small groups, or as a mingling activity. Monitor and collect examples of good language use and errors for feedback at the end. Include some feedback on the content of the activity as well, e.g. Which things were similar for them? Did anything surprise them?

wordbooster

30–45 mins

> This **wordbooster** is best done at this point in the lesson as some of the phrases appear in the lesson that follows.

life events

- For **exercise 1** see the **language point** on the right.
- The practice in using link words in **exercise 2** puts the vocabulary into context. It's important for general fluency (helping learners to speak in longer, connected chunks), and they can also use these link words in the **extended speaking** activity at the end of the unit. Notice that there will be a range of possible answers; in class feedback ask students to call out their sentences for others to check if they are correct.

professions

- As an extension to **exercise 1**, ask students to say what their own jobs / professions are or will be in the future. See also **ideas plus** on the right. The vocabulary here is quite straightforward, but you will need to highlight the pronunciation of the jobs and professions in **exercise 2**, especially the word stress.
- **Exercise 3** provides an opportunity to practise the words and express opinions. Students can include any extra jobs and professions they have come up with previously. Monitor the pair work in **exercise 4**, and at the end, you can open the discussion out to the whole class.

we'll meet again

exercise 1
1 the past
2 often
3 isn't / doesn't happen
4 it's not true now
5 I used to work, I never used to work, I didn't use to work

exercise 2
1 We used **to** have a lot of parties.
2 My sister used to go horseriding ~~yesterday~~. or My sister **went** horseriding yesterday.
3 correct
4 I used to take the bus to work, and it **was** always late. or I **usually** take the bus to work, and it's always late.
5 correct
6 I used to play tennis. I play**ed** on Saturday afternoons. or I **usually** play tennis. I play on Saturday afternoons.

exercise 5
My brother and I never used to go to parties on Friday nights.

exercise 6
<u>Chris used to</u>: go to salsa bars, go to the beach, go to a mountain north of Caracas, go walking, play baseball, have barbecues.
<u>Liz used to</u>: go out for drinks or pizzas with her students, share a flat with an ex-student, play the clarinet, be in a jazz band, go skiing, go horseriding

language point *used to* + verb

Used to + verb does not necessarily have equivalents in other languages. Here are some typical problems:

- students sometimes mistakenly use *used to* to talk about how long something happened, or how many times it happened:

NOT ~~I used to work in the bank for ten years~~. I **worked** in the bank for ten years.

NOT ~~She used to go there three times~~. She **went** there three times.

- Students confuse *used to* (past states and habits) with *usually* (present or past states and habits). NOT ~~I used to come to school by bus now~~. I **usually** come to school by bus now.

- Pronunciation: learners often say /~~juːsɪtuː~~/, instead of /juːstuː/. In addition, *to* is pronounced /tə/ before a consonant, e.g. *used to work* /juːstə wɜːk/, but before a vowel, it is pronounced in its full form /tuː/, e.g. *used to eat* /juːstuː iːt/.

ideas plus myself in pictures

Choose a time from your youth and on a large piece of paper, draw yourself at that time (different hair, clothes, size, etc.) and a few things to show the differences in your life then, e.g. the house you used to live in, a game you used to play, (but which you don't now). Show the class your sheet, and tell them that this is you at the age of ten. Elicit some sentences about yourself – e.g. *you used to have short hair / you used to play tennis*. You can confirm or deny what they say, and say a little about it, e.g. *Yes, my hair was very short because at school we had to have short hair*. Then give students topic prompts (as in the table in **exercise 1**) to produce their own drawing. Put them in groups to share their experiences as in **exercise 2**.

---

exercise 1
1 university
2 a dentist; a DJ
3 six months in Japan; a year in Spain
4 married; a job as a waiter
5 Daniel last summer; Cathy through a friend
6 abroad; in television

exercise 2 possible answers
I got a job in TV, and after that I married a DJ. After I left school, I worked abroad. I spent six months in Japan, and then I got a job as a waiter.

language point common errors

We have focused on this particular vocabulary in **exercise 1** because learners made a lot of errors with these forms in trialling.

- They said *I ~~knew~~ Julio last summer*, when they meant *I met Julio last summer*;
- They said *I ~~finished my studies~~* when *I left school / university* is more natural.

We also found that many students weren't familiar with these forms:

- work **in** (*a field*, e.g. television)
- *get a job* **as** *a* (*waiter*)
- **become** *a* (*doctor / vet*)

exercises 1 and 2
<u>m</u>edicine;
<u>l</u>aw;
<u>e</u>ngineering;
<u>j</u>ournalism;
<u>b</u>anking;
<u>IT</u> (pronounced /aɪ tiː/)
<u>b</u>usiness;

ideas plus jobs alphabet

This activity is a fun alternative to a straightforward brainstorm. Divide the class in half, and then into small groups. Give half the class letters of the alphabet from A to L; the other half M to W. (There aren't many jobs beginning with X, Y or Z.) Each group writes their letters vertically on a piece of paper. They have five minutes to think of a job / profession for as many of their letters as possible. Tell them to move on if they can't think of a job for a letter ('k' and 'q' are very difficult unless you accept *king* and *queen* as actual jobs) and let them use dictionaries. At the end, collate their answers on the board, or make posters for a wall display.

Many thanks to *Jane Hudson* for this activity.

twelve

reading friends reunited
75–90 mins

talk about Internet chat

read a cartoon and practise **natural English** phrases

read and talk about Friends Reunited

revise the present perfect and past simple

role play meeting old friends using **natural English** phrases

lead-in

- Your learners may or may not be Internet users. In **exercise 1**, 'chat' is in inverted commas because it is being used in a specific way: exchanging messages in an Internet chatroom. If they don't chat online, you could ask them to talk more generally about when / how they use the Internet. For more Internet terms, see the **language point** on the right.
- The photos set the context for the article about 'Friends Reunited'. For most learners, the scene in the pictures will be obvious, but if it isn't, you may need to explain that there are websites on the Internet where you can find out about old school friends.
- After practising the dialogues in **exercises 4** and **5**, you could ask students in pairs to invent some surprise announcements, perhaps about people in the class if appropriate, e.g. *Mario has ten children; Carla's going to be on TV tonight*. Everyone finds a new partner, tells them the news and gets a reaction using one of the **natural English** phrases.

read on

- **Exercise 1** is a gist reading task, while **exercise 2** requires learners to read for more detailed information.
- Before students begin talking about **exercises 2** and **3**, it would be sensible to ask if they know of or use any similar websites. There are sites which link up people through workplaces, clubs, military service, etc: you don't need to restrict the discussion to old school friends. While students are sharing their ideas in **exercise 4**, listen and make notes for feedback. Open up the discussion at the end to the whole group. For a follow-up suggestion, see **ideas plus** on the right.

grammar present perfect and past simple revision

- Students will need to use a range of tenses in the **extended speaking** activity at the end of the unit, so this is a chance for some consolidation and revision. They have already studied the past simple and present perfect (see **units one, three, seven** and **nine**), but it would be unrealistic to expect learners to use these forms consistently accurately at this level. **Exercises 1** and **2** are a reminder of the form and use of these tenses. If students are still unclear about the concepts, particularly of the present perfect, you could use a time line to clarify rule B in **exercise 2** (you will find one in the **language reference**, **unit nine** *p.167*). You can also contrast past simple and present perfect (for experience) using time lines: e.g.

  _____x_____x_____NOW   _____2004–2005_____NOW (2006)
  POLAND   POLAND

  I've worked in Poland (We don't know when)   *I worked in Poland last year.*

- For **exercise 3**, you could also photocopy the words in the wordpool and cut them up: give each pair a set of words to rearrange into questions, which they should write down. Do class feedback on the questions they produce, writing them on the board. Students can add questions they hadn't thought of in their notebooks. Ask pairs to write appropriate answers next to their questions in **exercise 4**. Once you have checked that these are correct, the students can use them for pair drilling, perhaps as a **test your partner**. See also **workbook**, **expand your grammar** short responses *p.60* for more practice of these tenses.

speaking it's your turn!

- Students focus here on a conversation (meeting up with old friends) which they will find very useful for the **extended speaking** activity at the end of the unit. See **troubleshooting** on the right.
- When students practise the dialogues in **exercise 2**, in addition to practising the correct sentence stress, it is important that they sound interested and happy to see the old friend; exaggerate the intonation yourself to demonstrate. **Exercise 3** should be light-hearted so don't intervene too much here.
- The language in the jumbled conversation in **exercise 4** brings together the past simple / present perfect with ways of showing surprise. Sometimes, short dialogues are worth memorizing because they integrate useful examples of grammar and predictable patterns. We think this is one such case.
- Once students have memorized the dialogues in **exercise 5**, they can act them out for another pair or ask them to adapt the conversation, changing names, times, jobs, etc. See also **workbook**, **expand your vocabulary** see *p.63* for an extension activity.

we'll meet again

exercise 2
1 false
2 false
3 false

exercise 3
I don't believe it!
That's incredible.
Wow!

exercise 4
go to **listening booklet** *p.38*

language point Internet language
- *on the Net* on the Internet
- *chatroom* (n) area on the Net where people can exchange messages
- *surf* (*the Net*) (v) look at different places on the Net (also used for TV channels)
- *e-mail / e-mail* (n) or (v): *send me an e-mail* or *e-mail it to me*
- *attachment* (n) a computer file or document you send with an e-mail
- *website / webpage* (n) place on the Net where you find information about a subject / organization
- *have access to the* (*Inter*) *net* have the opportunity or right to use the Net
- *online* (adj) connected to the Internet, e.g. *you can buy tickets online*

exercise 1
c

exercise 2
| 1 true | 3 false | 5 false |
| 2 false | 4 true | 6 true |

ideas plus using the Internet

If your class have access to the Internet, you could encourage them to look at one of these English-speaking sites, e.g. **friendsreunited.co.uk**, or **Classmates.com** in the USA. If you are a native speaker, you can register yourself, which will enable your learners to read some of the personal biographies that old classmates have written. Some of these will be accessible to your learners, as they will give simple biographical details not unlike the sort of thing they will be inventing in the **extended speaking** activity at the end of the unit. (e.g. *After I left school, I spent a couple of years working in ... I got married two years ago and now ...*)

exercise 1
2 Have you ever lived there?
3 I saw him with Jane yesterday.
4 I've lived in Paris all my life.
5 She's been at our house since the weekend.
6 They bought their car two years ago.

exercise 2
rule A: sentences 1, 3, 6   rule B: sentences 2, 4, 5

exercise 3 (including possible answers to **exercise 4**)
When did you become a doctor?	Two years ago. / Last year.
Why did you become a doctor?	I don't know.
When did you get married?	In May. / Last year.
Did you enjoy the film?	Yes, I did. / No, I didn't.
How long have you lived in Poland?	Since last year. / For three years. / Five years.
Have you lived in Poland?	Yes, I have. / No, I haven't. / No, never.
Have you worked at that hospital?	Yes, I have. / No, I haven't. / No, never.
How long have you studied English?	Since last year. / For three years. / Five years.

exercise 1
go to **listening booklet** *p.38*

exercise 4
Susie   Well, I'm a journalist.
Mark   Wow! I don't believe it! Me too.
Susie   Who do you work for?
Mark   'The Times'. I got a job there when I left university. How about you?
Susie   I work for 'Sports Weekly.'
Mark   Oh, so how long have you been there?
Susie   Oh, about two years.
Mark   Incredible!

troubleshooting present perfect continuous

The phrase *What have you been doing?* in the **natural English** box in **exercise 1** potentially throws up a new grammatical structure. However, we feel that at this stage, it is best learnt as a chunk or an expression (rather like the way we teach students *Would you like ...* at elementary level without getting involved in grammatical explanations, long before they learn conditionals). It is a very common question, and can be answered without necessarily resorting to the present perfect continuous in the response, e.g. *Oh, well, I left university and then ...*

twelve

extended speaking school reunion   60–75 mins

read about old school friends

invent information about a character's past

prepare questions using **natural English** phrases

role play a conversation with old friends

write about your character for a website

- It is important at the beginning of this activity to let learners read the left-hand column or tell them what they are going to do in the lesson, or put it on the board. This will enable them to get the whole picture. You should also give them time to look back at the **don't forget!** boxes which occur at the end of each section in the unit.

collect ideas

- For adapting this **extended speaking** activity to the level of your class, see the **troubleshooting** on the right.
- **Exercise 1** sets the scene, and gets students to anticipate suitable questions for the activity. Alternatively, you could ask students if they have been to a school reunion. What was it like? Who did they meet? Did any old schoolfriend have an interesting history? Or, you could show a photo of someone in your family (about school leaving age) and explain who it is; say you saw him / her ten years ago, but the family moved to Canada; you met again recently, and tell the students all the things he / she has done, and how he / she has changed.
- It might be helpful to set the date when the profiles in **exercise 2** were originally written. For example, if it is 2005 now, explain that these three schoolfriends finished school and last met in 1995. Students can say who they would like to meet, either in groups, or as a whole class.

invent a character

- It's important to make it absolutely clear that students will be playing the role of one of the characters, but ten years older. If they work with a partner who wants to be the same character, they can brainstorm ideas together in **exercise 3**. Organize the students into same-character pairs, then go through the prompts in the box. Make it clear that they need to think about logical developments for the character they have chosen. For example, Kas might end up having something to do with sport, or perhaps he / she decided to study when he / she was older. You don't need to insist that they think about every category, but they need to have quite a clear profile in order to do the role play.
- **Exercise 4** gives students a chance to practise what they plan to say in a controlled way; this will build confidence, especially for weaker students.
- **Exercise 5** is there to remind students that they will be engaging in a two-way conversation: the role play is not intended to be two monologues.
- Reminding students how to greet old friends, as in **exercise 6**, should get the role plays off to a good start; otherwise, they might take a while to get into the role play.

role play

- For ideas for bringing the role play to life, see **ideas plus** on the right. It would be a good idea to start this off by demonstrating what to do with a (strongish) student in the class. Greet them warmly by name, ask what they've been doing, etc. Don't do too much; just enough for the class to get the point.
- During the role plays in **exercises 7** and **8**, monitor and make notes for feedback at the end. When they have done the role play once, you could bring the class together and give them some feedback. Are they doing it in the right way? Do they need to interact more? Are they showing interest? Don't give feedback at this stage on language errors (save that for later), but intervene if you feel the general performance can be improved. At this stage, you could feed in some ways of bringing the conversation to a close, e.g. *It was lovely to see you / We must meet again.* Then go on to **exercise 9**.

Want to know more? Go to **how to ...** use the learners as a resource (task repetition) *p.172*

writing

- **Exercise 9** provides a writing model for the profiles they will write in **exercise 10**. If you prefer, you could ask learners to write a short profile about themselves to cover the last five or ten years of their life.

| 1 When / After | 2 and then | 3 After | 4 Two years ago | 5 Next year |

we'll meet again

twelve review student's book p.121   45 mins

Want to know more about how to use the reviews? Go to the introduction, *p.10*.

vocabulary professions

- Make it clear that students have to produce professions, e.g. *teaching, law*, and not jobs, e.g. *teacher, lawyer*. They can work or compare with a partner. For a quick follow-up, see if they can produce the related jobs within one minute.

1 IT	3 medicine	5 engineering	7 journalism
2 law	4 banking	6 teaching	8 business

vocabulary activities

- Some dictionaries have study / topic pages with illustrations of sports, hobbies, musical instruments, etc. e.g. *The Oxford Student's Dictionary of English* (for intermediate level); *The Oxford Advanced Learner's Dictionary*. Students could refer to them for this exercise.

exercise 1 possible answers
1 go to the beach / the cinema / the theatre
2 play the clarinet / guitar / piano
3 play football / baseball / tennis
4 have a barbecue / a drink / a meal / a shower / a walk
5 go skiing / horseriding / swimming / shopping

grammar *used to* + verb

- This is another memory game. First students describe pictures of people in **exercise 1** (*p.121*), and then have to produce sentences about them twenty years later (the pictures on *p.147*) using *used to* (*do*) in **exercise 2**. Describing the pictures on *p.121* will familiarize them with the details and make the *used to* (*do*) exercise on *p.147* easier. However, if students are having problems finding the last couple of sentences, let them look back at the original pictures to help.

exercise 2
The man used to have a beard, but now he doesn't.
He used to play football, but now he's a referee.
He used to be thinner, but now he's fatter.
The woman used to have dark hair, but now she's got grey hair.
She used to be a dancer, but now she's a dance teacher.
She never used to wear glasses, but now she does.

natural English

- Using the example, show students that they have to add a word <u>and</u> organize the words into sentences, although they may find it easier to organize the words first and then think about the missing word.
- After **exercise 2**, students could practise saying the sentences and even respond to create mini-dialogues.

see **natural English** boxes in **unit twelve** for answers.

go to **wordlist** *p.141*

---

troubleshooting level of challenge
In the trialling for this **extended speaking** activity, we found that most students enjoyed it very much, though it has to be said that it is quite challenging for weaker classes, or for some (but by no means all) teenage students who found it hard to invent characters because of lack of imagination or experience. If you have a weaker group, keep it simple. You might consider doing it in a more controlled way: for example, the class brainstorms together information about two of the characters in **exercise 3**, then you practise the conversation as a dialogue building activity with the group, and then finally they try it in pairs.

ideas plus bringing role plays to life
Get everyone up on their feet for this role play, and make sure they find a different character to talk to. One way to ensure this happens is for students to have a label with their name on. You could make this really come to life by turning it into a class reunion: perhaps set it in the old school building, have some music and plastic cups (of water) to simulate a party atmosphere.

test yourself!

Want to know more? Go to the **introduction** *p.9* for ways of using the **test yourself!**

1 go; play; get
2 teaching, medicine, law, engineering, journalism
3 Wow! That's incredible!; I don't believe it!; I can't believe it!

1 never
2 more
3 left; spent
4 still

1 I used to go to the beach ~~last week~~. or I **went** to the beach last week.
2 I **saw** it three days ago. or I've seen it **before**.
3 It's lovely **to** see you.
4 Me **neither**.

113

thirteen

in unit thirteen ...

reading speed dating
p.114

wordbooster
p.116

listening how to... describe people
p.118

extended speaking find your perfect partner
p.120

test yourself!
p.121

review
p.121

wordlist
p.142

talk about common interests using **natural English** phrases

read and discuss an article about speed dating

focus on conditional sentences with *would*

talk about the organization of a speed dating event using *would*

reading speed dating

90+ mins

lead-in

- The topic of **exercise 1** overlaps with others in previous units, so try to pair up students who don't usually sit together. However, the aim of this section is to introduce the phrase *have sth in common* so students should, in any case, be getting something new.

- When learners have completed **exercise 4** orally, you could ask them to write down a few sentences. This would also be an opportunity to revise *both* (from **unit one** of the **student's book**) and *neither* (from **unit one** of the **workbook**).

read on

- The article is about a new trend in the UK for people to meet members of the opposite sex. Your learners might also be interested to compare other features of 'dating' in the UK. See the **culture note** on the right.

- We have kept **exercise 1** at a theoretical level as the topic may be a sensitive one for some learners. However, you know your class best. If appropriate, they could extend the exercise and talk about where they met their current boyfriend / girlfriend, or husband / wife / partner.

- After you have worked on the two comprehension tasks in **exercises 2** and **3**, you can ask learners for their reaction to speed dating in **exercise 4**. We think most learners will have a view on the subject, and this might also be a suitable time to incorporate other more general issues, e.g. Is it OK for teenagers to come home when they like? Should people wait until their mid-twenties before they seriously think about marriage? The choice of topic will again depend on the age, attitude and circumstances of the students in your class.

- **Exercise 5** returns to the article to highlight some useful prepositional phrases which might otherwise go unnoticed. Make sure students write these phrases down in their notebooks. For some of them, they could add further examples, e.g. *by e-mail / post / phone; at the end of the evening / afternoon / meeting; talk to each other / write to each other*, etc.

grammar conditional sentences with *would*

- Introduce **exercise 1** by clarifying the hypothetical nature of the situation. For example, ask them if they have been to a speed dating event. If the answer is 'no', then it should be clearer to the group that the situation is not a 'real' one, but just one in which they have to use their imagination. If some learners are not sure about the word 'imagination', you could either translate it or tell them it's just a 'fantasy' (a word many learners know from their first language).

- For potential problems with this structure, see the **language point** on the right.

- As with most grammar presentations, it is a good idea to move round and monitor as much as possible if learners are being asked to write anything down, e.g. **exercise 2**. This helps you to see who is confident about the form, and who isn't. Similarly, if learners are struggling to think about answers, e.g. in **exercise 3**, you can ask them to exchange ideas with a partner, and so you have another opportunity, this time to hear whether the students are confident about the concept. Alternatively, you can do **exercises 2** and **3** as a class using the board if you prefer. Whenever you sense they are finding an exercise difficult, go over it before continuing with the next section; it is vital to carry the learners with you and not leave them struggling some way behind.

- If you feel the group would benefit from further controlled practice after **exercise 5**, go straight to the **language reference** and **practice exercises** on *p.171*.

looking for love

exercise 2
a lot
quite a lot
much

exercise 1 possible answers
They can meet at work, on holiday, or at a sports club. They can meet by accident or be introduced by a friend. Nowadays, people often meet each other via the Internet or by joining a dating agency.

exercise 2
1 How does it work?
2 What type of people will I meet?
3 What if I don't know what to say?
4 How can I get to know someone in three minutes?

exercise 3
| 1 true | 3 false | 5 false |
| 2 true | 4 false | 6 true |

exercise 5
| 1 at | 3 At | 5 At; after |
| 2 to | 4 by | 6 at |

culture note dating in the UK

It is difficult to generalize, but serious dating in the UK generally starts around the age of 15-16. At this age teenagers start going to clubs and parties on a regular basis, but most parents would still expect them home by midnight at the latest.

By the age of 18 most teenagers would be spending more time together in clubs and pubs, and they would probably stay out later. This is also about the time that teenagers start having holidays with friends rather than their parents, although they may have holidays with both.

They don't usually start thinking about marriage or a long-term partner until they are in their twenties.

exercise 2
positive	*if* + subj + past simple tense, subj + 'd / *would* + verb
negative	*if* + subj + past simple tense, subj + *wouldn't* + verb
question	*if* + subj + past simple tense, *would* + subj + verb

exercise 3
1 imagining / thinking about the situation
2 present / future time

exercise 5
2 wouldn't know; went
3 spoke; would feel
4 wouldn't be; were
5 felt; would you take
6 would you wear; went
7 would you feel; met
8 enjoyed; would you go

language point conditional sentences with *would*

As with the first conditional, a common error for some nationalities is to use *would* + verb in both clauses (e.g. *If I would see him, I would tell him*). Some learners also find it difficult to grasp the idea of using the past tense to talk about the present or future time.

The contraction *I'd* /aɪd/ is difficult to hear for some learners, and it may be misunderstood as *I had*.

One of the major problems, however, is in choosing between a real (first) or unreal (second) conditional. This is difficult, partly because the distinction in English can be quite fuzzy, depending often on the speaker's attitude / point of view (both forms may be possible); and also because the conceptual difference may not exist in other languages, e.g. Japanese. For this reason, we have chosen not to contrast the two conditionals at this level, but instead to wait until the intermediate level to tackle this problem. In this lesson, the use is clearly hypothetical, so you shouldn't need to explain the difference between first and second conditional.

thirteen

speaking it's your turn!

- If you have quite an imaginative class and also feel they may have had enough controlled practice of conditionals for one lesson, you could finish with an alternative activity. See **ideas plus** on the right.
- If you use the activity in the **student's book**, it's up to you how much you want learners to work through the questions systematically using a second conditional each time, or whether you are happy to let them take a freer approach and possibly drift away from the structure if they are very engaged in the discussion. After so much controlled practice, we think it is probably wiser to allow a freer approach in **exercise 3** and treat it as a communication activity. It is also worth bearing in mind that it is perfectly natural in spoken English to switch between a conditional structure and a present tense. This happens all the time, e.g. *I* **would invite** *boys and girls of the same age, more or less, because you* **don't want** *to go out with someone who is a lot older or younger.*
- Monitor the activity, and at the end, do feedback on the content: each group could summarize their discussion, for example, and you can then do feedback on their language use.

wordbooster

30–45 mins

> This **wordbooster** should be done at this point in the unit as the vocabulary is needed for the lesson that follows.

describing character

- We would expect learners to be familiar with some of these items in **exercise 1**, but not many will be part of their productive vocabulary, and some present problems of pronunciation, e.g. the diphthong /eɪ/ and the /ʃ/ sound in *patient* /ˈpeɪʃənt/ and the /ʃ/ sound in the final syllable of *ambitious* /æmˈbɪʃəs/.
- **Exercise 3** highlights a difficulty with connotation. See **language point** on the right.
- Learners at this level are generally not very good at using adverbs to qualify adjectives, so the language in the **natural English** box in **exercise 4** will require practice, which is provided in **exercises 5** and **6**. The meaning of *quite* is more complex than the paraphrase we have given, but we feel it is suitable for this level. You can also use the cline (*not friendly / not very friendly / quite friendly / very friendly*) below the **natural English** box to reinforce the concepts.

likes, dislikes, and interests

- *Love*, *like*, and *hate* can all be followed by *-ing* or the infinitive, but the infinitive form sounds more theoretical; and in any case, as *enjoy* can only be followed by *-ing*, it is easier if you stick to the *-ing* form for all of these at this level.
- After learners have done **exercise 2**, you could try the **ideas plus** on the right for a bit of fun. For more work on the *-ing* form after these verbs, go to the **language reference** and **practice exercises** on *p.171*.

looking for love

> **ideas plus** roleplay
>
> If it is culturally appropriate, and you have a reasonable balance of males and females in the group, you could set up your own speed dating role play in class. If possible, organize the furniture so that pairs are sitting opposite one another. Then give them five or ten minutes to think of questions they would like to ask the people they talk to. Suggest that learners think not only of initial questions, but also follow-up questions depending on the reply. Remember they only have three minutes to make an impact, although they can repeat the same questions with each person.
>
> When they start the role play it will be more fun if you have a whistle or bell which you use after three minutes to indicate they must move on to the next person. The number of people they interview will depend on the time available, but it would be nice to have at least three interviews.
>
> It would be insensitive at the end to ask students who they would like to see again, but you could have a more general discussion with the group about some of the more interesting questions and answers.

exercise 1
1 friendly   3 hard-working   5 kind   7 ambitious
2 impatient 4 shy   6 funny 8 organized

exercise 3
a unfriendly; impatient; lazy; selfish; disorganized
b friendly; patient; hard-working; kind; funny; easy-going; organized
c shy; extrovert; serious; ambitious

exercise 4
go to **listening booklet** p.40

> **language point** connotation
>
> Some descriptive adjectives can have a positive or negative connotation, depending on context. Compare:
>
> - She's very **ambitious**, so I think she'll do well.
>   I don't trust her. She's so **ambitious**, she'll say anything.
> - You can never have any fun with Jim. He's so **serious**.
>   Carole's a really **serious** student. She's a fantastic member of my class.
>
> You may need to clarify this point and give further examples.

exercise 1
2 cooking
3 playing computer games
4 sunbathing
5 washing up
6 cycling
7 driving
8 dancing
9 going to the gym

> **ideas plus** vocabulary practice
>
> Students need six or eight small bits of paper. On each one they write the name of an activity which they either like or dislike, e.g. *swimming, housework, homework, tennis*, etc. They work in groups of three, mix up all their slips of paper and put them face down on a desk or table. Each student takes it in turns to pick up a piece of paper and respond immediately using the target language from **exercise 2**, e.g. *I really love swimming* and the other two have to add their responses in reply, e.g. *Me too* or *It's OK* or *Oh, I hate it*. This activity works best if done at a good pace.

thirteen

listening how to ... describe people

75–90 mins

- describe people using **natural English** phrases
- **focus** on vocabulary for describing appearance
- **talk** about people's age using **natural English** phrases
- **listen** to someone describing the character and appearance of a colleague
- **focus** on defining relative clauses
- **write** a description of yourself

lead-in

- You could start by giving an example of someone from your students' country for them to guess, e.g. *He's tall. He's got a beard. He's a footballer.* Monitor as students write in **exercise 1** and correct where necessary. If someone can't think of a famous person, whisper a name to them.
- For the **natural English** box in **exercise 2**, see **language point** on the right.

vocabulary describing appearance

- There are several areas of difficulty with this lexical area. See the **language point** on the right.
- Although we have included phonemic script for a number of items in **exercise 1**, you will still need to highlight the pronunciation, e.g. the silent 'd' in *handsome* /ˈhænsəm/. The different diphthongs in *h<u>ei</u>ght* /haɪt/ and *w<u>ei</u>ght* /weɪt/ also cause problems. Students are given further practice with the vocabulary in **exercises 2** and **3**.
- When learners have completed the **natural English** box in **exercise 4**, you could extend the phrases by adding *early, mid* and *late*, e.g. *in his early twenties, mid thirties, late forties*, etc. If you add this refinement and students use them in **exercise 5**, there is more likely to be some disagreement with regard to the ages of the four people, and therefore more practice of the target language.
- **Exercise 6** gives students the opportunity to personalize the language they've learned so far.

listen to this

- Set the scene for the listening by referring to the picture and explaining that these two people are colleagues; one is asking the other about another colleague in the same company.
- The two recordings in **listen carefully** and **listening challenge** are linked, so it may be advisable to work through **exercises 1–5** as they are in the **student's book**, and then consider doing the activity in **ideas plus** on the right. Alternatively, if you you want to break up the two recordings, you could do the **ideas plus** activity after **exercise 2**.

grammar defining relative clauses

- This is an introduction to a structure which is developed more at the intermediate level. **Exercises 1–3** test basic problems of meaning and form; the emphasis you place on each will depend on the nationality of your students. If you used **ideas plus** in the previous section, **exercise 1** may be unnecessary. It depends on your learners and their knowledge of relative clauses: see the **language point** on the right.
- When learners read out the corrected sentences they agree with in **exercise 4**, encourage them also to discuss the answers. Why don't they agree with certain statements?
- The practice learners get in **exercises 5** and **6** corresponds very closely to the types of relative clause learners will need to produce in the **extended speaking** activity at the end of the unit. If they are able to manipulate these sentences correctly, that is more than enough at this level.

writing

- If you have the slightest doubt that this activity may be too personal or sensitive for some of your learners, omit it. Alternatively, you could keep the profile but amend it. See **troubleshooting** on the right.

looking for love

exercise 2
1 c   2 a   3 b

exercise 3
go to **listening booklet** *p.40*

language point *like*

Learners have already encountered *What is sb / sth like?* on several occasions in this book, but in the **natural English** box they have to use it alongside the other uses of *like* as both preposition and verb. You may also need to remind them that *like* as a verb here can be followed by a noun, e.g. *tennis*, or an *-ing* form, e.g. *playing tennis*. (See **wordbooster** from this unit.)

---

exercises 1, 2 and 3
<u>Carla</u> is very pretty. She's medium height and slim with shoulder length dark hair.
<u>Ana</u> is very pretty. She's tall and slim with long blonde hair.
<u>Robert</u> is very handsome. He's tall and slim with short blond hair.
<u>Eric</u> is quite good-looking. He's short and a bit overweight with short brown hair.

exercise 4
19; 20 and 29; between 40 and 49

language point describing appearance

- *Blond(e)* is one of the few words in English that can have a 'feminine' ending, i.e. *blond* for a man and *blonde* for a woman because it comes from the French language where they have masculine and feminine forms of adjectives. However, *blonde* occurs much more frequently.
- *Slim* is a positive way of describing someone who is *thin*. *Thin* is a difficult word in that it can have a positive or negative connotation. A person may say they 'want to be thin', but saying that someone else is 'very thin' is a criticism.
- *Overweight* is a more positive way of saying someone is fat, and would often be prefaced with '*He / she is a little bit overweight*'.
- Adjective word order also gets quite complicated, but at this level the only general rule you need is that 'length' goes before 'colour', e.g. *short, fair hair*.

---

exercise 1
He's in his late twenties, very tall with long, blond hair.

exercise 2
1 no
2 because David has a free room in his house, and Bob wants to move
3 because his flat is very expensive and a long way from work
4 because Margaret knows everyone

exercise 4
1 David   2 are serious   3 smoke

ideas plus describing someone

The recording is based on a common form of communication, i.e. trying to identify someone that both speaker and listener may know, but not by name. For example:
A *I gave it to David.*
B *David?*
A *Yes, you know the tall guy – the one who works in the library.*

This brings together the vocabulary of the previous section (adjectives to describe people) and the grammar coming up in the next (defining relative clauses). Ask each person to think of someone they both probably know, and describe them using the model above: one physical description, e.g. *she's got dark hair*, and one defining fact, e.g. *she works in reception*. In pairs, they try to identify them i.e. '*You know, she's got dark hair – the girl who works in reception*'.

---

exercise 1
a false   b false   c true   d true

exercise 2
we use *who* to refer to people; we use *which* to refer to things; we can use *that* for people or things in defining relative clauses.

exercise 3
1 I don't like children **who** are noisy.
2 I like people who ~~they~~ are ambitious.
3 I like men who are rich ~~men~~.
4 I enjoy films **which** have a happy ending.
5 I like people **who** speak English slowly.

language point defining relative clauses

A number of languages don't distinguish between personal and non-personal pronouns, so there is likely to be confusion in the choice of *who* or *which* (using *that* for both might be a short-term way round the problem). In other languages e.g. Japanese, relative pronouns don't exist, so relative clauses will be difficult. Go to the **language reference** and **practice exercises** *p.172* or the **workbook** *p.67* for more practice.

---

troubleshooting adapting sensitive material

Put up categories on the board but omit those which may be too personal, such as age or size. Or, use the categories in the **student's book** but make it absolutely clear that learners are free to omit some and add others, e.g. about their jobs or even their background if they wish. You could also restrict the public display of the profiles by doing it in smaller groups, although this may make it too easy for students to guess who wrote each one.

119

thirteen

extended speaking find your perfect partner　　60–75 mins

read two people's profiles and discuss them

invent a profile yourself with a partner

describe your profile to at least three others to find the best partner

invent your 'perfect partner' and describe them

- It is important at the beginning of this activity to let learners read the left-hand column, or tell them what they are going to do in the lesson or put it on the board. This will enable them to get the whole picture. You should also give them time to look back at the **don't forget!** boxes which appear at the end of each section in the unit.

collect ideas

- The statements in **exercise 1** may or may not generate much discussion. If they do, it is a bonus; but if they don't, just move on.
- You need to set the scene very carefully for **exercise 2**. Dating agencies may be relatively unknown in some cultures, and learners also have to be very clear that they are the managers of this dating agency and not the clients.
- When we trialled this activity, we found that the groups who got a lot out of the discussion in **exercise 3** were the ones who read the information carefully and really considered the possible implications. There were also a lot of disagreements. Some students felt that Tomas was too tall for Maria, others that Maria was too serious for Tomas. For some learners their different interests was thought to be a real obstacle, while others felt they had a lot in common as they were similar ages, both involved in travel, both spoke more than one language, etc. Some went as far as to suggest that if Tomas loved his family, he must be a kind person and so Maria would like him (kindness being a quality she admires). So, give learners plenty of time to prepare for **exercise 3**.

create profiles

- Move round and help the pairs with ideas as well as language during **exercise 4**. Furthermore, if the pairs are going to split up for **exercise 6**, it is essential they both write down all the details of their profile. We don't want students just reading out what they have written, but if they don't write it down in the first place they are highly unlikely to remember all of it.
- When each pair has completed their profile in **exercise 4**, get them first to practise it with each other in **exercise 5**, so that they are able to explain more or less everything without referring to their notes.
- If you have fewer than twelve students in the class, you will have to make a decsision about how best to organize the activity. See **troubleshooting** on the right.

find a perfect partner

- For **exercise 6**, instruct students to mingle and find other As or Bs to talk to. Each student can then describe their profile three times and find out about three possible partners. (If you have a smaller group, it will probably just be a single group with individuals explaining their profile to other students.) Monitor throughout, and make notes for feedback at the end. If after the first discussion you think you need to give the class some feedback, that would be fine, but it would need to be relatively short and would really only be necessary if students weren't communicating very well.
- The final part of this activity in **exercise 7** puts learners in a situation where they are talking hypothetically and so they should be able to use *would* here, e.g. *I think they would be good together / get on well because …* After this stage, give learners feedback on language: plenty of encouragement for good language use as well as some errors to correct.
- In **exercise 8** learners are again talking hypothetically, but this time, about themselves. Most learners we have worked with would be happy to do this and view it as a bit of fun, but if you feel it isn't suitable for your class, don't do it. Instead, you could ask the pairs to think about the characters they have created: What would be a good first date for them? Ask them to think about a suitable place, time, activity, etc.

looking for love

thirteen review — student's book p.138 — 45 mins

Want to know more about how to use the reviews? Go to the introduction, p.10.

grammar conditional sentences with would

- Put the first question on the board. (*What would you do if you ... (lose) your passport on holiday abroad?*) Ask students to complete it: check the concept and form, i.e. Are you imagining the situation? (Yes.) Is it probably going to happen? (No.) *Lost* is in the past form. Are we talking about a situation in the past, or now / in the future? (Now / the future.) Then tell students to complete the rest of the sentences. Go over the answers.
- **Exercise 2** gives students a chance to rehearse their answers and practise reading the questions aloud. For **exercise 3**, encourage them to choose five random questions, not just the first five, otherwise the guessing activity in **exercise 4** will be too easy.

exercise 1
1 lost	3 felt	5 left	7 went; was	9 rang
2 didn't understand	4 saw	6 broke	8 found	10 gave

vocabulary describing character

- If students can't answer a clue by themselves in **exercise 1**, they can work with another student doing the same clues i.e. A students can work together as can B students.
- Put students into A / B pairs for **exercise 2**. They read the clues which they have completed, but not their answers, to see if their partner can get the answer. Make it clear students shouldn't show their partner the clues but they can take it in turns to read their clues aloud. At the end, they should look at the answers they couldn't solve, and see if they can work out the question in purple squares as this might help with any missing answers. Go over any problems at the end.

Student A
1 hard-working	5 serious	9 lazy
3 organized	7 selfish	11 kind

Student B
2 shy	6 easy-going	10 ambitious
4 extrovert	8 friendly	12 impatient

Question: What is he like?

natural English & vocabulary describing people

- Tell students to think of someone in the class and complete the table individually.
- **Exercise 2** can be done in pairs or quickly as a whole class. Check pronunciation of these questions, then demonstrate the activity in **exercise 3**. Think of someone in the class and get students to ask you about them: they should be able to guess who it is. During the mingling activity, monitor and make notes for feedback.

exercise 2
1 How old is he / she?
2 What does he / she look like?
3 What's he / she like?
4 What does he /she like doing?

go to **wordlist** *p.142*

---

troubleshooting small groups

If you only have eight or ten students, you will have to compromise in some way. You could ask learners to prepare their profiles individually in **exercise 4**. The drawback is that they lose out on the negotiation of their profile with a partner, and possibly have fewer ideas as well; the advantage is that there will still be a number of different profiles to discuss in **exercise 6**.

The alternative is to keep the pairs in **exercise 4**. The disadvantage is that they will probably only have two profiles to choose from in **exercise 6**.

Finally, with pair activites, you always have the problem of what to do with an odd number of students. Here we would suggest that the best option is to have one learner (a strong student) creating a profile on their own. You can then spend a bit more time with this student in **exercise 5**.

test yourself!

Want to know more? Go to the **introduction** *p.9* for ways of using the **test yourself!**

1 friendly; organized; ambitious; impatient; kind, serious, selfish
2 black hair; tall and slim; a handsome / good-looking man
3 in; At; in; At; to

1 which / that
2 quite
3 very
4 like

1 If you **went** to Prague, I'm sure you'd love it.
2 I don't like boys **who** shout a lot.
3 Do you enjoy **working** there?
4 If I **had** a lot of money, I'd spend it.

121

fourteen

in unit fourteen ...

reading where shall we stay?
p.122

wordbooster
p.124

listening how to ... get through an airport
p.126

extended speaking hotels
p.128

test yourself!
p.129

review
p.129

wordlist
p.143

---

talk about places you've stayed in using **natural English** phrases

read and talk about hotels in Japan

focus on present and past passives

write a letter of complaint using passive forms

---

reading where shall we stay?

90+ mins

lead-in

- The **lead-in** starts with a short personalized speaking activity about holiday accommodation. See the **troubleshooting** box on the right.

- In the **natural English** box in **exercise 3**, *that* is a demonstrative pronoun. It refers back to a past time, event, or period which has already been mentioned; e.g. in conversation 1, *that* refers back to *stay in a really expensive hotel*; in conversation 2, *that* refers to *rent a holiday villa*. This may have an equivalent in your learners' mother tongue. If not, write the first dialogue on the board (from the **listening booklet**), and draw an arrow from *that* to *stay in ... hotel*.

- In **exercise 5** you might want to adapt the prompts (places to stay) to your teaching context. Are there other places where people stay in the country you are in? In Spain and Portugal, for example, there are *paradores* and *hostales* and in France, *gîtes* and *pensions*. You may also need to clarify the meaning of items such as *bed and breakfast* through translation. The practice dialogue in this exercise is a classic example of present perfect for experience followed by past simple for additional information / at a specific time. You can encourage them to continue their conversations beyond three lines by demonstrating with one student first in front of the class.

read on

- Before students start **exercise 1**, spend a little time together talking about the pictures. Are they familiar with the labelled items: *robe, mats*? Then give them time to read the articles and match them with the comments.

- If you have Japanese learners in your class, it would be genuinely interesting to ask them what they think of these texts, as they are authentic website articles written by Westerners. Do they think the information is accurate? Are there other kinds of hotel? Other learners in a multinational class may have questions to ask them.

- Students can compare ideas for **exercise 2**. Don't worry about pronunciation of the Japanese names unless you have a Japanese learner in your class who can correct you! Then give the class a chance to react in **exercises 3** and **4**. Do a quick class feedback on their views. For a different speaking activity, see **ideas plus** on the right.

grammar present and past passives

- Now that your learners are approaching intermediate level, they should not have too much trouble manipulating past and present simple passive forms. For more information on passives, see the **language point** on the right.

- For **exercise 1**, you could write the sentences on the board and ask the concept check questions yourself if you prefer.

- After **exercise 2**, ask the students to say the sentences. Make sure they use weak forms for *are* /ə/, *was* /wəz/ and *were* /wə/.

- When students have done **exercise 3** and you have checked the answers, you could add extra practice. Working in pairs, students take turns to read out a sentence, and they discuss whether it is always true or sometimes true in their experience. For more practice, you will see that the **writing** activity below includes passives, and you can also direct students to the **language reference** and **practice exercises** on *p.172*.

service with a smile

exercise 2
Nick: in Scotland; when his brother got married.
Emma: Ibiza; a couple of years ago.

exercise 3
When was that?   Where was that?

---

troubleshooting learners' experience

Most learners will have some experience of staying away from home or going on holiday, but if some of your class have never done this, here are some things you can do:
- Ask learners to put up their hands if they have had this kind of experience, then pair up students so that one has experience and the other hasn't; or put them in threes.
- Encourage students who have never stayed in a hotel to ask questions so that they get some communicative mileage out of it.
- Adapt the activity so that they talk about staying with a member of their family.

---

exercise 1
A a gaijin house   C a capsule hotel
B a ryokan

exercise 2
1 a capsule hotel   4 a gaijin house
2 a gaijin house   5 a ryokan
3 a ryokan   6 a capsule hotel

---

ideas plus speaking

To provide speaking practice, put this table on the board for students to copy and complete.

Where could these people stay in your home town? Complete the table. Give reasons.

a Japanese student for a few days' holiday
    Place 1_____ Why? _____
    Place 2 _____ Why? _____
an Australian teacher working for six months
    Place 1_____ Why? _____
    Place 2 _____ Why? _____

Put them in small groups to discuss their answers.

Each group then thinks of another visitor with a specific reason for coming to their town. They give their idea to another group to decide where they should stay and why.

---

exercise 1
1 b – someone who works in the hotel
2 b – the things that the people do

exercise 2
PRESENT SIMPLE
    Futons **are put** on the floor for guests.
    A ryokan **is owned** and run by a family.
PAST SIMPLE
    Dinner **was brought** to us in our room.
    We **were served** tea.

exercise 3
1 are given   4 is cleaned   7 is included
2 is taken   5 is made   8 were provided
3 is served   6 are given   9 were washed

---

language point present and past passives

We tend to use the passive more commonly in written English, and it is relatively infrequent in spoken English, apart from certain common phrases, e.g. *I was born / brought up in ...* In addition, the use of *by* + agent is less common than shorter forms, e.g. *She was taken to hospital* is more likely than, *She was taken to hospital by ambulance*. In some languages such as Italian, Spanish, and Arabic, passive forms are generally used much less; in others, such as Japanese, it is sometimes used in a different way: Japanese: *He was stolen his money* = English: *His money was stolen*.

For some nationalities, passive forms may exist, but students are easily confused about the uses of the verb *be*, e.g. *was made* (passive) being confused with *was making* (active, continuous).

123

fourteen

writing

- The present and past passives are used in a realistic written context here, and the letter provides a model for the students' own writing. They should read the letter through first to get the gist, e.g. Ask them 'Was he happy with the hotel?' before they start filling the gaps. **Exercise 1** checks that they understand where to use active and passive forms, and **exercise 2** checks understanding of the text.

- In **exercise 3**, you may wish to spell out the differences in letter layout from that of your learners' culture. The address of both sender and recipient may be in a different place; the greetings may be different; and in some cases the sender's name may appear elsewhere.

- For **exercise 4**, you might prefer students to work alone, or to write their letters for homework. If so, they can bring their letters to class the following day and compare with their partner (**exercise 5**). This can be a useful opportunity for some peer correction, and you could allow time for them to go over their letters, ask your advice and make corrections. Collect the letters at the end to correct and give back.

- For an extension activity, see **ideas plus** on the right. For more letter writing practice, see **natural English** pre-intermediate **reading and writing skills resource book** *pp.26, 34 and 46*.

wordbooster

30–45 mins

> This **wordbooster** can be done at this point in the unit or just before the **extended speaking** activity.

hotel rooms and bathrooms

- Students working together should be able to label some of the items in **exercise 1**, and those they don't know they can find in a dictionary. For more information about hotel facilities, see the **culture note** on the right.

- With these items, many of the problems are to do with pronunciation: the /θ/ sound in *toothbrush* and *toothpaste* is difficult; *soap* /səʊp/ is sometimes confused with *soup* /suːp/; *towel* /ˈtaʊəl/, *razor* /ˈreɪzə/, and *iron* /ˈaɪən/ are not pronounced in the way they are written; *mineral water* / ˈmɪnərəl ˈwɒtə/, *toilet paper* / ˈtɔɪlət ˈpeɪpə/, and *hairdryer* /ˈheədraɪə/ are often wrongly stressed.

- The focus on countable / uncountable nouns in **exercise 3** will be useful when they study the vocabulary in the **natural English** box in **exercise 4**, i.e. *another* + singular countable noun, *some more* + uncountable noun or plural countable noun. Practising these requests in **exercises 5** and **6** will be very useful for the **extended speaking** activity at the end of the unit.

- For more work on compound nouns, refer students to the **language reference** and **practice exercises** on *p.173*.

verbs often confused

- Many learners have problems with these pairs of verbs; often because in their own language, they are expressed through one verb only. Once students have completed the sentences in **exercise 1**, let them collaborate in pairs. This may sort out many of the difficulties in meaning before class feedback. You might need to do quite a bit of concept checking during the feedback to make sure that students are clear on the differences. See **language point** on the right.

- **Exercise 2** gives students further practice in discriminating between the pairs of verbs and can be done alone, then students can compare answers.

service with a smile

exercise 1
1 booked
2 asked
3 arrived
4 was given
5 were taken
6 was cleaned
7 is served
8 wasn't served

exercise 2
He was given a room next to the kitchen; the bags were taken to the wrong room; there was no soap in the bathroom; the room was cleaned once in three days; on two days, breakfast wasn't served until 7.45;

exercise 3
In a formal letter:
write your address at the top, on the right
write the date under your address
write the address of the person you are writing to on the left
begin Dear Sir (or Dear Madam)
end Yours faithfully

ideas plus role play
You can use the letter to provide more oral practice of the passive forms in a realistic context. Set the situation: you have written the letter to the manager, but not yet received a reply. You decide to telephone the manager. To your surprise, the manager says he has not received your letter, so you have to explain the problems again. The manager has to react appropriately and apologize for the different problems, and offer compensation.

When you divide students into guest and manager pairs, the guest will have quite a lot of information to memorize. While they are doing that, speak to the managers and ask them to plan different forms of compensation that that they can offer, e.g. money back, a free meal, or night at the hotel.

---

exercise 1
1 towel
2 toothbrush
3 toothpaste
4 toilet paper
5 razor
6 hairdryer
7 soap
8 iron
9 minibar
10 mineral water

exercise 3
<u>Countable</u>: toothbrush, towel, razor, hairdryer, minibar, iron
<u>Uncountable</u>: toothpaste, toilet paper, mineral water, soap

exercise 4
go to **listening booklet** p.42

exercise 5
We use *another* with singular countable nouns; we use *some more* with uncountable nouns and plural countable nouns.

culture note hotel facilities
Large international hotel chains are often similar in the facilities they provide in the bedrooms, but in smaller hotels and guest houses, there are often cultural differences. For example, in the UK, tea and coffee-making facilities are nearly always provided, even in a B&B. In some hotel rooms, there is a trouser press, and guests can request an iron / ironing board, or in larger hotels, use a laundry service. You only find flowers and fruit in hotel rooms if requested for a special occasion. Minibars are not provided everywhere. Bathrooms usually have a bath, sometimes with a shower as well, but bidets are rare. And finally, in a B&B, you might get a duvet rather than sheets and blankets.

---

exercise 1
1 bring   2 take   3 borrow   4 lend   5 told   6 said   7 left   8 forgot

exercise 2
1 I'm sorry I'm late, but I **left** my homework on the bus.
2 Can you **lend** me some money until tomorrow? or Could I borrow ~~me~~ some money until tomorrow?
3 correct
4 correct
5 correct
6 My doctor **told** me to stop smoking. or My doctor said ~~me~~ to stop smoking.
7 correct
8 His teacher **said** that he was very clever. or His teacher told **me** that he was very clever.

language point verbs often confused
For *bring* and *take*, you can make it clear that when you **come** to class (i.e. to the place you are in now), you *bring* your book, and when you **go** home (i.e. to another place, not here) you *take* it with you.

For *borrow* and *lend*, act out a situation where you *borrow* a student's pen (use it then give it back) and explain that you *borrowed* it, and the student *lent* it to you.

For *tell* and *say*, point out that *tell* is followed by a person, i.e. *tell her / me / them*, etc. whereas you *say something*, i.e. *she said the train was late*.

For *forget* and *leave*, stress that you *leave* something in a place, e.g. *She left her purse on the table*, but you *forget* to bring or take something e.g. *I forgot my coat*.

fourteen

listening how to ... get through an airport
75–90 mins

study vocabulary relating to airports

make requests using **natural English** phrases

listen to a check-in conversation, and a flight enquiry

role play an airport situation using **natural English** phrases

vocabulary airports

- The vocabulary in **exercise 1** is straightforward. You could point out to students that *suitcase* is countable, but *luggage* (or *baggage*) is uncountable in English; this is not the case in some other languages. *Scales* (meaning a weighing machine) on the other hand, is a plural noun, i.e. it always has an *s*, like *trousers, scissors, sunglasses*, etc. Check students' pronunciation of the items, especially the ones given in phonemic script.

- In **exercise 2**, once students have matched the words, you can check understanding by asking questions. Where do you wait for the plane? Where can you sit on a plane? Which phrase means an airport building? etc. Highlight the word stress in these compound words (see the **answer key**); and ask students to mark the stress and practise saying them aloud.

- **Exercise 3** is a comprehension check, and also provides a simple story in which to memorize the items. You could use this exercise in different ways. Once students have filled the gaps correctly, you could give them a few minutes in pairs to practise reading and memorizing the text (it is a very predictable script). They keep saying it and testing each other. Then, they shut their books and try to write it down. Another approach is for student A to shut their book and student B to read the text aloud, pausing when they get to a gap which A must complete orally.

- **Exercise 4** is a chance for some personalization. For more on the requests in the **natural English** box in **exercise 6**, see **language point** on the right. For more practice on *could* for requests see **language reference** and **practice exercises** *p.173*.

listen to this

- This listening activity should be a useful one for anyone travelling by plane where English is needed. It also acts as a model for the role play which students will do at the end of the lesson in **speaking it's your turn!**.

- You could start this section with a prediction activity to help arouse interest and aid the first listening. See **ideas plus** on the right.

- In **exercise 2**, more than one answer is possible in terms of logic. However, this activity will make students familiar with the prompts / stages, and provides a framework for the comprehension task that follows in **exercise 3**. **Exercise 4** checks understanding in more detail.

- The phrases in the **natural English** box in **exercise 6** are useful generally for students, and will also be useful in the role play and **extended speaking** activity at the end of the unit. However, they are difficult to practise in a controlled but natural way. Focusing on them in the **listening booklet** transcripts as suggested will raise their profile.

speaking it's your turn!

- For general information on how to approach this role play, see **troubleshooting** on the right.

- Your role here is to manage the activity. Organize students into pairs to work together preparing the roles. Monitor as they do this and help where necessary. If you have an odd number of students, have one group of three preparing a role, and then make sure that they take turns to do the role play. Reorganize the students into A / B pairs, and monitor the conversations. If you like, do some quick feedback when they have done it once: be supportive, but point out any major language problems. They can then keep the same role, but just find a new partner and do it again. Then ask them to swap role cards, plan alone quickly, then do it again. (Although they will be playing a different role, they should be very familiar with the activity and not need to plan with a partner a second time.) At the end, you can record some pairs doing the role play, or ask a pair to act it out. Give feedback on their performance.

service with a smile

exercise 1
1 trolley
2 queue
3 hand luggage
4 passenger
5 check-in desk
6 scales
7 suitcase

exercise 2
<u>ter</u>minal <u>one</u>; <u>passport</u> con<u>trol</u>; <u>boarding</u> card; de<u>par</u>ture lounge; <u>aisle</u> seat; gate <u>twelve</u>

exercise 3
1 check-in desk
2 queue
3 suitcase
4 scales
5 aisle seat
6 boarding card
7 passport control
8 departure lounge

exercise 6
go to **listening booklet** *p.42*

---

language point politeness

Learners are sometimes amused by the polite formulae used in requests in English, but it is sensible to learn them. These polite forms may help to make up for any deficiencies in pronunciation caused by inappropriate intonation. <u>Do stress to your students that native speakers often mistake inappropriate intonation for rudeness or directness.</u> At the same time, it's important to ensure that these are used in a relevant context: an overly polite request to a friend for something trivial might sound like sarcasm. In the practice in **exercise 8**, point out that these are requests to strangers. When you are asking someone to put themselves to some trouble on your behalf, *Could you possibly ...?* is more appropriate than just *Could you ... .*

---

exercise 1
He can't find his ticket.

exercise 3
he gives her his passport; he asks for a window seat; he puts his luggage on the scales; she asks about his hand luggage; she asks some security questions; she gives him the flight information

exercise 4
1 no
2 15 kg
3 three
4 16A
5 gate 11
6 a good flight

exercise 5
The flight is delayed 30–40 minutes.
It's delayed because of a problem with the luggage.

exercise 6
go to **listening booklet** *p.42*

---

ideas plus prediction

Tell students to look at the picture of the traveller and tell them that he's just arrived at the check-in desk. With a partner, can they think of five things that the check-in person or the traveller will say? They can note these down. At the end of the listening (after **exercise 4**) ask them to look again at their notes. Did they hear any of their ideas?

---

troubleshooting role playing

Some learners are nervous of role play because they think they have to play a character different from themselves. In this airport role play, they are simply playing themselves as a passenger or being a check-in person, which doesn't require any specialist knowledge. Make it clear that they will play both roles, and that it could be useful to them in the future. Notice too that each role card gives students some planning suggestions: the passenger has to think of their own requirements, so they can adapt it to their own situation, and the check-in person needs to plan their prompts. Planning what to say with another student playing the same role can help confidence.

Most pre-intermediate classes should manage this role play well. However, if your class needs a great deal of support, you could work through the role play first as a dialogue build: the group can look at the two role cards together, and you can elicit what each person could say. Practise it as a class, then ask them to role play it in pairs. This would mean the activity was very controlled and less spontaneous, though. In that case, in the following lesson, you could use the role cards again, this time asking each student to plan what to say on their own, and then role play in pairs. This may produce a freer more creative exchange second time round.

fourteen

extended speaking hotels

60–75 mins

read and talk about hotel notices

prepare a role play in a hotel

act out situations in a hotel reception

discuss the role play

- It is important at the beginning of this activity to let learners read the left-hand column or tell them what they are going to do in the lesson, or put it on the board. This will enable them to get the whole picture. You should also give them time to look back at the **don't forget!** boxes which occur at the end of each section in the unit.

collect ideas

- In this **extended speaking** activity, students will do a series of short role plays in a hotel, both as receptionists and guests. **Exercise 1** sets the scene for the lesson, and gives students an opportunity to give their opinions. Tell them to look at the notices, then ask what they think about the first one (breakfast times). This should elicit some reactions before they discuss their ideas in pairs.

prepare the role play

- Divide your class in half so that students can work on the same role card as their neighbour. The role cards guide them quite carefully to complete questions, requests and problems and then think up their own. It is very important to clarify that As are guests in the hotel; they are not casual callers asking for information – so they shouldn't be asking for a room, or the price of the rooms, etc. However, you could make it clear that they have only arrived that day, which will enable them to make a number of legitimate requests for information about the facilities. Both guests and receptionists will prepare questions so that when they swap roles in **exercise 4**, they will have all their prompts ready.
- You might decide to set the role play in a specific context – for example, a hotel in your town that the students all know. This could make the questions about the local area more realistic. See **troubleshooting** on the right.
- At a relevant point, encourage students to start practising their questions together, and monitor / correct their pronunciation.

role play

- You could give each learner a label to indicate whether they are guests or receptionists. Alternatively, if possible rearrange the seating in the classroom, with receptionists standing / sitting around the edge of the room and guests in the middle: they can then go easily from one receptionist to another. Let the guests find a receptionist and start their role play. Each role play will only take a minute or two, but they can try their questions on different receptionists – as many as they like. As you monitor the first role play or two, make notes, but if there are specific problems that you want to feedback before too long, call the class together and deal with them. However, if things are going well, don't interrupt.
- At a relevant point, tell the class to swap roles (**exercise 4**) and rearrange the class as necessary. Monitor and make notes.
- **Exercise 5** gives students a chance to reflect on their role plays; at the same time, this should be quite light-hearted. You could have a class vote on who made the best receptionist.

listen

- You can use the listening at this point, or if you prefer, you can use it earlier in the lesson: either before **exercise 2**, to set the scene, or before **exercise 3**, as a model. If your students' conversations were longer than these, so much the better.

exercise 7

GUEST'S PROBLEM	RECEPTIONIST'S SOLUTION
1 He needs directions to the concert hall.	He shows him on a map.
2 She needs an umbrella.	He lends her one.
3 He's left his key in his room.	He gives him a spare key.
4 She needs a hairdresser for her son.	There's one on the first floor.

service with a smile

fourteen review student's book p.139   45 mins

Want to know more about how to use the reviews? Go to the introduction, p.10.

vocabulary hotel rooms and bathrooms

- Exercise 1 should be fairly easy in terms of remembering the words but pronouncing them correctly will be more difficult. When you go over the answers to exercise 2, make sure learners are also saying the words with the correct stress, e.g. putting the stress on the first syllable of *toothpaste* but on the second syllable of *shampoo*.

exercise 1
1 shampoo, 2 mirror, 3 razor, 4 toothpaste, 5 toothbrush, 6 shower curtain, 7 soap, 8 washbasin, 9 shower, 10 toilet paper, 11 toilet, 12 bath, 13 towel, 14 hairdryer

exercise 2
1 toothbrush, toothpaste
2 washbasin, razor, toilet paper, toothpaste
3 shower, towel
4 toilet
5 soap
6 hairdryer

vocabulary airports

- In exercise 2, make sure students don't simply look at each other's answers; they must read out their sentences in order. This will give them some oral practice.
- Students can do exercise 3 in pairs, and when they do the mingling in exercise 4, let them talk freely. Monitor and make notes for feedback at the end.

exercise 1
1 d, 2 h, 3 b, 4 f, 5 c, 6 a, 7 g, 8 e

grammar present passive

- In exercise 1, students are only asked to provide one answer, but there may be several and if they want to write more, they can.
- For exercise 2, go through the example carefully so they know exactly what they have to do. At the end you could elicit some exchanges around the class. Keep the pace fairly rapid and tell students to shout out if they think an answer is wrong.

exercise 1 possible answers
2 kiosk, post office, some shops (depends on the country), 3 kitchen, bathroom, laundrette, 4 car park, garage, street, 5 cinema, theatre, library, classroom, buses, etc. (depends on the country), 6 airport, shops, banks, post office (depends on the country), 7 factory, 8 hotel, sports centre, swimming pool, gym, 9 school, university, hospital, 10 restaurant, hotel (depends on the country)

natural English

- After exercise 2, learners can practise the short dialogues in pairs.

see natural English boxes in unit fourteen for answers.

go to wordlist p.143

---

troubleshooting planning questions

Monitor carefully when students are preparing, and try to encourage them to produce realistic questions. (For instance, *Can I use the TV?* is not a very realistic question, whereas *How do I use the TV?* or *Can you show me how the TV works?* is a more likely question, given that TVs / videos in hotels or hotel rooms sometimes have rather complicated remote controls.)

You will also notice that students are likely to spend some time negotiating together how to express their questions. This is to be encouraged: they are rehearsing language and will want to get it right. Look at the examples below of two learners from our trialling data who are 'polishing' a question.

A *Have you got my message? Have you got ...?*
B *I have any message?*
A *Have you got ...?*
B *Do you have any message?*
A *Have you got any message?*
B *I need in this question, 'have you got any message for me?'*
A *OK.*

They still need to make *message* plural, but they have found a good question to suit their needs.

test yourself!

Want to know more? Go to the introduction p.9 for ways of using the test yourself!

1 toothpaste, razor, soap, towel, toilet paper, hairdryer, shampoo
2 desk, card, seat, luggage
3 another, some more, another, some more

1 served
2 queue
3 Could
4 that

1 Can you **lend** me a pen? or Can **I borrow** ~~me~~ a pen?
2 Breakfast is include**d** in the price.
3 I've **left** my money at home.
4 Could you **bring** me the books from over there?

129

one wordlist

natural English

asking people to be quiet
Shut up! _____
Quiet! Be quiet! _____
Shh! _____
Could you be quiet, please? _____

what's ... like?
What's (your flat) like? _____
What's (her new boyfriend) like? _____

showing interest
Wow! _____
Really? _____
(That's) interesting! _____
(That's) fantastic! _____

possessive 's
Robert's boss _____
Emma's ex-boyfriend _____

both
They both come from Spain. _____
They're both journalists. _____
Both of them speak English. _____

how about you?
How about you? _____
And you? _____

wordbooster

relatives
father / mother _____
brother / sister _____
son / daughter _____
uncle / aunt _____
grandfather / grandmother _____
brother-in-law / sister-in-law _____
son-in-law / daughter-in-law _____
nephew / niece _____
cousin _____
stepfather / stepmother _____
parents _____
grandparents _____
relatives (also relations) _____

talking about you and your family
an only child _____
a close family _____
on my own _____
strict _____
argue a lot _____
get on very well with sb _____
ten years old _____
family celebration _____
single parent _____
get married _____

glossaries
darling (n) _____
kiss (n) _____
dad / daddy ☺ (n) _____
granny (n) _____
mum / mummy ☺ (n) _____
boring (adj) _____
turn up (v) _____
date (n) _____
upset (adj) _____
unreliable (adj) _____
spend (time) _____
furious (adj) _____

two wordlist

natural English

have + noun

	your language
(What time do you) have breakfast?	_____
(Where did you) have lunch yesterday?	_____
(What did you) have for dinner last night?	_____
(Shall we) have a coffee?	_____

a lot, much, many, any

We eat a lot of (cheese).	_____
We don't drink much / a lot of (tea).	_____
We don't eat many / a lot of (biscuits).	_____
We don't eat any (frozen food).	_____

saying sorry

I'm sorry I'm late.	_____
I'm really sorry about that.	_____
I didn't have time to do it.	_____
That's OK. Don't worry.	_____
Don't worry. It doesn't matter.	_____

offering food or drink

Would you like something to eat?	_____
How about something to drink?	_____

talking about a picture

I think he's / she's saying, ' … '	_____
I think he's / she's asking, ' … '	_____

vocabulary

food

rice	_____
pasta	_____
bread	_____
instant coffee	_____
chick peas	_____
aubergine	_____
olives	_____
spinach	_____
courgette	_____
carrots	_____
red pepper	_____
onion	_____
frozen peas	_____
grapes	_____

wordbooster

restaurant language

	your language
starter	_____
main course	_____
dessert	_____
wine list	_____
Here's the menu.	_____
Are you ready to order?	_____
I'd like …	_____
I'll have …	_____
Enjoy your meal.	_____
Is everything all right?	_____
Could I have the bill?	_____

extreme adjectives

awful	_____
disgusting	_____
horrible	_____
terrible	_____
delicious	_____
wonderful	_____
gorgeous	_____
brilliant	_____
fabulous	_____

three wordlist

natural English

your language

the best / worst thing about ...
The best thing about (living in a city) is ... _____
The worst thing is ... _____

once, twice, etc
Have you ever ... ? _____
No, never. _____
Yes, once. _____
Yes, twice. _____
Yes, a couple of times. _____
Yes, a few times. _____
Yes, lots of times. _____

a five-minute walk
How long does it take to get there? _____
It's a five-minute drive. _____
 a ten-minute bus ride. _____
 a twenty-minute walk. _____
It's five minutes by car / by bus / on foot. _____

asking where things are
Excuse me, ... _____
 is there a (post office) near here? _____
 where's the nearest (bank) ? _____
 how far's (the station) ? _____
There's one down the road. _____
It's over there. _____

a great / horrible place
a great place to live _____
a horrible place to work _____
an expensive place to stay _____
It's opposite the pizza place. _____

vocabulary

prepositional phrases
on the edge of town _____
right in the centre _____
quite near the centre _____
in the countryside _____
very close to the centre _____
round the corner from the hotel _____

your language

at the end of the road _____
opposite (the bank) _____
on the corner _____
next to (the post office) _____
down the road _____
just outside / behind (the cinema) _____

wordbooster

describing towns
car park _____
factory _____
park _____
market _____
library _____
(night) club _____
doctor's surgery _____
petrol station _____

noisy / peaceful _____
clean / polluted _____
safe / dangerous _____
quiet / lively _____
ugly / attractive _____
relaxing / stressful _____

distance and time
quite near _____
not very far _____
quite a long way _____
a long way _____

glossaries
refugee (n) _____
pale (skin) (adj) _____
privacy (n) _____
celebrity (n) _____
shaving (n) _____

132 Photocopiable © Oxford University Press 2005

four wordlist

your language   your language

natural English

this / that; these / those
I like this one. _____
I hate that one. _____
I like these. _____
I quite like those. _____

can / can't afford
I can't afford that car. _____
I can't afford to go on holiday. _____
Can you afford it? _____

wear / carry
She's wearing (a jacket). _____
Do you usually wear (glasses)? _____
She's wearing (a ring on her finger). _____
She's carrying (an umbrella). _____

talking about size
What size are you? _____
What size do you take? _____
It's / They're the wrong size. _____
It doesn't fit. _____
It's a bit big / small. _____
They're a bit long / short. _____

vocabulary

shopping
What size are you? _____
Could I try these on? _____
Do they fit? _____
Have you got them in a bigger size? _____
What do you think of them? _____
Where do I pay? _____
They're too tight. _____
Over there, at the counter. _____
They look good on you. _____
The changing room's over there. _____
I'm a (size) 28. _____
Here you are. _____

wordbooster

clothes
top _____
jumper _____
shirt _____
jacket _____
tie _____
jeans _____
skirt _____
suit _____
belt _____
cap _____
tights _____
socks _____
trainers _____
high heels _____
necklace _____
bracelet _____
ring _____
umbrella _____
briefcase _____

phrasal verbs
take sth off _____
try sth on _____
take sth back _____
pick sth up _____
hang sth up _____
turn sth on _____
put sth on _____
turn sth off _____
put sth down _____

glossary

discount (n) _____
haggle (v) _____
tell a lie _____
(10%) off (prep) _____
stall (n) _____

five wordlist

natural English

your language

how do you spell ... ?
I don't know how to spell ... _____
How do you spell ... ? _____
You spell it with double F. _____

asking for permission
Can (we borrow the cassettes)? _____
Yes, of course. _____
Is it OK if (I use the printer)? _____
Yeah, no problem. _____
No, I'm sorry, you can't. _____

what / when you like
You can wear what you like. _____
You can study what you like. _____
You can eat when you like. _____

saying if things are true
(I think) that's (usually) true. _____
I'm not sure (about that). _____
I don't think that's (usually) true. _____
(I'm sure) that's not true. _____
It depends. _____

giving instructions / advice
Remember to (write clearly). _____
Don't (speak to other people). _____
Always (make a plan). _____
It's a good idea to (arrive early). _____

vocabulary

study centre
bookshelf _____
computer _____
file _____
video _____
cassette _____
CD _____
cassette recorder _____
headphones _____
photocopier _____

wordbooster

your language

verb + noun collocation
take an exam _____
go to school _____
wear a uniform _____
join a club _____
leave school _____
miss a lesson _____
pass / fail an exam _____
revise for an exam _____
make progress _____

school and university
nursery school _____
primary school _____
secondary school _____
college / university _____
state school _____
be (five) years old _____
at the age of 16 _____
it depends on ... _____
... until you are 18. _____

glossaries
hit (v) _____
carry on (v) _____
it's (her) fault (n) _____
liar (n) _____
routine (n) _____
pack (v) _____
breathe (v) _____
confidence (n) _____

six wordlist

your language

natural English

a bit + adjective, a bit of + noun
a bit cloudy / warmer _____
a bit of rain / time _____

guessing
What's this? _____
I'm not sure. _____
It might be … _____
I've no idea. _____

what sort / kind of…?
What sort of food do you like? _____
What kind of car do you drive? _____

vague language around, about, or so
around 25 degrees _____
about 5cm of snow _____
an hour or so _____

vocabulary

parts of a country
in the north _____
in the south _____
in the east _____
in the west _____
in the north-east _____
in the south-west _____
on the north / south / east / west coast _____
in the centre _____
on the border _____
in the mountains _____
the capital _____
an island (off the coast) _____

your language

wordbooster

weather conditions
There will be … _____
  some sunshine. _____
  a lot of cloud. _____
  some wind. _____
  some fog. _____
  some snow. _____
  a lot of rain. _____
It will be … _____
  sunny. _____
  cloudy. _____
  windy. _____
  foggy. _____
It will … _____
  snow. _____
  rain. _____

climate and temperature
temperature _____
wet / dry _____
showers _____
rise (v) / fall (v) _____
icy _____
heavy rain _____
thunder and lightning _____
(minus) five degrees _____

glossary

wheel (n) _____
rock (n) _____
vet (n) _____

seven wordlist

your language

natural English

anyway, so anyway
Anyway ... _____
So anyway ... _____

link words and phrases
First / First of all ... _____
After that / Afterwards ... _____
Then / And then ... _____

have a good / bad time
I'm having a good time. _____
I had a terrible time. _____
Have a great time! _____

uses of get
Can you get here by 7.00? (= arrive) _____
Did you get my e-mail? (= receive) _____

asking how to say things
What's this called in English? _____
How do you say ... in English? _____

vocabulary

phrases with go
go for a run _____
go for a walk _____
go for a picnic _____
go for a meal in a restaurant _____
go sightseeing _____
go shopping _____
go skiing _____
go swimming _____
go and see a film _____
go and watch a match _____
go and see a friend _____
go and buy something _____
go to a wedding _____
go to a party _____
go to a disco _____
go to a meeting _____

your language

wordbooster

irregular verbs
steal / stole / stolen _____
bite / bit / bitten _____
run / ran / run _____
break / broke / broken _____
throw / threw / thrown _____
fall / fell / fallen _____
hurt / hurt / hurt _____
catch / caught / caught _____
hit / hit / hit _____

phrasal verbs
lie down (on a bed) _____
take off (planes) _____
(cars) break down _____
turn up (= arrive) _____
fall over sth _____
run away _____
stand up _____
set off (on a journey) _____

glossary

field (n) _____
picnic (n) _____
wave (v) _____
helicopter (n) _____
land (v) _____
take off (v) _____
(un)fortunately (adj) _____
fire alarm (n) _____
evacuate (v) _____
delay (n) _____
smash (v) _____

eight wordlist

natural English

suggestions

We could (go to the beach).
Yes, good idea / lovely.
How about (going for a walk)?
Hmm, maybe.
What about (having a pizza)?
I don't like (pizza) very much.

it's popular / common

(Football) is extremely popular.
(Gardening) isn't very popular.
(Cookery programmes) are quite common.

be going to + verb

I'm going (to the dentist).
Are you going (shopping)?

all day / night / week / the time

(I was at the beach) all day.
(It's going to be sunny) all week.
(The dog was barking) all night.
(We speak English) all the time.

invitations

Would you like to (go out)?
Yes, great / I'd love to.
Do you want to (come shopping)?
I'd love to, but I can't.

making arrangements

Where shall we meet?
When shall we meet?
Shall we meet outside?
Why don't we meet at (7.30)?
How about 7.30?
Yes, fine.

vocabulary

verb + noun collocation

accept / refuse an invitation
make an appointment
make an arrangement
invite friends (for dinner)
book a table
make a booking
make plans

wordbooster

time phrases

three days ago
the day before yesterday
last night
tonight
all tomorrow afternoon
tomorrow evening
the day after tomorrow
this week / weekend
this Sunday
all day Tuesday
next Monday
next week
in ten days' time
the week after next

glossary

Easter (n)
ha, ha, very funny ☺.
kids ☺ (n)
abroad (adj)
no way ☺
gathering (n)
shopping mall (n)
soap opera (n)
window shopping (n)
designer boutique (n)

nine wordlist

                                              your language   your language

natural English

still
Do you still work at the bank?   _____
My brother's still at school.   _____

use of *long*
Have you lived here long?   _____
Have you had your shoes long?   _____

there's ... it's got ...
It's got (a large kitchen).   _____
There's (a garage).   _____
There are (three car parks).   _____

vague language *thing(s)*
Can you pass me that thing, please?   _____
That's a difficult thing to do.   _____
The best thing about my job is ...   _____

wordbooster

homes
ground floor   _____
hall   _____
toilet   _____
stairs   _____
living room   _____
dining room   _____
kitchen   _____
patio   _____
garden   _____
first floor   _____
landing   _____
bedroom   _____
bathroom   _____
balcony   _____
garage   _____

adjectives describing homes
warm   _____
cold   _____
clean   _____
dirty   _____
beautiful   _____
ugly   _____
modern   _____
traditional   _____
unusual   _____
ordinary   _____
tidy   _____
untidy   _____
light   _____
dark   _____
small   _____
spacious   _____

glossary

get (sth / sb) ready   _____
cheerful (adj)   _____
well-behaved (adj)   _____
complain (v)   _____
let sb do sth (v)   _____

ten wordlist

your language   your language

natural English

really
It was really interesting. _____
I'm really worried about it. _____
I'm really frightened of it. _____

what's the matter?
What's the matter? _____
I've got a headache. _____
Oh, no. _____
What's wrong? _____
I don't feel very well. _____
Oh, dear. _____

accepting and refusing suggestions
How / What about 3.30? _____
Yes, that's fine / great. _____
I'm afraid I can't. _____
Sorry, that's no good. _____

fillers in conversation
Right, … _____
OK, … _____
Let me see, … _____
Hmm / Er, … _____
Well, … _____

vocabulary

sleep
fall asleep _____
wake up _____
dream (v) about sth _____
have a dream (n) about sth _____
have a nightmare about sth _____
wake sb up _____
talk in your sleep _____
sleepwalk _____

-ed / -ing adjectives
excited / exciting _____
interested / interesting _____
relaxed / relaxing _____
surprised / surprising _____
worried / worrying _____
bored / boring _____
embarrassed / embarrassing _____
frightened / frightening _____

verb patterns
phone sb _____
ring sb _____
e-mail sb _____
tell sb sth _____
ask sb sth _____
thank sb _____
text sb _____
write to sb _____
speak to sb _____
talk to sb _____

wordbooster

aches and pains
a terrible headache _____
stomach ache _____
toothache _____
a pain in my leg / arm / foot _____
I feel sick. _____
My foot / arm hurts. _____
I don't feel very well. _____

glossary
according to sb / sth (prep) _____
injury (n) _____
survive (v) _____
terrified (adj) _____
weapon (n) _____

eleven wordlist

your language   your language

natural English

leaving out words

Everything OK? _____
Got a pen? _____
Ready? _____
Don't know. _____

I (don't) agree / it depends

I agree with you / that. _____
I think it depends. _____
Sorry, I don't agree with you. _____

use of *work*

I've got a lot of work this week. _____
When do you start work? _____
I get the train to work. _____
I haven't got a job. (NOT ~~a work~~) _____

what if ... ?

What if the taxi is late? _____
What if the train isn't on time? _____
What if no one comes? _____

vocabulary

work and working conditions

run a company _____
boss _____
busy _____
a lot of work _____
lunch break _____
salary _____
earn _____
a job _____
working hours _____
nine to five _____
share (an office) _____
three of us _____
get on well with sb _____
have a good (working) relationship _____

wordbooster

office jobs

telephonist _____
accountant _____
secretary _____
receptionist _____
personnel manager _____
sales manager _____

relationships

(be) (no) good at sth _____
fall in love _____
jealous of sb _____
have an argument _____
lazy _____
split up _____
afraid of sb / sth _____
go out with sb _____
get upset _____

glossary

get lost _____
had better do sth (v) _____
Hi there! 🌀 _____
get the sack 🌀 _____
client (n) _____
monitor (v) _____
gossip (n) _____
sensible (adj) _____
split up (v) _____

text vocabulary

in your own time _____
hours on end _____
in moderation _____
in a relationship _____

twelve wordlist

your language   your language

natural English

me too / me neither
A I like it. _____
B Me too. _____
C Really? I don't. _____
A I don't like it. _____
B Me neither. _____
C Really? I do _____

showing surprise
Wow! _____
I don't believe it! _____
I can't believe it! _____
That's incredible! _____

greeting old friends
How are you? _____
It's lovely / great to see you. _____
What have you been doing? _____
What are you doing now? _____

asking about the past and present
What happened to (your sister)? _____
Are you still (interested in cars)? _____
Do you still (play a lot of football)? _____

vocabulary

activities
go to the beach _____
go clubbing _____
go skiing _____
go horseriding _____
play the clarinet _____
play baseball _____
have a barbecue _____
play cards _____

wordbooster

life events
leave school / university _____
become a (doctor) _____
spend (time) in ... _____
get a job in (banking) / as a (waiter) _____
get married _____
meet sb through (a friend) _____
work abroad / in television _____

professions
go into (a profession) _____
become (a teacher) _____
teacher / teaching _____
doctor / medicine _____
lawyer / law _____
engineer / engineering _____
journalist / journalism _____
banker / banking _____
computer programmer / IT _____
businessman / businesswoman / business _____

glossaries

I wonder (v) _____
fee (n) _____
worldwide (adj) _____
spare room (n) _____
curious (adj) _____
get in touch (with sb) (v) _____

thirteen wordlist

your language

natural English

have (got) sth *in common*
We've got (quite) a lot in common. _____
We haven't got much in common. _____

***quite / not very* + adjective**
He's quite ambitious. _____
She's not very patient. _____

asking about people
What's she like? _____
What does she look like? _____
What does she like doing? _____

describing age
She's in her teens. _____
He's in his twenties. _____
They're in their forties. _____

vocabulary

describing appearance
pretty _____
good-looking _____
handsome _____
short _____
medium height _____
tall _____
slim _____
overweight _____
short hair _____
shoulder-length hair _____
long hair _____
blonde / blond hair _____
brown hair _____
dark hair _____

wordbooster

describing character
(un) friendly _____
(im)patient _____
lazy _____
hard-working _____
shy _____
extrovert _____

your language

kind _____
selfish _____
serious _____
funny _____
ambitious _____
easy-going _____
(dis)organized _____

likes / dislikes and interests
eating chocolates _____
cooking _____
computer games _____
sunbathing _____
washing up _____
cycling _____
driving _____
dancing _____
going to the gym _____
I (really) love + noun / -ing _____
I (quite) like + noun / -ing _____
I enjoy + noun / -ing _____
I don't like + noun / -ing _____
I hate + noun / -ing _____

glossary

dating (n) _____
get to know sb _____
couple (n) _____
travel agent (n) _____
a while (n) _____
funny (adj) (= strange) _____

text vocabulary

sit at a table _____
talk to sb / each other _____
at the end of … _____
by e-mail _____
at first _____
after a while _____
look at sb / each other _____

fourteen wordlist

your language   your language

natural English

when / where was that?
A I went to Greece.
B When was that? _____
A We found a nice hotel.
B Where was that? _____

another / some more
I'd like another (towel), please. _____
Yes, I'll get you one. _____
I'd like some more (soap), please. _____
Yes, I'll get you some. _____

requests
Could I (have your passport, please)? _____
Sure. _____
(Sorry,) Could you (lend me a pen)? _____
Yes, of course. _____
(Excuse me,) Could you (possibly)
   (move your bag)? _____
Here you are. _____

taking time to think
Just a moment / minute ... _____
Let me think ... _____
I'm not sure – let me see ... _____

vocabulary

airports
trolley _____
queue _____
hand luggage _____
passenger _____
check-in desk _____
scales _____
suitcase _____
terminal (one) _____
passport control _____
boarding card _____
departure lounge _____
aisle seat _____
gate (number) _____

wordbooster

hotel rooms and bathrooms
towel _____
toothbrush _____
toothpaste _____
toilet paper _____
razor _____
hairdryer _____
soap _____
iron _____
minibar _____
mineral water _____

verbs often confused
bring / take _____
lend / borrow _____
tell / say _____
forget / leave _____

glossary

own (v) _____
run (a business) (v) _____
guest (n) _____
provide (v) _____
essential (adj) _____
futon (n) _____

teacher development chapters

how to ... do pair and group work — *p.146*

how to ... practise grammar — *p.153*

how to ... motivate low level learners to write — *p.160*

how to ... use the learners as a resource — *p.167*

how to ... help learners understand natural speech — *p.174*

how to ... do pair and group work

1 Why do pair and group work?
2 Individuals, pairs, groups, or whole class?
3 What can learners do in pairs and groups?
4 Class management
5 Troubleshooting

1 Why do pair and group work?

When people join a language class, they expect to spend some of their time working individually on tasks set by the teacher: completing grammar and vocabulary exercises, answering comprehension questions, writing down information from the board, etc. And they will expect to spend much of their time listening to and working with the teacher as she explains new language, asks questions, checks answers, elicits opinions, and so on. This is generally how learners expect to use their time, and many will be less prepared for classrooms in which they are asked to work with a partner or in small groups, where the teacher may not be listening to them some of the time.

think!¹
Do you use pair and group work in your classes? If so, why? If not, why not? If you don't use pair and group work, write down three reasons why it might help. Then read on.

We know some teachers are reluctant to let their students work in pairs and groups, and this seems most apparent when teachers have to manage very large classes (anything from 20 to 100 students). With these numbers, there is no denying that the teacher cannot monitor all the pairs / groups effectively in any single activity, and there is the danger that certain students might wander off the subject, revert to the L1 in the case of monolingual classes, or just not do the activity at all. These are causes for concern, and if the teacher starts to feel that they are no longer in control of the students or the lesson, they may consider pair and group work too risky.

We can sympathise with teachers who feel like this, but we still believe that pair and group work has so much to offer in almost every teaching situation we are aware of. Here is a list of some of the key benefits:

advantages

- Pair and group work maximises the opportunities for students to engage in oral practice and communicate. In large classes where opportunities for oral practice might be very restricted, this is even more important.
- It helps students to realize that they can work independently of the teacher, and they can learn from other students and help each other.
- It usually creates a good atmosphere in class and helps to build rapport among class members. For some learners, going to a language class is a social activity, and through pair and group work, they will get to know each other better and feel more positive towards the class.
- It varies the focus of attention in the classroom and creates a change in pace.
- Close monitoring of pair and group work provides the teacher with important knowledge and information about the students and how they are performing. This may be valuable for future lesson planning and can also help the teacher to build a rapport with their students.
- It allows students to gain confidence by checking answers and rehearsing things to say before speaking more publicly in open class.
- It frees up the teacher to work with one or two pairs who may need extra attention.

2 Individuals, pairs, small groups, or whole class?

If the teacher remains the only focus of attention and all classroom activities are directed through them, there is the danger of lessons becoming rather monotonous. As we have already said, pair and group work changes that focus and can give lessons both variety and a change of pace. It is equally true that too much pair and group work will create its own monotony. Worse still, if endless pair work without a clear purpose is also accompanied by an absence of effective feedback, some learners may feel that classroom time is being spent, and perhaps wasted, on activities that they could be doing themselves in the coffee bar. It is, therefore, essential that teachers have a clear reason for putting students in pairs and groups, and back this up with careful monitoring and feedback.

Pair and group work has a place, but there are times when the lesson is most effective when the teacher is working together with the whole class. This type of interaction provides shared experiences which help to create a sense of belonging. As we said earlier, it is also the type of classroom experience that most learners expect, so they may find it comforting and reassuring.

Working individually also has its advantages. It allows the teacher the opportunity to help individual students without disrupting a working pair, and to some extent, it allows students to work at their own pace and in their own way. This will be particularly valuable if your lessons are quite long. Listening to the teacher and talking to other students are both demanding activities which require a lot of concentration, and some students will certainly benefit from the opportunity to sit back and work alone.

> ### think![1]
> If you were a language student, which activities below would you prefer to do:
> a individually?
> b with a partner?
> c in a small group of three or four?
> d with the whole class?
> Why?
>
> #### Activity 1
> You have studied some language for asking for / giving directions. You are now going to practise asking for / giving directions based on a street map.
>
> #### Activity 2
> A matching activity. You have ten new vocabulary items on the left hand side to match with their definitions on the right.
>
> #### Activity 3
> You have just listened to and studied the beginning of an informal telephone conversation (about 8 lines) between two friends. You are now going to practise a similar conversation.
>
> #### Activity 4
> You have filled in a questionnaire giving opinions about the education system in your country. You are now going to find out if other students have different answers.

Activity 1
This seems ideal for pair work. Most conversations of this type would be on a one-to-one basis, and in the classroom this would be very easy to set up. Students will also get the intensive practice they need in pairs, and even more so if it is done as a class mingle in which they work in different pairs.

Activity 2
We think this activity is best done individually. Matching exercises require concentration. Students have to juggle the different words and definitions at their disposal, and they also need to focus on the written word and work with the layout. Speaking to someone at the same time could be distracting and frustrating. However, they often like the opportunity to compare ideas with a partner when they have completed the exercise. This gives them a chance to satisfy their curiosity, to talk through any problems in a non-threatening context (i.e. not in full view of the class), and of course, to use the target language. They can then work with a partner to practise the pronunciation of the words – learners often give this a much higher priority than teachers – and test each other.

Activity 3
For this activity, it is difficult to imagine anything other than working with a partner. A dialogue practised on your own isn't much fun, and with a partner you will have a sense of real conversation, which you can repeat until you are satisfied. You will also be able to listen to your partner and perhaps learn from them or be able to help them.

Activity 4
This would be very suitable for small groups because there is more likely to be disagreement among three or four people than there will be with just two, so the discussion will probably be longer, more varied, and more animated. Doing the activity as a whole class would have the disadvantage that some learners may say very little or nothing at all (class discussions are often dominated by a few confident learners). However, we would like the opportunity after the small group discussion to find out what others think, so working with the whole class may be the most rewarding way to conclude the activity.

To sum up, pair work, as we have suggested above, is extremely useful for short activities which focus on specific language, and it has the advantage of being very easy to set up as learners don't have to stand up, move furniture, etc. Small group work provides a different kind of interaction, and it is important for learners to practise their English in such groups, as well as on a one-to-one basis with a partner. Group work offers a different kind of challenge. It may be harder in that the conversation will move faster and be more unpredictable, and in a chatty group, individuals may need to raise their voice or interrupt in order to have their say. On the other hand, participants do have the option of taking a back seat at times.

3 What can learners do in pairs and groups?

Here is a small selection of activities which benefit from being done in pairs.

comparing answers
To practise specific language items, learners usually work alone on a gap fill, matching or sentence completion exercise. However, if they compare their answers in pairs before class feedback, they have the chance to check and amend their answers and help each other where necessary. Pair work here also provides an opportunity for some oral / pronunciation practice, and allows time for you to monitor and help individuals.

peer teaching / testing
You can set up a simple peer teaching exercise as follows.

> – Divide the class in half: A students and B students.
> – Give each group different sentences with errors to correct (i.e. A's and B's sentences are not the same). Here is an example of A's sentences from the pre-intermediate **student's book**, unit two:

> **student A** Correct the errors in these sentences. Check your answers.
>
> 1 We eat a lot of spaghettis.
> 2 These pasta are really nice.
> 3 Do you eat many bread?
> 4 I don't like coffees.
> 5 How much sugar are there?
>
> Read out the incorrect sentences to your partner. They have to correct them.

how to ... do pair and group work 147

> **student B** Correct the errors in these sentences. Check your answers.
>
> 1 Can I have a toast?
> 2 Would you like some biscuit?
> 3 We don't need much olives.
> 4 Cheese are good for you.
> 5 I don't eat many butter.
>
> Read out the <u>incorrect</u> sentences to your partner. They have to correct them.
>
> - A students work in pairs on their sentences, and B students work in pairs on their sentences (*p.142*).
> - Give each group a photocopy of the correct answers to check their sentences.
> - A students then find a B partner. They read out their incorrect sentences for their new partner to correct orally.

from pre-intermediate **student's book**, unit two **pairwork** *pp.148 and 142*

This technique provides a simple twist on a fairly standard exercise, i.e. the students become the teacher when they work with a new partner. Doing the activity orally at this stage also provides a greater challenge. You can use this technique with many standard controlled practice activities.

information gap

In an information gap activity, learners are supplied with different information and need to communicate in pairs in order to complete the activity. The information gap can be real, e.g. Students A and B have to find out certain facts about each other's family, or it can be created artificially for the purpose of language practice, e.g. this role play from the **student's book**, **unit ten review**, in which a patient (Student B) has to cancel an appointment with the receptionist (Student A) at a doctor's surgery. They each have a role card with different information on it, which introduces an element of unpredictability and realism into a commonplace situation.

> **student A**   RECEPTIONIST
> It's FIVE minutes before your patient / client's appointment. They're going to ring you.
>
> **Think! What are you going to say?**
> – greetings
> – listen and respond
> – explain that you are full this morning
> – suggest other times / days
>
> **You answer the phone.**

from pre-intermediate **student's book**, unit ten **review** *p.101*.

> **student B**   PATIENT / CLIENT
> It's FIVE minutes before your appointment. You've got a problem. Ring the receptionist.
>
> **Think! What are you going to say?**
> – say your name, and who your appointment is with
> – explain the problem, e.g. you're in a meeting, or your car has broken down
> – say sorry
> – try to make another appointment for this morning
>
> **Now phone the receptionist. He / She will speak first.**

from pre-intermediate **student's book**, unit ten **review** *p.149*.

planning and rehearsing

Learners can work in pairs to plan, rehearse or write out short conversations, incorporating language they have recently studied. A good example of this is the **extended speaking** activity in **student's book, unit four** shown below.

invent a conversation

4 With a partner, look at all the pictures. Do you understand the story? If not, ask your partner.

5 Invent the conversation with your partner. Write it down.

6 Practise it until you can say it without looking.

act out your conversation

7 Work with another pair. Act out your conversations. Are they the same or different?

from pre-intermediate **student's book**, **extended speaking** activity *p.41*

In our experience, the process of negotiating the correct / appropriate language in the dialogue involves a great deal of genuine communication which goes beyond the simple content of the dialogue.

predicting

In pairs, learners make predictions about what they are going to read or hear, based on some information you have given them. For example, they are going to read an article about a terrible train journey from London to Paris. They think of five problems that might have occurred, compare with another pair, then tell the class. These predictions can be written on the board and provide a very useful initial reading task: were the problems mentioned in the article? In this instance, everyone is getting an opportunity to contribute, and learners who are less able to predict may be getting some support from those who can. Here is another example from the pre-intermediate **student's book**.

listening challenge

4 Stephen's got a car for the first time. With a partner, think of four ways his life is now different.

5 (9.3) Listen. Were your ideas correct? Does Stephen talk about any other differences?

from pre-intermediate **student's book** p.86

Here are four activity types which are more suited to group work at lower levels:

brainstorming

Group work is very useful for brainstorming as you get a greater diversity of ideas. For instance, if you want students to produce some written guidelines on how to practise English outside the classroom, you can give them some discussion prompts first.

try it out

1 You are going to write an advice sheet on how to practise English outside the classroom. Think about the following areas and make notes in the table.

	How to improve
Grammar	
Vocabulary	
Pronunciation	
Listening	
Speaking	
Reading	
Writing	

2 Now talk in small groups and share ideas.
3 In groups, write your advice sheet. Put it on the wall for other groups to read and comment.

Allow them a couple of minutes to think on their own, before putting them in groups to pool ideas. In that way, they will come to the group work with something to contribute, and the discussion will flow more freely. Students can then begin to organize their ideas together, and start to write a joint advice sheet.

discussion

Discussion activities are usually more successful in small groups. There is likely to be a greater diversity of opinions among three or four people (than just two), and therefore the probability of a more interesting and animated conversation. Sometimes a discussion may begin in pairs then develop into groups. For instance, in the pyramid discussion below:

- learners first discuss a topic in pairs, e.g. *Everybody should go to university*, and agree on their views
- then they re-form as a group of four to discuss their conclusions. The group must also reach a consensus
- then they re-form into a group of eight, and so on.

There is one important consideration with any group work activity which invites students to pool information, generate ideas, or give opinions. In our experience, learners benefit considerably from having time to think and plan their ideas, and even to rehearse ways of expressing them on their own, before group work. The group activity itself then takes off more quickly because people have something to say and aren't struggling with both language and content simultaneously.

games

A number of games are designed for three or more players, e.g. Grammar Monopoly, but even games that can be played in pairs, e.g. Twenty Questions, are often more interesting in small groups. Most games become more competitive with a larger number of participants, but the main advantage is that games usually generate more noise, fun and excitement when three or more people are involved.

mingling

Here's a less structured activity which involves groups or pairs:

speaking it's your turn!

1 **Think!** Think about your own plans. Write down five things you are going to do, might do, or would like to do this week / weekend.

2 Find someone in the class with at least two similar plans.

Have you got any plans for this weekend?

What are you going to do this weekend?

Yes, I'm going to ...

from pre-intermediate **student's book**, unit eight p.76

Mingling allows learners to communicate with many different people, sometimes with students they rarely talk to, and often means an opportunity to practise specific language items many times over without seeming repetitive. It is also worth pointing out that this fairly simple activity has an outcome: they are comparing information in order to find others with similar plans. The principle of setting concrete aims and outcomes is an important one in pair and group work.

> **try it out** starting a lesson
> My learners come to class on two evenings a week, after work, and they don't have much exposure to English outside the classroom. When they arrive, they need a little time to tune in to English, and pair and group work is the ideal way of providing this. I generally have a few minutes at the beginning of every lesson where they have to use English in a relaxed and unthreatening way. Sometimes, I ask them to compare their homework answers with a partner, or play a quick vocabulary revision game in small groups using words on cards, or perhaps talk to their partner about what they did the evening before. These few minutes can also be a useful way of absorbing latecomers. I always monitor during this time, taking the opportunity to make contact with individuals, assess what they are saying, and decide what feedback to give. I find it creates a pleasant atmosphere and purposeful start, and my learners seem to like it.
> Marianne, Lyon

4 Class management

Class management of pair and group work involves:

- **setting up:** organizing the pairs / groups and giving them instructions
- **monitoring:** listening to the pairs / groups during the activity and guiding / giving support / making notes
- **winding down:** bringing the activity to a close and providing feedback.

Let's look at these in turn.

setting up

If your learners are not used to working independently in pairs or groups, it is worth spending time to explain how such activities can help them (look back at section 1 of this chapter).

1 knowing your aim

Firstly, an activity should have a learning aim. In some cases, this will be linguistic, e.g. learners have intensive oral practice of specific language; in others it will be communicative, e.g. learners develop their fluency in a freer, more extended activity. Where students are exchanging information, pooling ideas or giving opinions, it is more motivating for them if the activity has an outcome which is not simply linguistic. For example, in **unit five** of the pre-intermediate **student's book**, learners read an article full of advice for students taking exams. After working on general comprehension of the text, students do the following tasks.

> 4 Think! Choose the three most important pieces of advice, and one or two you don't think are important.
>
> 5 Compare in groups. Agree on the three most important pieces of advice. Do you have any other advice?

from pre-intermediate **student's book** p.50

For **exercise 5** students must reach agreement on the three most important ones. In other words, they have to reach an outcome in which there is consensus. It is very important to make the aim explicit at the start of the activity so that students will know what they have to achieve by the end.

> **think!**[2]
> Can you think of a concrete outcome for these speaking activities?
> a In small groups, learners tell each other what their family eats in a typical day.
> b In small groups, learners compare their opinions on a questionnaire about public transport in their town.
> c In groups, students talk about how much housework they do.

go to **answer key** p.152

2 physical organisation

From a class management point of view, it is easier in pair work if learners work with the person next to them, and as they have often chosen who they want to sit with, this is likely to be a comfortable arrangement for most of them. You will need to be alert to pairings which might indicate problems. For example:

- if you are teaching employees from a single company, it may not be desirable to pair up a junior employee with their boss
- with multinational classes, there may be a reason for keeping certain nationalities apart
- in some classes there may be female students who are uncomfortable with certain male students, and vice versa.

Some unlikely pairs may be a great success. Instinctively you may not think it wise to mix older and younger class members, but we have had teenagers who not only behave in a more adult way working with older students, they also feel more secure and less inhibited in this situation.

Initially, let students build their confidence with a limited range of partners. Monitor closely and praise students who are working well together. Keep a mental check of those who work well together and those who don't. Gradually move the pairs around and monitor the different dynamics. You need to accept that it is rare to have all the pairs performing equally well, but it is important to ensure that you don't have an under-performing pair together all the time. As a general rule, we don't organize different pairs all the time (it's disruptive and too time-consuming), but we like to vary the pairs some of the time:

- to allow students to do the same activity again but with a new partner
- to see how learners perform with different partners
- to rearrange pairs where the 'chemistry' doesn't work
- to share around a problematic learner
- to provide variety

There are several simple time-saving ways to change pairs around: work with the student on your left or right; work with the student in front of you / behind you. If students are sitting in a horseshoe arrangement, move one student on the end to the other end of the horseshoe. If you have an odd number of students in the class, there will always be one group of three. This doesn't matter as long as it's not the same three all the time.

150 how to ... do pair and group work

In group work, you may group learners who are sitting near each other for minimum disruption. Friendship groups may also work well together provided they don't form cliques and turn the class into separate factions. If you find a group isn't working well together, bear it in mind for the next group activity and change the groups around. Here are two simple ideas for rearranging groups.

- If you have say, 15 students, and you want five groups of three randomly organized, go round the class giving each person a letter: A, B, C, D or E. Then tell all the As to sit together, and so on.
- You can do the same thing with fifteen pieces of coloured card: red, green, blue, etc. Let students take a colour, then tell them to sit with others with the same colour.

Group size can be a crucial factor in the success of an activity. We tend to keep groups to three or four because larger groups can intimidate less confident learners and they allow fewer opportunities for everyone to speak. From the learner's point of view it can also be difficult to see and hear everyone when the group is quite big, especially if you have a noisy class.

It is interesting to experiment with the composition of the groups; you may need to try a number of options before getting the right mix.

3 clear instructions

If your learners have never worked in pairs or groups before, choose activities which are easy to set up, and if necessary, give the instructions in the students' mother tongue. Gradually move towards instructions in English, which will provide listening practice with a real purpose, and students will acquire some very useful language (*first of all, listen to each other, when you've finished, go on to the next one*, etc.).

If you're worried about giving instructions, here are a few tips:

- Tell the class the end result of the activity in one sentence, e.g. 'You're going to tell a partner the story of a film you like very much.' (See **knowing your aim** above)
- Give instructions in the students' mother tongue first if you have a particularly weak class. For lower levels, start with simple activities with simple instructions and gradually move on to more complicated ones.
- Give the instructions on a 'need to know' basis. Explain the first stage they have to do, let them do it, and then give the next instructions as required; otherwise students can get overwhelmed and you run the risk of losing their attention.
- Use demonstration or examples to check learners understand your instructions, especially with lower levels. For instance, if the activity asks learners to think of five things to do in a park, ask the whole class to come up with one or two ideas only as an example, then put them in pairs to think of five more. This is essential with a large class, where you may not be able to monitor all the pairs effectively once the activity is underway.
- Give the students a time limit for the activity as this will allow them to manage their own time.
- As a final check, as soon as learners have started working in pairs or groups, spend a minute quickly going round to see if they are doing the right thing. Don't interfere at this stage, but if more than one pair or group hasn't understood the instructions, it may be quicker to call the class's attention and clarify what to do; otherwise just deal quickly with any problem of understanding with the relevant pair / group.

monitoring

When you have checked the learners are doing the activity correctly, you can monitor more generally and respond to individual problems or queries, without getting too involved. You should sit where you can hear most of the group, or move round quietly. While you monitor, make notes for feedback at the end; include examples of good language use or performance as well as important errors. At this stage you should also be paying careful attention to the dynamics of the different pairs / groups. With a large class you must obviously try to ensure that you monitor more or less equally, so if you were unable to listen to a particular pair or group last time, make sure you listen to them this time. The type of monitoring you do will depend on the activity.

Want to know more? Go to intermediate **teacher's book**, **how to ...** monitor and give feedback *p.156*

winding down

Pair and group work is most successful when students are engaged, focused, and learning from the activity – and when it takes 'the right amount of time' from their point of view. However, pairs and groups can't all work at the same pace; some will finish earlier than others, so be prepared for this. You can often provide something simple for them to do while the others are finishing. For example, if they have been asked to think of four reasons for doing something, you could ask them to think of two more. With certain oral activities it may be relevant to ask learners who finish early to write down some of their ideas (try to find time to go back and look at what they have written). They might also benefit from listening to the other pairs / groups who are still working.

A common problem is letting activities go on for too long. You don't want to lose the momentum of a good activity by allowing animated talk to slow down to a whisper before you stop the activity. Don't intervene when the whole class is clearly still engaged in the activity, but be prepared to finish at a point when most pairs / groups are reaching the end, and don't expect everyone to finish. If you've given a time limit at the start, try to keep to it but allow some flexibility. If you have over- or under-estimated time, don't worry; just observe how students are working and adjust accordingly. A one-minute or two-minute warning before you stop can be very useful for learners and often livens up the pace.

It is important to bring the class together after pair and group activities. At this point, you can ask pairs / groups to report back on what they discussed, and you can also give your own feedback on the ideas discussed and the language they used (both good language use and errors).

Want to know more? Go to intermediate **teacher's book**, **how to ...** monitor and give feedback *p.156*

5 Troubleshooting

Different teaching situations throw up different problems. These are some of the most common ones we have encountered with relevance to pair and group work activities.

PROBLEM: My students either don't want to speak in English or are too embarrassed to speak in English.

With a few exceptions, we have not encountered students who don't want to speak in English. However, we are familiar with students who feel embarrassed about speaking English, especially with learners they feel are better than they are, or learners who share the same mother tongue. We think it is worth pointing out that talking quietly to a 'supportive' partner is probably the easiest and least threatening way to start speaking in English; and the more you do it, the easier it gets. Start with simple controlled activities, and aim from the outset to develop among your learners a positive and supportive attitude. Try to match less confident learners with people who won't overwhelm them, and give lots of praise when they do speak in English – whether it is accurate or not! Be very firm with any student who laughs at someone else's English.

> **PROBLEM:** If I put students in pairs, they talk in their first language all the time.

With monolingual classes you will have to be very pragmatic. Some students will find it hard to relinquish their first language, so try to be tolerant with these students while coaxing them to use English more and more. It will be particularly important with this type of student that the activity is clearly achievable, and some students may find it easier if they are not working with a close friend or someone who is clearly better than they are. Again, give lots of praise when they use English. You can introduce fun penalties and prizes to further encourage the use of English in class e.g. for certain stages of the lesson like a fluency activity, if the students use their mother tongue, they get a black mark. The student with the most number of black marks has to buy the teacher tea in the break.

There is also the positive contribution that the use of the mother tongue can have. Students may sometimes revert to the L1 as a necessary tool to repair or clarify a particular message, thereby allowing the activity to continue, largely in English. Finally, it's worth bearing in mind that some English and some mother tongue is far better than no English at all.

> **PROBLEM:** My students say they don't want to do pair and group work because they will start copying other learners' mistakes.

Mistakes are not a disease, but an important part of the learning process. Everyone makes mistakes, and practice is the best way to reduce them. By pointing out successful language use in feedback, e.g. correct use of some recently taught grammar or a very useful phrase, you will help to make learners more aware of the positive influence of other learners.

> **PROBLEM:** My classroom isn't big enough for students to move around, and the furniture is very inflexible.

This can certainly inhibit group work, but students can do pair work activities sitting where they are, and no furniture has to be moved. For variety, you could ask learners to sit in a different place at the beginning of each lesson, so that over a period of lessons or weeks they will work with a range of students. You could also think about doing activities standing up. As learners are seated for most of the lesson, many welcome the opportunity to stand up and stretch their legs. The advantage of this is that learners can work in pairs or groups without having to move chairs or desks.

> **PROBLEM:** When my class are working in pairs or groups, the teachers next door complain about the noise.

If pair and group work in your classroom creates a lot of noise, it suggests that your learners are involved in what they are doing! However, you need to be sensitive to your neighbours. Make sure you keep an open channel of communication with other teachers to prevent it becoming a problem between you, and obviously avoid noisy activities if a test or reading activity is going on next door. You can also ask your students to speak a bit more quietly if noise levels are becoming excessive.

conclusion

In this chapter we have discussed:
- the reasons for including pair and group work, along with individual and whole class activities
- a selection of classroom activities that are suited to pair and group work
- class management procedures which help to make pair and group work successful
- troubleshooting common problems

If you have been suspicious of pair and group work in the past, we hope this chapter will have encouraged you to try it out. If, on the other hand, pair and group work is something you use regularly, we hope the chapter will have helped you to reflect on your current practice and encourage further experimentation.

follow up

Harmer J 2001 *The Practice of English Language Teaching* (third edition) Longman
Hadfield J 1998 *Classroom Dynamics* Oxford University Press
Malamah-Thomas A 1987 *Classroom Interaction* Oxford University Press
Nolasco R and L Nolasco 1987 *Conversation* Oxford University Press
Seligson P 1999 *Two heads are better than one* English Teaching Professional 11

answer key

think![2] *p.150* possible outcomes
a Find the family who eats the most meat / fish / vegetables, etc., or the family with the healthiest diet, or the family which is most similar to your family, or find four similarities and differences.
b In each group, decide on the single most important issue, then compare with the other groups, or decide on two important changes you would like to make to public transport. Alternatively, each group could write a short summary of the majority opinions for other groups to read and discuss.
c Each group must agree on who does the most or least housework.

how to ... practise grammar

1 What is 'good' practice?
2 Bringing controlled practice to life
3 Staging practice activities
4 The role of the teacher

1 What is 'good' practice?

Does practice make perfect in language learning? No, not always. There are times when repeated practice seems to have little or no effect on some learners' ability to use new language accurately or fluently. Equally, there are occasions when recently encountered language passes into productive use with no specific practice or intervention on the teacher's part. However, for most learners, most of the time, practice is essential, but to make the best use of limited classroom time, we also have to give careful consideration to the quality and appropriateness of the practice we provide.

The following list is not exhaustive, but it outlines some of the important features that good practice should contain. Bearing in mind that learners need different types of practice at different stages in their learning, we would not expect many practice activities to fulfil all of the criteria below: the essential ingredients will depend on the stage of learning your students have reached.

practise what we teach

> **think!**[1]
> What is the purpose of this exercise?
> **Complete the sentences with the correct form of the present perfect.**
>   1 I ____ (work) here for three years and I really like the job.
>   2 She ____ (not see) her brothers since last May.
>   3 He ____ (not take) any exams for six months now.
>   etc.

This exercise requires students to think about the construction of the present perfect, but is not asking them to consider why the tense is used. In other words, the exercise tests <u>form</u> but not <u>meaning</u>. This is perfectly valid provided the teacher does not believe that meaning is being tested or practised. In very controlled exercises, it is easy to ensure that learners are at least focusing on the form and / or the meaning of the target language. As understanding deepens and performance improves, practice needs to expand accordingly, with more language choice and more learner freedom. For example, we usually test the past continuous initially at sentence level, contrasting it with the past simple, before moving on to a practice phase where we might ask our students to use the structure in some kind of narrative. At this point it is not uncommon for learners to manage to construct a logical and largely accurate story without using the past continuous at all. This could be for two possible reasons:

- our failure to devise a suitable vehicle for use of the past continuous.
- the learners are not yet able to incorporate the structure productively when they have so many other language decisions to make.

In future you may also decide that the narrative needs more structure and the learners need more guidance to encourage use of the target language. We can't expect all practice activities to be successful, but we need to be aware of what we want an activity to practise, and we need to be able to recognize, when the activity has been completed, whether it has achieved that aim.

quantity vs. quality

We should try to ensure that practice provides learners with many opportunities to use the target grammar. Volume of practice can help learners to produce the language more rapidly. This is easier with some structures than others. It is relatively straightforward to find realistic contexts for quantity practice of, say, the present simple (e.g. talking about daily routines) or past simple (e.g. talking about what you did last weekend). To achieve the same with the past perfect simple or continuous is not so easy, as these forms are less likely to occur both naturally and frequently within a single passage or conversation. Moreover, there is no guarantee either that repeated practice will lead to improved performance, especially if the practice is decontextualised and fairly mechanical. Repeated practice may become counter-productive and encourage learners to use the targeted item more often than is appropriate. Learners who have had lots of practice with the past perfect, for example, often over-apply it in story-telling tasks. Sometimes there has to be a trade-off between quantity and quality, in which case quality should prevail.

challenging but achievable

If practice activities are consistently too difficult, learners will find them demotivating, and this is likely to have an adverse effect on their learning. But if they are too easy, they will soon become boring. Practice should aim to be sufficiently challenging to maintain interest, but always achievable so that it is confidence building. It's a difficult balance to get right because as students become more proficient, the level of challenge needs to rise accordingly. It is probably wiser to err on the side of being too easy in the initial practice, but learners need to be stretched as they become more confident and proficient.

learner scope

Most teachers have to contend with the reality of mixed ability classes. Even when students all start at roughly the same level, it isn't long before several different levels emerge. Practice activities that are achievable for weaker students may be easy for stronger learners, and vice versa. One way to combat this problem is by providing grammar practice that allows learners to tackle an activity at different levels of complexity. For example, here are two forms of practice for comparative adjectives:

how to ... practise grammar   153

1 a series of sentences in which learners have to choose between the two forms, e.g. *I arrived later/ more late than the others.*
2 In pairs, students make sentences comparing other people in the class using comparative adjectives.

The first task is for recognition, and has a simple right / wrong answer in each case, so if weaker learners are able to do it successfully, it is unlikely to provide sufficient challenge for stronger learners. The second activity requires student output / production, and with its potential for many different answers, it allows students to produce responses whose relative length or complexity matches their ability. A strong student may write that *Paulo's English is more accurate than mine* or *Dino wears smarter clothes than me.* But a weaker student will also have completed the task successfully if they are able to say *Paulo's taller than Junko* or *Marek's older than Edith.*

Allowing learners opportunities for individual creativity may not be a priority just after presenting some new grammar, but it should figure prominently as practice develops and learner differences start to emerge more clearly.

interest

Practice activities have a linguistic aim which learners should recognize and appreciate. However, if the aim remains purely linguistic and students are put through a series of similar activities, their attention may begin to wane, and learning may be less effective. To sustain interest and engagement – and probably facilitate more effective learning – it helps to have a communicative aim as well.

> **think!**[2]
> If learners are expanding prompts into questions to practise question forms, which of these prompts will produce the more generative question?
> a What time / lesson start this morning?
> b Where / you go for your last holiday?

The first question will produce an answer that everyone in the class already knows, so why should anyone want to ask it? The second question will not only have answers that others don't know, it may also generate a different answer from every student in the class and lead on very naturally to more questions with a genuine communicative purpose:

Where did you stay?
Who did you go with?
Did you have a good time?
etc.

Having an exercise with a communicative aim doesn't mean suddenly throwing learners into a lengthy activity: it simply means finding appropriate prompts to stimulate the learners to produce relevant language.

variety

Providing variety of practice is important for two reasons:
- students need different forms of practice at different stages. At the beginning, practice will have a more obvious linguistic aim, its focus will be restricted, and it shouldn't be too challenging. As practice progresses, students need activities with more language choice and more scope for creativity.

- too many activities of the same type will eventually become boring. If, for example, you are providing a sequence of three practice activities, try to ensure that at least two require student output, and at least one has an additional communicative aim such as exchanging personal information or solving a problem. Try to make all of them different in some way: oral vs. written practice, individual vs. group practice, paper-based and paperless practice, etc.

2 Bringing controlled practice to life

In this section we are going to look at some of the most common exercise types which are used to test / practise language, and focus on ways in which controlled exercises can be made more interesting and often transformed into freer and more expansive forms of practice.

> **think!**[3]
> Look at the exercises below.
> 1 Do these exercise types provide volume of practice?
> 2 Do they allow for learner creativity?
> 3 Do they have a linguistic and a communicative aim?
> 4 Are they interesting for students to do?
>
> 1 Fill the gaps with the correct form of the verb.
>   e.g. 1 I _____ (be) in this class since last year.
> 2 Transform the sentences from active to passive.
>   e.g. 1 They make these cars in Wales.
>   These cars _____.
> 3 Correct the errors.
>   e.g. 1 The ticket office gave me all the informations.
> 4 Match the sentence halves.
>   e.g. 1 I spoke   a the doctor about my problem.
>   2 I told   b to the doctor about my problem.
> 5 Put the words in order.
>   e.g. 1 he/ late/ class/ for/ is/ always

While these exercises may vary in focus and the degree of student output, they are all similar in that they are controlled tests. They all have a single right answer, restrict learner creativity and offer limited or no language choice. One consequence of this is that learners are unlikely to get many answers wrong, thereby making them achievable and good for confidence building. There is no denying some students have an immense appetite for exercises like these which are quick to do, relatively easy and provide them with positive feedback. Sentence level exercises are also relatively straightforward for teachers to construct. It would be easy to write ten examples for each exercise, and they can also be given for homework. In other words, these exercises have value, but as they currently stand, it is limited value. The aim in each one is purely linguistic, the scope for learner output is very restricted, and the level of interest is limited. They need to be followed up by more expansive forms of practice in which the new language can be personalized and placed in a more meaningful context.

On the next page are some ideas for providing more generative and meaningful practice from controlled exercises.

> **think!**[5]
> As you read the descriptions below of different activities, think about the exercise types. Which do you do often? Which do your learners find useful and / or enjoyable? Are there any you don't do? If so, why?

gap fill

Gap fill exercises can sometimes be transformed into a type of information gap, which is more interactive, and can then be used for personalized practice. Here is an example designed to practise question forms. The class is divided into two halves, A and B. Each half is given the same exercise, but different words are blanked out in A and B copies. For example:

student A

example
____What____ 's your best friend's name?

1 When _____ you first meet him / her?
2 _____ 's he / she like?
3 How often _____ you see him / her?
4 _____ old is he / she?
5 What _____ he / she do?
6 _____ do you get on well?
7 Where _____ he / she live?
8 _____ does he / she live with?
9 What _____ you do together?
10 Has he / she _____ any children?

I'm just curious!

student B

example What ___'s___ your best friend's name?

1 _____ did you first meet him / her?
2 What _____ he / she like?
3 _____ do you see him / her?
4 How old _____ he / she?
5 _____ does he / she do?
6 Why _____ you get on well?
7 _____ does he / she live?
8 Who _____ he / she live with?
9 _____ do you do together?
10 _____ he / she got any children?

A students work together to complete their gaps, as do B students. A's then find a B partner and have to read their questions aloud. Only by interacting with each other in this way can each pair find out if they have filled the gaps correctly. This part of the exercise focuses on accuracy in question forms.

In the next stage, the students can use the questions to interview their teacher and / or other students about their best friend. The exercise now has a communicative purpose (to find out about their partner's best friend), with scope for learners to speak at length if they so wish and also think up more questions to ask. If students find the activity motivating, they will become more concerned with communicating a message than monitoring how it is constructed.

> **Also suitable for:**
> 'information gap' conditional questions, e.g.
> A *What _____ (do) if you saw somebody stealing food in a market?*
> B *What would you do if you _____ (see) somebody stealing food in a market?*
> 'information gap' zero article statements, e.g.
> A *_____ is more important than money.*
> B *Health is more important than _____.*
> For the zero conditional example above, students may use different abstract nouns which could lead to some interesting discussion.

discrimination exercise

This type of recognition exercise is simple and quick for learners to do, but it can be extended for student output if the target sentences are presented in a real-life context which can lead to discussion. In the activity below, the examples are set in the context of the classroom. Although the linguistic choice is limited, there may be some disagreement, which will provide an interactive element. Reading the sentences to a partner provides controlled oral practice. You can also ask learners to make up similar sentences about the class or school / place of study which they pass to another pair to answer. This provides further learner output, and is a very useful way for the teacher to monitor the students' ability to use the structure.

> 3 Underline the true answers for your class.
>
>   1 We can / can't smoke in the classroom.
>   2 We have to / don't have to speak English most of the time in class.
>   3 We can / can't use dictionaries in class.
>   4 We have to / don't have to sit in the same place every lesson.
>   5 We have to / don't have to do homework three times a week.
>   6 We can / can't speak in our own language in class.
>   7 We can / can't bring drinks into the classroom.
>   8 We have to / don't have to do a test every month.

from pre-intermediate **student's book**, unit five *p.47*

> **also suitable for:** *-ed / -ing* adjectives, e.g.
>   1 *Do you think learning English is interested / interesting?*
>   2 *Do you feel embarrassed / embarrassing if you make mistakes in English?*

true / false statements

Statements containing the target structure which students have to change or discuss are another useful form of personalized practice. For instance, you can provide sentences for students to make true for themselves, like this:

   never
I ~~often~~ work late in the evenings.

   usually
I ~~never~~ go to bed before midnight.

etc.

how to ... practise grammar

The activity above can be done orally in pairs, or students can write the answers alone then compare. Alternatively, they can try to guess which statements are true for their partner.

In the activity below, students work in small groups and have to find out whether the statements in the questionnaire are true for their group. In order to do this, there will be a high volume of practice as students will need to use the target structure repeatedly, (i.e. the present continuous for future). The activity provides quite controlled practice of question forms and short answers and high frequency collocations, but it does require learners to really listen to each other and process the answers.

> **Work in small groups. Ask questions to find the answers to the questionnaire. Write T (true) or F (false).**
>
> *example*   **A** Are you working late tomorrow?
>   **B** No, I'm not.
>   **C** Yes, I am.
>
> | IN OUR GROUP ... | TRUE OR FALSE? |
> |---|---|
> | – somebody is working late tomorrow. | _____ |
> | – everybody is coming to the next lesson. | _____ |
> | – nobody is staying at home tomorrow evening. | _____ |
> | – somebody is going on holiday next month. | _____ |
> | – everybody is going home after the lesson. | _____ |
> | – somebody is doing some sport this weekend. | _____ |
> | – everybody is going shopping this weekend. | _____ |
> | – nobody is getting married this year. | _____ |
> | – somebody is moving house this year. | _____ |
> | – nobody is taking an exam this year. | _____ |

from pre intermediate **student's book**, review eight *p.83*

also suitable for: other tenses; modals of obligation or ability

substitution drills

In classic substitution drilling, the teacher provides a sentence, e.g. *I've had three coffees today* and then a prompt, e.g. *she*. The class repeats the sentence incorporating the new word and any necessary changes, i.e. *She's had three coffees today*. The teacher continues to give prompts and the class provide appropriate sentences. Here is a variation on the teacher-led drill which increases the practice each student gets because they do it in pairs.

> **4 With a partner, take turns to change the sentence below, using the words given. Don't write anything.**
>
>   *I never used to go out on Sundays.*
>
> 1   we   We never used to go out on Sundays.
> 2   Mondays   We never used to go out on Mondays.
> 3   they   7   stay at home
> 4   Friday nights   8   never
> 5   always   9   go to parties
> 6   she   10   my brother and I
>
> **5 Write down the last sentence. Compare with another pair.**

from pre intermediate **student's book**, unit twelve *p.114*

Like all drills, it tests form and pronunciation rather than meaning, and there is no scope for creativity or personalisation, but the exercise can be fun. By handing over control to the learners it is also more flexible than a classic teacher-led drill. If you feel your learners have a good grasp of the forms, you could do this drill with pairs racing each other to find the final sentence (it's very difficult to do this activity without saying all the sentences). If your learners are less confident, they can work in pairs and proceed at their own pace without being rushed. It is important to plan your prompts carefully for the students, however, to ensure that they produce natural, logical sentences.

also suitable for: most forms of tense practice.

mime

A type of practice activity with a visual element is miming. In the activity below, students in pairs are given sentences to mime for another pair or for the class.

> **A pairs**   Act out these sentences for B pairs. You can't speak – you have to mime. Practise your actions for each sentence.
>
> 1   I was having my lunch when somebody phoned me.
> 2   I was driving to work when the police stopped me.
> 3   When I was taking a photo, somebody stole my bag.
> 4   I was having a shower when I heard the fire alarm.
> 5   I was waiting for a bus when somebody asked me the time.

> **B pairs**   You have to act out these sentences for A pairs. You can't speak – you have to mime. Practise your actions for each sentence.
>
> 1   I was watching TV when somebody broke the window.
> 2   I was changing some money at the bank when I met an old friend.
> 3   I was working on my computer when the phone rang.
> 4   When I was running for the bus, a dog ran after me and bit me.
> 5   When I was sitting in the garden somebody threw a ball at me.

from pre-intermediate **student's book**, unit seven **pairwork** *p.141* 'B pairs' sentences *p.142*

Firstly, the pairs rehearse their mimes. During this stage, they will use a range of language, not just the target language, while negotiating how best to do the mimes. They then find a B pair and act out a sentence. The B pair have to say what happened / was happening: in other words, produce an accurate past continuous / past simple sentence. They may have to make some guesses (especially if the mimes are rather ambiguous), which will add to the volume of practice. The activity provides challenge and is game-like, everyone is engaged and this results in some lively interaction with a physical element in the classroom. Pairs can make up their own sentences to mime, or invent sentences for other students to mime; this will further demonstrate their awareness of the concepts.

also suitable for: *too* + adjective / *not* + adjective + *enough* e.g. *the soup's too salty; the trousers aren't long enough.*

Separable phrasal verbs, e.g. *she picked the book up; he threw the paper away.*

try it out ten things

This is an adaptable framework relying entirely on the learners' experience, which provides high volume controlled practice.

1 Ask students in pairs to write down **ten things** you do in a restaurant, e.g. *You sit at a table / ask for the menu.* (Do an example together first.) Set a time limit of say, three minutes, but if they need more time, let them have it. Monitor, help and correct where necessary. Students can use dictionaries, but if so, they may need more time.

2 Tell students to find a new partner. They take turns to say a sentence, e.g. *You order from the menu*. If a student says a sentence which their partner hasn't got, they get a point.

3 At the end, students read out the sentences which were different from their partner's.

This example practises the present simple, but it also provides considerable practice in noun + verb collocations, as do the contexts below. You can therefore feed in or correct these.

Here are some more structures for pair practice:

ten things ... you **can do** at a wedding / on a beach / in a park
you **have to do** when you're organizing a party
you **should do** to improve your English

Here are some structures for students to prepare alone before comparing with a partner:

ten things ... you**'ve done** this week / this month
you**'re going to do** at the weekend
you**'d like to do** before you get old
you **used to do** when you were younger
you **would do** if money wasn't a problem

Tina, Bath

3 Staging practice activities

Staging the practice so that the length and complexity of the activities proceed at the appropriate pace for your learners is quite a challenge. If we are too cautious and restrict learners wholly to a diet of controlled gap fills or drills, they will never get a chance to use the language for a real communicative purpose. Consequently they may remain obsessed with correctness and never achieve any real fluency. At the other extreme, if we ask students to launch straight into a free practice activity before they have had a chance to grasp the forms and concepts, they are likely to feel frustrated by their own inaccuracy.

It makes sense, therefore, to stage students' learning so that practice activities which immediately follow newly presented grammar do not demand too much attention to form and meaning at the same time. There is no blueprint for staging practice, but as a general rule:

– recognition (e.g. underlining or matching) precedes production

– practice in isolation before in combination (e.g. practise present perfect first before contrasting it with past simple)

– control before freedom and creativity.

Let's look at a staged set of activities designed to help learners use *will* for spontaneous decisions and offers. We are assuming that learners have already studied the meaning, form, and pronunciation of *will* (see **natural English** pre-intermediate **student book**, unit four *p.36*, grammar **exercises 1-3**.) The first form of practice below (**exercise 4** in the **student's book**) is very controlled: learners only have two choices so they are free to concentrate on the difference in concept between *will* and the present simple (learners often make the mistake of using the present simple instead of *will* here).

4 Complete the sentences with *'ll* or nothing (-).

1 **A** I think you need to contact her.
  B Yes, you're right. I _____ e-mail her now.

2 **A** Do you meet her a lot?
  B Yes, I _____ see her every day.

3 **A** Does she reply to all the letters she receives?
  B Yes, but I _____ type them.

4 **A** The boss is busy.
  B OK, I _____ phone her later.

from pre-intermediate **student's book**, unit four *p.36*

The next activity in the sequence, **exercise 5** below, requires more output by the students: they have to produce the correct form *I'll ...*, and they also have to create logical and coherent responses to the stimuli they are given.

5 Complete the dialogues. Use *I'll*.

1 Look, it's going to rain. OK, _____.
2 What would you like to drink? Er, _____.
3 I need to get to the station quickly. Fine, _____.
4 I can't do my homework. Don't worry, _____.

from pre-intermediate **student's book**, unit four *p.36*

how to ... practise grammar   157

The dialogues are quite restricted but they are designed to elicit verbs which frequently co-occur with *will* with this meaning, e.g. *I'll help you, I'll take my umbrella, I'll have a coffee*, etc. By producing the responses, it will help learners to memorize useful lexical chunks. This activity is still controlled, but there is more choice for the learner in terms of lexis, and when they compare their sentences with a partner, they may discover that they have different but equally valid responses. In question 3, for example (*I need to get to the station*), learners might come up with different responses: *Fine, I'll take you / I'll give you a lift / I'll call a taxi*. In other words, they can learn from each others' responses.

Finally, at the end of the lesson, learners have the opportunity to use *will* in another context where it would arise naturally in offers and spontaneous decisions*. The simple role play and guided dialogue in **'it's your turn!'** below illustrates to the students how the language point can be used. The item has to be used in real time, and as part of a communicative activity with a specified outcome: buying and selling possessions. The other language around the target item should be within the learners' grasp, and the activity should be achievable. Practising first with a partner in **exercise 2** gives students a chance to rehearse the conversation – time to think and rehearse is an opportunity for monitoring and attention to accuracy – and by the time they get to the mingling activity in **exercise 3**, it is hoped that their use of *will* is now becoming a little more automatic. They may even feel they can take more risks in their conversations.

---

speaking it's your turn!

1 You're going to sell three of your things (your book, your pen, etc.). Choose three things and decide a price for each one.

  examples   my jacket – €80   my pencil – 30 cents

2 Try to sell your things to a partner. They should try to get a discount.

  example A How much is your jacket?
       B It's €80.
       A €80! That's expensive. I'll give you €50.
       B No, but you can have it for €70.
       A No thanks, I'll leave it. / OK, I'll take it.

3 Move around the class. Try to buy things at a discount.

4 Tell the class what you bought. Who got the best price?

from pre-intermediate **student's book**, unit four *p.36*

It is important to stress that the sequence given above is just an example. Good staging depends entirely on your on-going evaluation of your learners' grasp of the target language. Some groups will need to spend more time on a particular type of practice, and inevitably, students in the same class will need different amounts of practice; this is when practice allowing individual scope for different levels of complexity becomes a priority.

* At the back of the student's book, there is a bank of practice exercises alongside the language reference. These provide additional controlled practice for the teacher to use with their class where necessary, say before the 'it's your turn' in this case. You can use the exercises with some of the students but not others, if you wish; they are simply there to be used at your discretion.

4 The role of the teacher

> **think!**[6]
> What kind of things do you do while your students are doing grammar practice activities? Think for a few moments, then read on.

In grammar practice activities, the main role of the teacher is to provide help and support. With activities directed by the teacher from the front of the class, this may mean correcting errors, but also giving learners time to think before they answer. If students are rushed into giving an answer, they are more likely to make mistakes and lose confidence. If someone is struggling to respond at this point, you can help by giving a hint or possibly starting off the correct sentence. However, when students are working in pairs or small groups, it is sensible to move round quietly and be available to help only where necessary. When they are working individually on a writing activity, you can see from their answers which students will benefit from your help.

monitoring and correction

How you provide help while monitoring grammar practice activities will depend largely on the aim of the activity and the students themselves. If the focus of the activity is accuracy – you want learners to select the correct meaning and / or produce the correct form – then they will need clear feedback. After all, opportunities to have mistakes corrected in a risk-free environment is one of the benefits of classroom practice. Here are two common correction techniques:

1 reformulate with the correct version. For example, if a student says, ' If I would go', you can repeat quietly, 'If I WENT'. This quick form of correction won't disrupt the activity and makes good sense if you judge the student will immediately recognize both the error and the correct version without any need for further explanation.

2 guided self correction. Repeat the error, but with a look on your face and / or an intonation pattern which clearly indicates to the student that a mistake has been made. By stressing the error, e.g. 'I GO yesterday', you can also highlight where the mistake has been made. In this case, there is clearly an invitation for the learner to correct the error themselves, and again this seems sensible if you are confident the student will be able to do so. Many learners find self-correction more satisfying than being corrected by others, and it may also have a more positive long term effect on their learning. However, it can be useful to call on other learners to help with the correct answer if the student is unable to find it him / herself.

Learners need to know when they are getting something wrong, but they also need to know when they are getting it right. This doesn't mean constantly stopping an activity in order to give praise, but a quiet 'good' or positive gesture, e.g. a thumbs up or nod of approval as you walk by, will let learners know that they are doing well. Such positive signs from the teacher are essential for student motivation; we all like praise.

With all grammar practice activities, whether accuracy-based or fluency-based, the way you respond to students will depend partly on them. Some learners respond well to correction; others less so. Some learners expect you to correct them; others are quietly pleased if you adopt a more tolerant approach to error. Some learners respond particularly well to praise; others might find it rather meaningless if it happens too often. This doesn't mean ignoring errors or giving praise for the sake of it, but using your experience and judgement to determine how best to help individual learners.

> **Want to know more** about monitoring and correction? Go to intermediate **teacher's book**, **how to ...** monitor and give feedback *pp. 156–161*.

conclusion

In this chapter we have

- selected criteria for features of 'good' practice
- looked at common exercise types for grammar practice with some suggestions for making this practice more interesting and expansive
- included an example to show how practice can be staged
- concluded with a brief look at the role of the teacher during grammar practice activities.

In particular, we hope this chapter will encourage you to think about ways you can adapt and extend exercises with purely linguistic aims and turn them into more expansive and communicative activities.

follow up

Thornbury S 1999 *How to teach Grammar* Longman

Ur P 1996 *A Course in Language Teaching* Module 6 Cambridge University Press

Ur P 1988 *Grammar Practice Activities* Cambridge University Press

Harmer J 2001 *The Practice of English Language Teaching* part 5 Longman

Swan M and Walter C 2001 *The Good Grammar Book* Oxford University Press

how to ... motivate low level learners to write

1 Why is motivation a problem with writing?
2 Product and process
3 Integrating classroom writing
4 Motivation through feedback

1 Why is motivation a problem with writing?

> **think!**[1]
> How would you feel if you had to write a magazine article, say, on the problems your learners have with writing?

We think most people would be, initially at least, daunted by the prospect of having to write an article for a magazine, even in their mother tongue. Writing is an acquired skill, and we have all, at some time in our lives, struggled with the difficulties of writing an extended piece of prose which someone might evaluate or criticise. To start with, there is the dread of the blank page and all those questions in our heads:

- Who exactly am I writing it for?
- How explicit do I need to be? i.e. Are the readers informed or not informed?
- Have I got any ideas? If so, how do I organize them?
- How do I express my ideas? i.e. What about my grammar, vocabulary, and style?
- How do I link my ideas together in logical, coherent prose?

It should be said that there are some people who relish this challenge and are very good at it; but for most of us it is exceptionally hard work and takes a lot of time to do well. Little surprise then if our learners find writing difficult, and especially in a second language where the written form of many words seems different from the spoken form, and where the conventions of style and layout in different genres are often so different from their own language.

In addition to the inherent difficulty of writing, there are other fears possibly induced by the classroom environment itself. Learners may receive praise or criticism for their efforts when they speak, but such comments from the teacher happen quickly in real time, and are usually soon forgotten. Writing, however, has permanence, and most learners believe, rightly or wrongly, that written tasks are set by teachers for the sole purpose of close inspection and evaluation – a view that is endorsed when they get their work back with a mark or grade. Of course, this may encourage the few learners who are good at it, but the prospect of such a task rarely motivates the majority.

We also have to recognize that most learners (and teachers) on general English courses don't necessarily view writing as a priority. Learners see the classroom fundamentally as the place to learn new vocabulary and grammar, and improve their speaking and listening. They feel that if writing is to play any part in the course, the logical place for it is homework. We have heard this opinion voiced by many learners over the years, and it reflects a widely held view that writing is, essentially, a solitary occupation; something you do, and need to do, on your own.

There may be other reasons why learners are not motivated to write, but there are at least three issues that need to be addressed in our approach to writing if we are going to make it a more enjoyable experience for the majority of learners:

- Does it need to be so difficult?
- Does it need to be judged?
- Does it need to be a solitary occupation?

One of the major debates in recent years has been the product versus process approach to writing. This debate also has relevance to the issues mentioned above, so we will consider it briefly now. We will also be considering these questions in different parts of the chapter.

2 Process and product

The <u>product approach</u> aims to get the learner to produce an original text based on a model text: the focus is on the product of writing. These texts are often designed to highlight particular features of written language, and they provide a framework for the learners' own writing with specific language they may need to use. Here is an example of a teaching sequence following this approach.

> 1 Learners read a letter of complaint (e.g. from a passenger to an airline about poor service). Comprehension is checked.
> 2 The text is analysed for specific features. These might include a focus on the layout of the letter, greetings and formulaic expressions, ways of linking clauses, the organisation of ideas, formality of style, etc. Learners focus on one or two features or more.
> 3 They then work on specific exercises to practise subskills. For example, they are given jumbled sentences from another letter of complaint to put in order (to help with the organisation of content); they practise linking clauses through sentence completion; they are given a similar letter which contains errors in layout to correct; and so on.
> 4 Learners use the framework of the letter (e.g. address layout, greetings, reason for writing, description of the problems, language used, etc.) to help them produce a parallel piece of writing, perhaps about poor service in a hotel or at a restaurant.

The <u>process approach</u>, as its name indicates, focuses on the process of writing itself, and attempts to reflect the way good writers go about writing. Their starting point is not a model text but a communicative purpose, and they certainly don't achieve the end result at the first draft. Here is an outline of the process one might go through when producing a piece of writing:

- In a pre-writing phase, time is spent brainstorming ideas and making notes.

- The writer then needs to consider the reader in order to clarify the main focus of the writing and their attitude to it. At this point, they will select and organize their ideas.
- They should now be in a position to produce a first draft.
- This needs to be reviewed and checked that ideas are coming across clearly and in a well-balanced way.
- This first draft stage is followed by further revision and re-writing.
- Other people may also be involved in reading and commenting on the later drafts, leading to further revisions as a result of their comments.

In other words, writing evolves over a considerable period of time; there are no quick fixes.

When a process approach is adopted in the classroom, learners work collaboratively in pairs and groups at different stages of the writing. Here is an example of a process writing activity, based on one from *Writing 3* by Andrew Littlejohn. Learners imagine they are looking into a room through a window, and they write a description of what they see.

1. Learners are given pictures of different rooms around the world.
2. They brainstorm vocabulary to describe rooms under different headings, e.g. size and shape, light, overall impression. They compare with other learners.
3. They look at different pictures of windows and try to imagine the room behind one of them. They make notes about the room, the objects in it, the person in the room and what they are doing, the sounds and smells in the room.
4. They write a first draft of their description using their notes. They can ask other learners or the teacher for help during this stage.
5. They exchange papers with another student. They read their partner's text and write questions to prompt more information, e.g. Tell me more about the old lady. What does she look like?
6. Learners give their papers back and try to include answers to the questions in their description (in other words, they redraft their text).
7. Learners read out their finished texts; the class have to guess which window they were looking through.

There is a final stage in which learners read each others' work and suggest improvements, e.g. improving the vocabulary range, the flow of the text, linguistic accuracy.

from **Writing 3** by Andrew Littlejohn (see **follow up**)

Each approach, both product and process, has certain advantages, and we feel there is no reason why teachers should not incorporate ideas from both approaches at different times, or for different purposes. Primarily, you need to consider your learners and what will suit them best.

think![2]
As you read the benefits of each approach listed below, think about a particular group you are teaching. Which points seem most relevant to them? Can you add any more benefits?

benefits of a product approach

- Many learners find it safe and reassuring. They are not expected to be creative or imaginative, although for some this may be frustrating.
- Some learners at this level still have problems with basic issues such as letter formation and spelling – therefore copying or modifying model texts slightly is a very useful exercise / learning technique.
- Learners get a validated framework and accurate writing sample which they can refer back to later.
- For certain types of writing activity such as business letters, models are necessary. Many discoursal features of writing are culture specific, so learners are unlikely to arrive at correct text types by guesswork.
- Model texts provide a vehicle for presenting language exponents which may be relevant and useful for the task. Many learners expect this kind of lesson framework and find it reassuring.

benefits of a process approach

- The collaborative element of process writing can go a long way towards removing some of the fears of writing, and make it a less solitary activity.
- Collaboration also provides a considerable amount of speaking practice with a real communicative purpose, which can be motivating and enjoyable.
- The approach hands control and responsibility to the learner, enabling them to develop a personal approach.
- It can reduce anxiety for learners who may feel they will be judged on their first efforts. With a process approach, the first draft is only the first step. In addition, the teacher's role is to facilitate more than to judge.
- Self-expression is encouraged, which is also good for motivation.

It is important to bear in mind your learners' previous learning experience and attitudes to collaborative writing. For some, process writing will be very liberating and enjoyable; others may prefer to write alone and require time and space to do so. With thoughtful class management, however, there is no reason why one or two individuals shouldn't work alone while others work together. A further consideration is that process writing takes up a lot of time and it might be advisable to spread it over different lessons.

There is nothing to stop you from using elements of both process and product approaches in a writing activity. For instance, you could start with a model letter, but still include collaborative drafting and redrafting of the learners' own letter. Alternatively, you could start with brainstorming ideas and initial writing, and introduce a model later for them to use for their own editing or future reference.

3 Integrating classroom writing

Here are a few suggestions for ways of including writing, using aspects of both product and process approaches, as an integral part of the lesson. We hope they will make writing a more enjoyable and motivating experience for learners who are usually reluctant to pick up their pens.

how to ... motivate low level learners to write

collaboration

The inherent difficulty of extended writing i.e. the pressure to 'put it all together' is one very good reason for collaboration. Two heads (or even three or four) are often better than one, so if learners can work together on a writing task, they can help each other with the content, the organisation of the content, and the drafting and editing of the content. The anxiety of working alone is removed, the fear of failure is greatly reduced (working together tends to diminish feelings of individual failure), and the chances of completing the task successfully are likely to increase. And as we have already said, collaboration involves speaking with a real communicative purpose. Here is a simple example from the pre-intermediate **student's book**:

1 With a partner, on a piece of paper write:
   - an activity
   - a place
   - the name of a famous person
   - an object
   - a question

> watching TV
> my house
> Jennifer Lopez
> a clock on the wall
> How much is it?

from pre-intermediate **student's book**, unit ten *p.94*

At this stage the learners don't know why they are writing down these things down, so there is no particular motivation to link them together. Then, they read a dream story:

> In my dream, I was watching The Simpsons on TV at home. The doorbell rang, and it was Jennifer Lopez. I was really surprised! She came into the house, sat down and watched it with me. Then she saw an old clock on the wall.
> She said, 'I want that! How much is it?'
> I said, 'You can't have it.
> It's my father's.
> Go away and leave me alone!'
> And then I woke up.

from pre-intermediate **student's book**, unit ten *p.94*

Learners pick out certain features of the language (e.g. the use of the past continuous and *really* + adjective), and then swap prompts (from **exercise 1**) with another pair. Each pair then writes a dream story based on the prompts they were given. Finally, the pairs read each other their dream stories, and say what they think of them.

As pointed out earlier, collaborative writing does not appeal to everyone and is sensitive to different learner styles. If you have learners in your class who still prefer to write on their own, you could put learners in groups of three to work together on the ideas and organisation of the ideas, then allow individuals to write their draft alone, while others work in pairs. They can join together again to read, discuss and edit their work, then perhaps separate once more to produce their second draft. As with any unfamiliar procedure, it is wise to start with small tasks, say in pairs, and build up gradually to larger collaborative activities with a variety of pairings and groupings.

multi-skills approach

Some learners want to do writing activities; others don't. You can reduce and possibly resolve this conflict by including writing as part of a multi-skills activity, i.e. learners may be prepared to do some writing if they can see that it is part of a larger activity involving other skills such as speaking, reading or listening.

In this example from part of the **extended speaking** activity in **unit six** of the pre-intermediate **student's book** *p.60*, learners work in pairs to produce a weather forecast. They have already studied the use of *will* for prediction, vocabulary connected with weather and geographical regions, adverbs, and comparative adjectives. The writing task also encourages learners to use *so* to link statements with consequences.

- First they listen to a weather forecast with a comprehension task.
- Then they draw a map of their country, divide it into two or three main regions, and decide what the weather will be like tonight and tomorrow, using weather symbols (which they have been shown).
- Following the discussion, they write the forecast together, and each person has to read and memorize certain parts of it.
- Finally, they present their weather forecast orally to the rest of the class.

Here is part of a weather forecast produced by two pre-intermediate Italian learners.

> Good evening and now the weather forecast.
> Tonight there will be a lot of snow coming in the north, so tomorrow it will be a good day to ski. In the morning more clouds are to be expected.
> In the middle it will be cloudy, and a bit foggy. Temperatures perhaps 15-20 degrees near the coast. So drive carefully!
> In the south, no sign of clouds, it will be sunny, and warmer than yesterday - over 20 degrees - so it will be a nice day to go to the seaside.
> The seas will be calm in all parts of Italy.
> Good night.

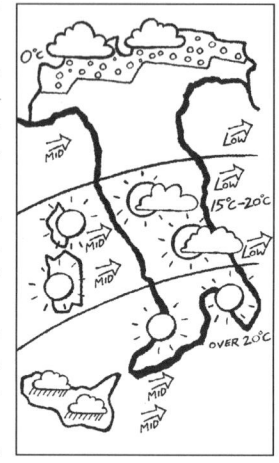

from **natural English** pre-intermediate research data

During this multi-skills activity learners have had listening practice and a discussion, produced a more formal oral presentation, and they have used recently presented grammar and vocabulary. As a result, they are unlikely to feel this is just a writing activity. At the same time, the written component is

how to ... motivate low level learners to write

an important part of the task: it is a genuine activity since weather forecasters have to script presentations carefully in order to include so much factual information within strict time constraints. As the writing forms the basis of the presentation to the rest of the class, we have also found that learners take it seriously and want to get it right.

Other examples that include writing as part of a multi-skills activity are:
- producing a TV or radio advertisement (write the text for the ad)
- producing a news story (write up the final story)
- producing a front page for a newspaper (edit other people's reports)
- designing a language school or holiday complex (produce a report)
- discussing a topical issue (write a discursive essay)
- interviewing a partner about a topic (write it up for a class magazine).

writing for a real audience
Consider the following teaching sequence:

creating a profile
Learners read profiles of two different people (overseas learners at English universities), who are interviewed about their current situation and future plans. In pairs, they analyse each profile, then roleplay the two original interviews, taking it in turns to be interviewer and interviewee. They are now very familiar with the profiles and are able to use them as a framework to complete sentences about their own situation and future plans.

The next step logically might be for each student to expand the sentences into a full profile of themselves. But it isn't. It is this:

> a You are going to interview a classmate in order to write a profile for your school website. Write five questions to ask your classmate about their experience and plans for the future.
> b Work in pairs. Compare your ideas and check your questions together.
> c Sit with the person you are going to interview. Ask your questions and make notes of your partner's answers. Quote something your partner says for the profile, e.g. *I miss seeing my friends every day.*
>
> *Theresa Clementson, Brighton, UK.*

Learners follow up the interview by writing the first draft of the profile <u>of their partner</u>. Then they check and edit their work, and show it to their partner. Together they check that the information is correct in both profiles and discuss possible improvements, before producing the final version of the profile for the school website or class magazine.

Writing about a partner rather than oneself introduces a new dimension: it means that each student is now producing a piece of writing for an interested reader (their partner), who will be motivated to ensure that the comments expressed in the interview have been accurately recorded. Imagine someone is writing a profile of you for a teacher's magazine. Wouldn't you read it with genuine interest and want to correct any inaccuracies? The other motivating factor here is that the final product is going to be displayed, in this case on a class website or in a class magazine; another reason to want to do well.

writing a notice
In real life, we may display things we have written for a purpose: to inform, to advertise, to elicit a response, etc. In the following activity, learners read shop window notices advertising a room to rent, or notices written by people looking for a room. They focus on the vocabulary used and complete notices using appropriate vocabulary. In the final stage, they produce written texts themselves. Here writing is used as part of a problem-solving activity: matching landlords with tenants.

> a Draft two notices.
>   1 You are looking for an English-speaking person to rent a room in your house or flat.
>   2 You are looking for a room, house or flat to share in an English-speaking country.
> b Exchange your notices with a partner. Compare your ideas and suggest any changes or improvements to each other's notices.
> c Rewrite your notices for display on a noticeboard.
> d Read other people's notices.
>   1 Choose the room, house or flat which appeals to you most.
>   2 Choose the best person / people for your room.
>
> *Theresa Clementson, Brighton, UK.*

Here are two examples of 'writing for a real audience' from the **natural English** pre-intermediate **skills resource book**:

writing an invitation
Getting learners to send messages to each other is a fun and authentic way to set up genuine communication within the classroom. Giving the exchange a real communicative outcome will help to motivate learners and lend the activity authenticity. In the lesson below, learners analyse invitations in e-mail, letter and text message form for relevant features of style and language function. They then get together in an 'ideas generation' phase i.e. deciding on the purpose or outcome of the message before choosing a suitable medium.

5 generating ideas
> a Work in pairs. You have something to celebrate. Decide what you are celebrating and what you want to do, e.g. give a party, go out for dinner, etc.
> b Decide the time, place, and any other details.

Writing task
> a You are going to invite a classmate to your celebration. Decide whether to write a letter, e-mail, or text message.
> b Write your invitation and 'send' it to your classmate.

from **natural English** pre-intermediate **skills resource book** *p.6*

writing a film review
In this lesson, learners work up to writing a film review, which their classmates will read. This turns what could be a rather 'flat' ending to a lesson i.e. finishing writing the review, into a genuine writing task with a real-life outcome. On the basis of

how to ... motivate low level learners to write

reading each other's reviews, learners are asked for a genuine response to the details and opinions given.

The lesson begins with a discussion to generate ideas and some input from a sample review:

Learners then focus on the way opinions are expressed in the review, and how different aspects of the film are described e.g. *It's set in ..., It is directed by ...*. They also work on ways of connecting the ideas into longer sentences before doing the writing task below:

Writing task

a Write a review of a film you have seen recently for your class magazine.

b Read other people's reviews.

1 Do you agree with their review? (if you've seen the film)

2 Would you like to see the film? (if you haven't seen it)

---

from **natural English** pre-intermediate **skills resource book** *p.50*

A number of writing tasks can be made more interesting and enjoyable if learners are writing to and for other learners, and exchanging correspondence, including e-mails. These could be:

- invitations and replies regarding social arrangements
- a set of instructions for someone else to carry out in class
- notices and messages for a classroom noticeboard
- descriptions of people and things for other members of class to guess
- a series of classroom rules for others to add to and amend
- the beginning of a story which others continue.

Some of the ideas above can be brought to life by providing learners with materials to write on (card, coloured paper), and by using word processing which helps greatly with editing, downloading visuals from the Internet for wall displays, etc.

The **try it out** idea below involves different elements from this section.

---

try it out images of childhood

I wanted learners to write a personal anecdote (an event from their childhood) as the culmination of some work on narrating.

Before the lesson:

- I asked them to bring to class a photo of themselves when they were young, and think of an event that happened during their childhood. They could check any new vocabulary in a dictionary and rehearse the episode in English before the lesson.

In the lesson:

- I showed them a photo of myself as a child.
- I told them a true story about the day I fell and broke my front teeth.
- At the end, I asked them firstly how the story made them feel and secondly about the structure of the story: scene-setting, the lead-up to the event, the event itself, what happened next, the consequence.

- I then put them in small groups to show each other their photos and ask questions. This produced a lot of genuine interaction. In pairs, learners told each other their stories while I monitored.
- We then went to the language laboratory, and learners recorded their own stories. (If you do not have access to a lab or listening centre, learners can record their stories on cassette recorders in class or even at home.)They listened to their recording and wrote down what they had said, correcting and changing the story as they went.
- Then, working with their original partner, they edited and corrected each other's stories.

After the lesson:

- I collected the stories, suggested further corrections, then learners typed up a final draft and put them on a wall display with a photocopy of their childhood photo.

They were motivated throughout, keen to read each other's stories, and the final results were excellent.

Jackie, Paris

---

diary writing

One final type of writing that has been used very successfully by several of our colleagues is diary writing. Traditionally, diary entries are a very personal form of writing and not usually intended for anyone except the diarist. Sometimes, however, learners find it very satisfying to keep a diary in English, which they only show to their teacher. The idea may be attractive because it provides the student with a channel of communication to the teacher and a way of getting feedback from them. Possibly, it may just be the novelty of it that is appealing. From our experience, teachers who use diary writing usually lay down certain guidelines for the learners, the most important being that this is not writing for evaluation: teachers read the diary entries and may respond by writing themselves, but they make very few language corrections. The principle behind diary writing is that learners can express themselves freely without fear of correction, and that they get into the habit of writing regularly. It should never be made compulsory – it only appeals to a minority in most classes – and learners can choose to disclose their entries or keep them private.

This is a type of writing that will take place largely outside the classroom, but to introduce it, you will need to allocate a little classroom time to it. Ask learners to get a small notebook, and start off with five minutes of diary writing in lessons over a week or two. Another option is for learners to start an e-mail diary which they send to their teacher, who responds accordingly.

4 Motivation through feedback

During the writing process, you will be helping learners with brainstorming and planning, and making suggestions. Afterwards they need to spend time looking through their work again, improving the grammar, use of vocabulary, spelling, linking, and so on. You might suggest a particular focus for their final editing, whether this is done alone or in pairs. At the end though, many learners will want some validation or appreciation of what they have done – your encouragement will be essential if you want to motivate learners to carry on writing – as well as supportive advice for improvements. But how much correction should you give? Understandably, learners want to have their mistakes corrected in order to improve, and their confidence in you may be undermined if they discover that you have overlooked some of their errors. At the same time, the sight of homework covered in red pen can be very discouraging, and there is a danger of learners becoming more interested in discrete errors of spelling, grammar or sentence construction than whether the text has the intended effect on the reader and fulfils the task. The key is to achieve the right balance of encouragement and guidance on global writing skills while attending to specific language issues.

writing samples for evaluation

Let's look at two pieces of written work produced by Spanish learners after trialling the **extended speaking** activity in **natural English** pre-intermediate, **unit nine**, 'From home to home', *p.90*. In the speaking activity, learners interviewed each other about their previous homes and the home they currently live in. As a follow-up activity, their task was to write about 'My home history' i.e. about their previous and current homes (in other words, to write a personal account of what they had already spent time planning and discussing). For trialling purposes, this assignment was given without any pre-teaching of grammar or vocabulary.

---

think![3]

Read both assignments. Which student do you think fulfils the above more effectively, and why?

Student A   Angel

My home history

I was born in and old house in Barcelona. It was built in the forties of the 19cth Century. It had 8 rooms and one big patio. It didn't have running water or central heating. in the winter I had ever cold but I remember when I played in the patio in the summer, also I remember I had ever different animals (dogs, cats, chickens, pigeons, guinea pigs, fishes, rabbits, ducks.)

It took 10 or 15 minutes to school and 5 minutes for Underground. Every day in the afternoon, when I finished de homework I played in a square near my house with other children.

I lived in this house since I was born until I had 15 years old. Then I lived in other house for 3 years, and then other, and other …

Student B   Carlos

My home history

I have lived in two different places. When I was young, I lived in my first house. My first house was big, the house was in a village, the village was between the mountains and the sea. In the house there were three bedrooms, two bathrooms there was a kitchen and a big living room. Outside the house, there were two parkin spaces, one swimming pool and a garden, in the garden there were some flowers and plants. Living in this house was fantastic because it was quiet and everyday the weather was hot.

When I was eleven years old I moved to the city. My father bought a flat in the centre. Today I live there. The flat is comfortable. There are three bedrooms and two bathrooms, there is a small kitchen one beautiful living room and one storeroom. The flat is in a good place because all day is sunny. in the building there are a lot of neighbours and a few are rude.

---

from **natural English** pre-intermediate research data
go to **answer key** *p.166*

It is important to consider the overall effect on the reader of a learner's piece of writing, and it is crucial to give them feedback on this – in the form of a general comment, for example, at the end of the piece of writing. In the case of Student A, more time to plan his assignment, talk to another student or the teacher about his plans and get feedback from them on his ideas might have helped him to focus the content of the writing more accurately before he wrote the draft. When giving learners feedback on task achievement, you could write some encouraging comments at the end of their work, and either write questions to help them think about content or make suggestions yourself. This might be used for a redrafting of the assignment or simply as a guide for future work, and might also incorporate feedback on more specific errors, which we will now discuss.

correction schemes

When it comes to a more detailed look at the learners' writing, you have a number of choices at your disposal. You can:

- write in the correct form above the error.
- underline errors, without indicating what type of error has been made, and ask learners to try to correct them.
- highlight the type of error the learner has made using a correction code. If you use a code, you will need to check that learners understand it.

Here is a code with an activity which checks understanding of the code and provides practice in improving a text:

Read a student's first draft. Use the correction code to rewrite the text. Then compare your text with your partner's.

[WW]*And* when he [T]*see* the [Sp]*prize* he knew he [P]*couldnt* buy ^*ring*. It cost £1,500 ~~pounds~~. The man couldn't [WF]*stops* thinking about the ring. He knew [Sp]*wood* love it [WO]*his wife*.

correction code

WW	wrong word
T	wrong tense
Sp	wrong spelling
P	wrong punctuation
^	something is missing
—	you don't need this word
WF	wrong form
WO	wrong word order

---

think![4]

For what reasons might you use (or not use) each of the ways of correcting suggested above?

go to **answer key** *p.166*

Using a code might suggest that you need to correct everything, which could certainly deflate low level learners in particular. It is important to look at learners' writing in context. What was the aim of the task you set them? Was it to develop a particular aspect of the writing skill, such as using an appropriate style, or organizing ideas? Was it to provide freer practice of particular language? Or was it simply to write personally and creatively? Whatever you decide, the feedback needs to match the task set. When you return learners' work, tell them how

how to ... motivate low level learners to write

you have corrected it. If you have just corrected selectively, that is to say the errors you consider to be most important, explain what you have done, and why. Trisha Hedge (1988) suggests handing learners a marking policy document, which explains how the teacher will help them during and after the writing process. If you do a lot of writing activities with your learners, you could consider writing a policy document of your own.

Giving learners feedback on their written work is a perfect opportunity to focus on their individual needs. Let's consider this issue for the two learners above.

> **think!**[5]
> Look at Angel and Carlos's writing again on *p.165*.
> How could they improve it? Choose <u>two</u> areas for each student.

go to **answer key** *p.166*

conclusion

In this chapter, we have discussed:
- the reasons why many learners are not very motivated to write in English
- product- and process-oriented approaches to writing, and the benefits of both
- ways of motivating low level learners to write, through collaborative writing activities, a multi-skills approach and by providing a real reader or readers
- how to approach the correction of written work

We hope the combination of collaborative writing tasks with supportive teaching frameworks and feedback will help to make writing more engaging, interactive and less daunting for learners. If you would like to devote more time to helping your pre-intermediate learners develop their writing skills, the **natural English** pre-intermediate **reading and writing skills resource book** provides a comprehensive range of stimulating activities.

follow up

Littlejohn A 1993 *Writing 1, 2, 3* and *4 Cambridge Skills for fluency* Cambridge University Press (the activity described on *p.00* is from unit 3, 'Through a window')

Hedge T 1988 *Writing* Resource Books for Teachers (*p.151*) OUP

Nunan D 1991 *Language Teaching Methodology* Chapter 5 Prentice Hall International (UK) Ltd

White R and Arndt V 1991 *Process Writing* Longman

Hadfield C and Hadfield J 1990 *Writing Games* Nelson

Haines S *Difficult, lonely and boring* in English Teaching Professional October 1998 Issue 9

answer key

think![3] *p.165*
Student A's work answers the task at the beginning and starts well in the first few lines – you get a good sense of the type of building he was brought up in. However, he quickly digresses into anecdotal detail about his pets and the playground. He links the old house to the later houses very well, but then abandons the task. Writing is demanding for a learner at his level, and he may be satisfied that he has done enough and produced a piece of personal writing.

Student B fulfils the task more effectively. He writes about both homes, describing the interior and exterior, and introduces the second home very well, explaining how they came to move. The ideas are logically organized. He briefly mentions his attitude to both homes, though this account is a little more impersonal than student A's text, and possibly less engaging.

think![4] *p.165*
Writing in the corrected form throughout as a matter of policy would deny learners the opportunity to try to correct their mistakes, and it's quite possible that they would glance at the feedback, put it in a folder and not think about it again. However, if an error involves language which is beyond the learner's competence, or they need a particular expression which they are very unlikely to know or be able to find, then supplying the correct form is sensible. For instance, in Angel's text, *in the forties of the 19cth Century* could be corrected to *in the 1840s*.

Underlining errors provides a little guidance, and is more of a challenge than using a correction code. You might do this if you think the learner is capable of identifying the type of error (e.g. putting 'see' instead of 'saw' in the correction exercise text from the example.) You are more likely to use a correction code if you feel that learners are able to correct the error, or can find out how to correct it, with the help of dictionaries or grammar books, for example. This approach provides guidance without telling learners the answer, so in theory they will have to put some effort into making improvements. For example, in Carlos's text, a link mark between his short sentences *I lived in my first house. My first house was big*.

There is a warning with correction codes, however: keep them simple. Too many abbreviations and symbols can be confusing.

think![5] *p.166*
As we said in the previous **think!** task, we think that Angel needs to brainstorm and select ideas which are more suited to the task, and this might also help him to pace himself so that he can write succinctly about his previous homes and have the stamina to continue to write about his current one. In addition, a language point which recurs is the use of *have* in place of *be* in lexical chunks such as *I ~~had ever~~ cold (I was cold); I ~~had 15 years old~~ (I was 15)*. Alternatively, you could focus on *ever* which he uses meaning *always*; or *other* for *another*. To extend his grammatical range, you might want to introduce *used to do* for reminiscences.

Carlos writes very carefully with good attention to accuracy, but he would benefit from some work on sentence linking – there are too many short sentences which can be neatly combined, and this would make his writing more sophisticated, e.g. *When I was young, I lived in a big house in a village between the mountains and the sea. It had three bedrooms, two bathrooms, a kitchen and a big living room*. He also needs help with punctuation.

how to ... use the learners as a resource

1 Putting the learners centre stage
2 Turning student output into lesson input
3 What can we learn from learner output?
4 Correction and reformulation

1 Putting the learners centre stage

In our constant search for teaching materials – whether it be listening or reading texts, videos, visual materials, language exercises, computer games or a role play – we are in danger of overlooking the most important and generative resource in the classroom: the students themselves. Of course, different types of material are needed to provide variety, and sometimes the material you have selected is the most natural and obvious way to learn or practise particular language exponents. However, it is the learners' personalities, knowledge and experience which make a class what it is; and their contribution to the lessons and to each others' learning, although difficult to measure, is absolutely crucial.

advantages of learner-generated output

Much learner-generated output will involve personalization, i.e. people talking about themselves and giving their opinions. Most learners are happy to do this, within reason. This may be because:

- their personal information is at their fingertips, so they don't need to consume vast amounts of material and memorize the information before they have something to say.
- personalized activities provide opportunities for learners to share experiences with others and find similarities and differences in their lives and outlook, which can help the rapport between learners (and the teacher) and add to the interest of the class.

People need to know about each other to make connections, so 'getting to know you' activities are not just about language use, but about developing relationships. Strange as it may seem, it is quite easy to make the classroom an unreal place. A friend of ours attending a language course in German was quite frustrated to find that after learning vocabulary to describe different jobs, the class were given role cards with false names and jobs in order to practise asking and answering questions about the jobs. He never found out what people in his class really did for a living, and didn't know how to say his own real job.

Putting the learners centre stage values their input and can help them to talk about what is of most interest to them. It also makes lessons more memorable, alive and fresh. The added bonus for the teacher is that learner-generated output doesn't involve producing a lot of material, although it does require thought and preparation.

risks

Learner-generated activities in the classroom are not without risks for you or the students.

For students:

- Personalized material may be sensitive. We can sometimes anticipate this problem, e.g. in the pre-intermediate **student's book**, **unit four**, students learn phrases to talk about clothes size, e.g. *What size do you take?* This language is clearly essential if you are buying clothes, but it became obvious that to provide practice of this language, we would have to be careful with the garments we asked learners to talk about; shoes were the safest option we could find.
- Controversial topics can cause offence. One measure we can take is to make it clear that learners do not have to talk about something if they don't want to. You might teach them useful ways to express this: *'I'd rather not talk about that / I'd rather not say'*.
- Talking about themselves in class may not be something they expect to do. In this case, introduce personalized activities very gradually, starting with simple information that anyone would be prepared to reveal about themselves, e.g. TV viewing habits, things they would take to a desert island. Be guided by their response, and make your aims clear.

For teachers:

- What students produce can be quite unpredictable, and you may have to deal with language or content issues which you didn't expect. 'Thinking on your feet' is not easy, particularly for inexperienced teachers.
- Anticipating how long learner-generated activities will take is more difficult, but that doesn't mean you shouldn't try.

> **think!**[1]
> Have you touched on any sensitive subjects in your lessons recently? How did you handle the situation? Think about a learner-generated activity you have done. How did you / the students cope with it?

finding out about your learners

With a new class, you will need to find out what interests them and what they are happy to talk about. You can start this off by revealing things about yourself. If you are prepared to give a lead, it will encourage students to do the same, and it can also help to develop class rapport.

> **think!**[2]
> Think back to the last lesson you taught. How much did you find out about your learners as individuals? How much did you reveal about yourself?

Topics in course books are usually 'safe', and should have general appeal. At pre-intermediate level, most learners can talk about their home and family life, their work / studies, their social lives, eating, etc. You will want to know what else interests them, and the easiest way to do this is to give out a list of topics and ask students to tick the ones which interest them most. You can include issues relevant to the local environment, and allow a blank space for learners to add their own topics. Learners can compare ideas in groups, and then feed back to you. Bear in mind that considerable linguistic skills and knowledge are required to discuss certain topics. While some lively debate might occur on a topical issue, it can also flounder as students struggle to express themselves, and some learners find topical discussion difficult. Nevertheless, everyone has something to say about themselves, which can help you to generate a great deal of productive talk at lower levels.

> **try it out** topic questionnaire
> Look at the topics in the map of **natural English** pre-intermediate **student's book**.
> Make a list of other topics you think might interest your class, and leave a space for them to add their own topics. Give it to your class to discuss. Do the results surprise you?

2   Turning student output into lesson input

Student output can be the basis for different types of interaction in a classroom, involving different degrees of control or freedom, and for varying lengths of time. It can be used as a way of presenting, practising, or revising language (grammar, vocabulary, lexical phrases, etc.), and as a means of providing longer classroom segments: in fluency activities learners may be talking about themselves for quite long periods without the restraints of target language.

Below, you will find some simple teaching frameworks which you can adapt for different linguistic purposes and use in different ways: as short, warmer-type activities, or more extended speaking activities. Some of the activity types described in this section are based on activities from **natural English** pre-intermediate **student's book**. We believe these are all suitable for pre-intermediate level, but there is no reason why you should not use them at higher levels, and some can be adapted for elementary learners. The emphasis throughout is on learner-generated rather than teacher-generated language, and on making the learner (rather than the material) the central resource in the classroom.

can I ask you some questions?

Consider the following sequence:

> 1 Alone, learners write down five questions to ask classmates on a given topic e.g. their family.
> 2 They show their questions to a partner who makes any necessary corrections. They add any different questions from their partner's list to their own list. Meanwhile, you monitor and suggest corrections.
> 3 They think about their answers to all the questions. This gives them time to plan what they are going to say and think about any language they might need.
> 4 As a rehearsal stage, they ask and answer the questions with their partner. You monitor and give feedback to the class (this might include a little correction, or encouraging them to talk at greater length, or asking follow-up questions to produce more natural conversation).
> 5 Students do the activity as a class mingle, speaking to at least three or four new partners, and have to find the person whose family is most similar to theirs. You monitor then provide feedback.

Your focus in this activity will obviously depend on your aims, which might be to produce accurate question forms, to work on certain tenses, practise specific lexis, etc. However, on the whole the topic is likely to dictate the language focus. For instance, if they are asking and answering about their home, they will need to use a range of tenses (*Where do you live? How long have you been there? Why did you move there? How long are you planning to stay?*)

proxy questions

In this activity, learners have to guess or invent answers to questions on behalf of another learner. Show learners how this works by demonstrating it yourself first with two students.

> 1 Students work in threes, A, B, and C. Each student prepares five or six questions, perhaps on a given topic such as their jobs (assuming they all work). They can compare questions and correct them as in the previous activity.
> 2 Student A now asks student B the questions. B has to answer the questions <u>as if they were student C</u>. If they don't know all the answers (and they probably won't), they should invent them. Meanwhile C listens and notes any answers which aren't true. Then students swap, and B asks C about A, etc. During this activity, you can monitor and note down points for feedback at the end.
> 3 Tell students that they should now go over the answers given and tell each other which were true and correct any inaccuracies in the information. They could also decide which student was the best at guessing or inventing.

This is another activity where the language focus is up to you and will depend on the topic. Students could ask questions about each other's education (which could involve past tenses and passive forms), future plans, likes and dislikes, etc.

making lists

Lists are a useful way of providing practice in particular language areas, based on personal experiences or knowledge of the world. You can exploit list-making as a warmer, or to generate examples of a language point. Here is an example:

> 1 In pairs, students write down ten things old people and young people in their country do at the weekends. You monitor and suggest corrections where necessary. (The list will obviously contain vocabulary to do with leisure activities, family routines, etc.)
> 2 They compare with another pair and decide on the top five activities.
> 3 You can feed in appropriate language here. For instance:
>   *X is very common / popular ....*
>   *Young people tend to ....*
>   *Older people generally ....*
> 4 Students produce a short presentation, using their ideas from the list and the language taught. Lists are a very useful way to practise specific grammar areas. For example:
>   – *We think parents / children / teenagers, etc* <u>should always</u> ... / <u>should never</u> ...
>   – *When we were young, we* <u>used to</u> ... / *we* <u>never used to</u> ...
>   – *In tomorrow's lesson, we* <u>might</u> ...
>   – *Places where you can hide money* (for prepositions)
>   – *Reasons why your town is better than anywhere else* (for comparatives or superlatives)

168   how to ... use the learners as a resource

draw it

It is important to impress upon learners that they do not need to be good at drawing to do this type of activity (indeed, they might feel more comfortable if your own drawing isn't terribly good when you show them what to do). Look at the following example from an **extended speaking** activity in the pre-intermediate **student's book**:

> 1 Put a sketch map of the area where you live on the board. Keep it very simple, putting crosses to indicate where certain places are, but don't label them. The places should include your home and any shops, parks or other amenities nearby.
>
> 2 Tell students this is your local area, point out your home, and encourage them to ask you about the other places. Try to develop what you say about the places: for example, if you live near a restaurant, tell them what kind of food it serves, whether it's popular / expensive / good, how often you go there, etc.
>
> 3 If appropriate, go back and focus on any specific useful language you / they used.
>
> 4 Students now draw their own sketch maps, marking six to eight places without labelling them. Give them time to rehearse what they are going to say. Help with vocabulary as required.
>
> 5 In pairs, students talk and ask about each map in turn.
>
> You can adapt this activity by getting students to draw a family tree, a sketch of their flat, or a room in their home, or to draw five things which are important to them.

from **extended speaking** pre-intermediate **student's book**, unit three *pp.32* and *33*.

creative planning

In this activity type, students have to produce creative plans e.g. to organize an event. Here are a few ideas:

– students in pairs create a profile of a hotel, using prompts, e.g. the hotel location, its name, the price range, the types of rooms, the services provided, restaurants and bars, etc. Once they have produced them, the information can be used as the basis for a role play: potential customers requesting information about the hotel.

– in a similar way, students in pairs design a café menu to include hot meals, cold meals, snacks and drinks, and possibly facilities or entertainments. Again, these can be used for role plays.

– pairs plan their ideal classroom or office (particularly if they are a business English group). They then present their ideas to other pairs.

– pairs plan a class night out at a place of their choosing and decide on the necessary arrangements (see pre-intermediate **student's book**, **unit eight** *pp.80* and *81*.)

Planning activities certainly require support frameworks to get the best out of them (guidelines, question prompts: see pre-intermediate **student's book**, **unit eight** *pp.80* and *81* for an example), but you can make the content relevant to the learners and the learning context. For example, a menu produced in the learners' own environment is not going to run into cultural differences, which might be the case if they use a menu in a British course book.

location, location, location

This is a useful framework for focusing on a range of student-generated language in a specific context. The focus might be functional exponents, vocabulary or grammatical structures.

> 1 Choose a location and write it on the board, e.g. a shoe shop. In pairs, students write down the following:
>
> | three questions a customer might ask | e.g. Have you got these shoes in a bigger size? |
> |---|---|
> | three things a customer might say | e.g. (I'm afraid) they're too tight. |
> | three things the assistant might ask | e.g. Are you paying in cash? |
> | three things the assistant might say | e.g. I'm sorry, we've only got them in brown. |
>
> Check students know what to do by eliciting a sample question / statement for each category before they work together. Monitor the pair work. Don't correct what they write, but provide help if students ask for it.
>
> 2 Pairs compare what they wrote with other pairs; together, they correct errors.
>
> 3 Bring the class together. Students write up the questions and statements on the board under the different headings. The combined language examples should be quite comprehensive. At this point, be prepared to feed in any language you think is needed, or make corrections. Students should make a record of this as their personal phrasebook.
>
> 4 Students do mini-role plays in the situation, using the language. Monitor and give feedback.

Once students have grasped the idea of this, you can use this lesson framework on a regular basis, changing the context: a railway station, doctor's surgery, hotel reception, etc. You can ask learners which contexts / locations they would like to concentrate on.

talk about it

For the activity below, provide a range of topics yourself, or ask learners to suggest them. For most learners at lower levels, descriptive topics are more straightforward: describe your family / favourite film / perfect day. At first, students may be worried about talking for a minute, but if you start with simple topics, they should have plenty to say and you can build up the length of time they speak.

> 1 Write ten suitable topics randomly on the board. Ask students (working alone) to think of two or three they can talk about for one minute. Give them time to think what to say about one of them.
>
> 2 Students work in groups of three. Student A tells B and C which topic they have chosen; A talks about their topic for one minute (B or C can time them). While listening, B and C think of questions to ask A at the end. After a minute, B and C ask A their questions.
>
> 3 Student B now talks about the topic they have chosen. As before, A and C listen and think of questions to ask.

During the activity, monitor and make notes for feedback at the end. You can ask students to assess which topics were easy to discuss, and why: this will help you to select topics in the future.

try it out personal sentences

With this activity, you, the teacher, are the starting point and have control over the language you introduce, but it then proceeds to a stage where learners generate personalised examples.

1. Dictate five sentences about yourself to the class, e.g.
   I've been teaching English <u>for ages</u>.
   I started working in (Spain) <u>when</u> I was 30.
   I passed my driving test <u>a long time ago</u>.
   <u>This time next week</u>, I'll be in New York.
   <u>I once</u> worked as a dentist's receptionist.
   Students compare them in pairs; let them check what they wrote by writing the sentences on the board.

2. Tell students that one sentence is not true. In pairs, they decide which one, and why. They tell the class; eventually you reveal which one isn't true.

3. Focus on specific language you want to teach or revise. In the examples above, the underlined time expressions and associated tenses are the focus, but you could adapt this for different language areas at different levels. Check understanding, and drill for pronunciation if you think this will be helpful.

4. Working alone, students write sentences about themselves, choosing from the given structures. Their sentences can be true or false. Monitor and help / correct where necessary.

5. Students read their sentences aloud in small groups. The group decides if they are true or false and discusses the true sentences, reporting back on interesting findings.
   Scott Thornbury, Barcelona, Spain.

3   What can we learn from learner output?

For each level of **natural English**, our starting point has been a wide range of extended speaking activities which we have trialled with multilingual groups studying in Britain and monolingual groups overseas. The main aim of this trialling has been to help us to identify the language syllabus that seemed most relevant to each level, but it has also been fascinating to observe and analyse so much different learner interaction and output. This section provides a few samples from that data with observations about possible implications for classroom practice.

task performance

The transcript below is of a conversation between two pre-intermediate learners. The stated aim of the activity was to find out how similar or different their families were. They had a framework of questions to help them, but they were free to explore any of the similarities and differences, and take the conversation in whichever direction they wished.

think![3]
Read through the transcript. Do you think the activity was successful? If so, why? If not, why not?

Conversation 1
A: Do you live with your family or your parents?
B: Yes I live.
A: Have you got any brothers or sisters?
B: No I haven't.
A: Do you spends a lot of time with your family?
B: Yes, a lot.
A: Have you got a lot of relatives?
B: Yes, a lot.
A: Do you see them a lot?
B: Yes, quite often.
A: When do you see them?
B: Weekends …at weekends…Saturday and Sunday.
A: Every week.
B: Yes.
A: What is your family like?
B: We are close family, all time.
A: Together.
B: Yes …and you live with your parents?
A: Yes, live with my parents.
B: And have you got any brother or sisters?
A: Yes, I have two brothers and two sisters.
B: What are their names?
A: My brother is Mohamed and Ali, and my sister is Fatima and Leila.
B: Do they live with you?
A: Yes, my brother and sister.
B: Do you spend a lot of time with your family?
A: Yes, I spend a lot of time with my family.
B: Have you got lots of relatives?
A: Yes, I have a lot of relatives.
B: And do you see them a lot?
A: Yes.
B: When?
A: I see them in my grandfather house.
B: Thank you. What's your family like?
A: Close family.

from **natural English** pre-intermediate research data

The conversation is clear, coherent and largely accurate, and they have fulfilled the task in that they now have information from which they can draw some conclusions about the similarities and differences between their families. But has it been an engaging and rewarding interaction for the two students? Compare it with part of a transcript of two different learners doing the same activity.

Conversation 2
A: Do you live with your parents?
S: No, I live with my friend.
A: But in your country?
S: Yes, in Korea. I met him military service.
A: How old are you when you meet your friend?
S: My friend? 21, 21 years.
A: Have you got any brothers and sisters?
S: Yes, I have got one brothers, one brother.
A: Only one brother.
S: Yes, my older brother.
A: How old is he?
S: 25 years.
A: 25 years. He is married?
S: No. Why?

> A: No, because 25 years...
> S: Usually Korean man usually married 28 or 29 or 30.
> A: What does he do?
> S: My brother work in military service.
> A: How long?
> S: 26 month. I work for 28 month because I was navy.
> A: What is he name?
> S: My brother's name is Kwang Min.
> A: And do you spend a lot of time with your family?
> S: No, because I live in London, my parents live in Korea.
> A: But in Korea, do you spend a lot of time with your family?
> S: When I was high school student, I spent a lot of time with my parents, but after I was university student I only slept in my home, my room. My house is a hotel. After I went to military service, I can't, I couldn't go to my home, only I stay on holiday.
> A: On holiday. And how often do you call your family?
> S: I call yesterday, I call my parents. Sometimes I call four weeks.
> A: When you are in Korea how often you call them?
> S: Never, because my parents call me, so I didn't have to call them.
> A: And do you write letters?
> S: Yes.
>
> from **natural English** pre-intermediate research data

These students in conversation 2 were from a different class, and one of the students, a young Polish woman called Anna, was in an elementary class, but their conversation lasted much longer than conversation 1; too long, in fact, to include it all here. From this extract though, it is clear they are engaged in the task, they are listening to each other, and fully prepared to move beyond the initial framework of the activity and take risks with the language in order to get the information they want. As a result of this there are more errors, but they are involved in real communication.

In contrast, the first couple seem more interested in monitoring the accuracy of their language. They are reluctant to follow up their initial questions – perhaps for fear of making mistakes, or perhaps they aren't sufficiently interested in their partner's answers. Either way, it is essentially a language exercise for them. It fulfils a purpose, but a limited one. The students are consolidating language they already know and, for the most part, using it accurately, but they are not using the activity to experiment with new language, and they are certainly not pushing themselves even close to the limit of their ability.

> **think!**⁴
> Look back again at the transcript for conversation 1. Can you think of any reasons <u>why</u> the activity wasn't successful? Then read on.

From this short extract it is impossible to know exactly why the activity with the first pair was less successful than it might have been. There are at least three potential reasons:

– the two learners don't work particularly well together
– they have not found the activity sufficiently motivating and / or they believe it is essentially a linguistic task rather than a communicative one.
– they have not been shown how to make the most of a learner-centred activity.

The first problem is an issue of class management. If the activity has worked well with other pairs, the teacher may decide to keep these two students apart for a period of time and monitor how well they work with other partners. For the second problem, if the activity failed to inspire others in the class, then it may be a question of material: the topic may not be very suitable for this particular group. On the other hand, it may not be the topic itself. If other students approached the activity in the same 'safety first' way as our first two learners, they may have thought the activity was too easy – lack of challenge can be a reason for poor motivation. For the third problem, as our second pair demonstrated, a learner-centred activity can be as challenging as you choose to make it. What our first pair may require is more guidance on how to extract the maximum benefit from an activity. You can do this by:

– demonstrating how the activity can be expanded. You interview a willing student, then go back over the conversation and elicit some of the follow-up questions used to keep the conversation going. Students can practise these until they can produce them automatically.

– encouraging students to take risks in classroom activities. Learners should realise that the classroom is one place where language can be repaired when it goes wrong; and if they don't experiment, they won't find out what they can and can't do. Teachers can't work miracles, but if we can give our learners the courage and confidence they need to push back the boundaries of their current competence, they will improve; and they will see that improvement.

4 Correction and reformulation

When learners have contributed freely in an activity and generated a lot of language, the next issue is: what do you do with this output? We believe that learners can benefit a great deal from teacher feedback at the end of an activity, and most learners perceive this feedback to be extremely relevant and useful. But what form should the feedback take?

Traditionally, feedback has largely consisted of correction of grammar, and to a lesser extent, of vocabulary mistakes. This seems to be an almost instinctive reaction. When we listen to learners, of whatever level, it seems that grammar errors are invariably the ones that register first and stand out. But while it is important to correct errors, it is equally important to consider improvements in their language based on things they didn't say, but perhaps should have said.

The following transcript is of three adult learners studying in Barcelona, and it is part of the trialling of an **extended speaking** activity in **unit three** of the **student's book** about transport problems in their town. Please note that for trialling purposes, there was no pre-teaching of any language relevant to the activity.

> A: No, the area is fresh because I live near Collserola and in ten minutes I on foot I arrive to the ... [unclear], yes.
> B: I live from to five minutes walking on the Carreteras de las Aguas. I live down the hospital Vall d'Hebron.
> A: Yes I know. But you are on the other hand of the Carreteras de las Aguas. I start at San Pedro Mártir and you at ... [unclear]. And you, Julio – what is the situation of the transport of your area?

> J: Yes, in my area there are some buses to Barcelona or the train station but the problem is the traffic. Every morning there are many, many traffic. It's a problem because I need about one hour to arrive of my work.
> A: Do you use to your car?
> J: No I don't use my car because I prefer you use the bus or train because I arrive to Barcelona more ... more relaxed about to arrive by car.
> B: In my area the traffic jam is only a problem where the bus are place.
> A: Yes, I don't have problem with traffic.

from **natural English** pre-intermediate research data

Listening to these students in 'real time', certain common grammar errors and mistakes with prepositions leap out at you – ~~many traffic~~ and ~~arrive of~~, for example. But when we transcribed and analysed the conversation (and others like it), we noticed more and more that the characteristics of the conversation which made it sound most unnatural were the learners' inability to manipulate common formulaic language:

- the facility in English to form a compound adjective using numbers and a time period , e.g. *a ten-minute walk to ...* (instead of: ~~in ten minutes I on foot arrive to~~ ...). The exact numbers and time periods are variable, but the pattern is frequent and predictable, as are many of the nouns which collocate with these compound adjectives, e.g. *a five-minute walk, a ten-minute drive, a fifteen-minute wait, a two-hour delay*, etc.
- the most common and natural way of describing the time required to get from A to B, i.e. *It takes (me) an hour to get to work* (instead of: ~~I need about one hour to arrive of my work~~).
- the most obvious way of asking someone to tell you more about someone or something, i.e. <u>What's transport like in your area?</u> (instead of: ~~what is the situation of the transport of your area?~~)

It has to be said that reformulations of this sort are far easier to make when you are working from a transcript. If you are able to record your learners, even occasionally, we would certainly recommend it. Transcribing the recordings would be a very time-consuming occupation for you, but that is where you can make use of your learners. Ask them to transcribe a small part of their conversation, and having done so, see if they can correct or improve what they have said. Even if you can't repeat the procedure very often, you might be surprised at how much mileage you can obtain from one short, recorded conversation.

We are aware this is not a luxury available to everyone, and in most situations teachers have to monitor and make notes while conversations take place in 'real time'. In these conditions it is easier to spot errors than it is to recognize the need for longer lexical chunks in place of a phrase of their own which, however stilted or unnatural it may sound, doesn't necessarily contain any grammatical mistakes. But if you can do this just once or twice, it can broaden the scope of feedback and shift the emphasis away from error, which can have the effect of making learners overly concerned with accuracy, and focus instead more on reformulation and improvement.

task repetition

One of the **extended speaking** activities we trialled for the pre-intermediate **student's book, unit seven** p.70, was a narrative which students have to construct from a series of pictures. One group who did this consisted of two young Japanese women, Natsuko and Tomomi, and a young Taiwanese student who called himself Jeremy. We knew this would be very challenging for them with no pre-teaching other than a few items of vocabulary (*bark, brick, bite,* and *smash*), so we let them work together as a group and help each other. This was their first attempt.

> **think!**[5]
> Read through the transcript below. What do you think the teacher should focus on after this first attempt? Then read on.

> J: They went to the park by car and he go with his dog and he take lunch box and I have sandwich and hamburgers.
> T: Champagne ...
> J: Champagne, sandwich and very peaceful, but later many people will come, will came, ... many people came here and one people played football and the dog is barking there ...
> N: They were fed up ... a man listening to music ...
> J: And a child shout very loudly, shout very loud ... they are fed up and they decide to go home.
> T: They went to car park ... they looked to a man, hold a brick ...
> J: They see ... they saw one people hold a brick and they will smash his car's window and they feel very scared ... and the dog barked ... and the man very scared.
> N: The man screamed, shouted ... Tom, maybe he was surprised and his dog bite, bit this guy.
> J: The man fight with ... the man with the brick ... and this man didn't stole, didn't steal anything.
> T: This man couldn't run away ... and the woman call the police and the police will come, will came and arrest them.

from **natural English** pre-intermediate research data

After this first attempt the teacher talked to the students about the story and ways in which they could improve it. He talked about the need to keep the story in the past tense – they were aware of making mistakes with the past simple – but also focused on two features of narrative which they could incorporate, even with their level of English. One of these was the need to 'set the scene' of the narrative, and the second was the dramatic use of direct speech, which can sometimes help lower level learners to get round a potentially difficult explanation. After some further guidance from the teacher, the group were keen to have another go ... and then another go. After the second attempt the teacher provided more guidance. This was their third attempt.

> T: It was a nice sunny day so Tom and Victoria decided to go to picnic in the countryside. They went to picnic by car with their dogs, his name is Jim. They had lunchbox and champagne, sandwiches and hamburgers.
> N: They found a nice place near the lake ... very peaceful.
> J: Felt relaxed, but later one family come and the man was playing football, the girl singing, the dog was barking and the man listen loud music.
> T: They were fed up. They decided to go home. They went to the car park, er ... a man hold a brick and smashed the window.
> J: The man will ... the dog bit the man and the man shouted ...
> T: Tom shouted, "That's my car. What are you doing?"
> N: Tom and this man had ... fighting, had a fight, then Jim bit the man and they couldn't go, run away, and the woman called the police, and the police came and arrest, arrested them.

from **natural English** pre-intermediate research data

172 how to ... use the learners as a resource

All three students worked extremely hard throughout the teaching sequence and what was interesting was their willingness, in fact their eagerness, to repeat the task several times. Admittedly this was a small group, so the students were getting a lot of individual attention, but it seemed to us that their enthusiasm was largely because they could see they were improving.

We know from our own experience and through conversations with other teachers that we are often reluctant to ask students to repeat activities too many times for fear that they will get bored. This does happen sometimes, but we may underestimate the satisfaction learners get from repeating a task – provided there is guidance and support each time to increase the likelihood of an improved performance.

To summarize the main points in this section:

- When initiating student-centred activities, don't assume your learners will automatically know how to make the most of them. Give them support and guidance.
- Try to nurture a classroom culture which is tolerant of error and encourages students to experiment and push themselves to the limit of their ability.
- In feedback, provide correction of error, but also think about ways to reformulate and improve awkward or unnatural English.
- Make sure feedback is on-going, and don't be afraid to give learners the opportunity to repeat tasks and see their improvement.

These observations will be fairly familiar to experienced teachers, but we found in the trialling that, perhaps by virtue of their familiarity, some of the most obvious classroom procedures were the ones which were easiest to overlook.

conclusion

In this chapter we have concentrated on the learner as the primary classroom resource, and suggested:

- a series of frameworks for classroom activities which use the knowledge and experience of the learners in the class
- a number of observations on how to utilize that learner output

Teaching is a demanding profession and course books serve an important function. At the very least, they can take the pressure off busy teachers by providing professional, ready-made material; for less experienced teachers, they provide a necessary structure and can serve as a teacher development tool. One should not overlook the fact that many students expect to use course books and can learn from them. At the same time, teachers shouldn't become slaves to the course book. We would recommend that they put the course book aside some of the time and create some space for learners, free of materials and technology.

follow-up

Campbell C and Kryszewska H 1992 *Learner-based teaching* Oxford University Press

Sheelagh Deller 1990 *Lessons from the Learner* Pilgrims / Longman

Thornbury S and Conte N *Materials-free teaching* in English Teaching Professional Issue 26 January 2003

Griff Griffiths and Kathy Keohane 2000 *Personalizing Language Learning* Cambridge University Press

how to ... help learners understand natural speech

1 Choosing listening material for the classroom
2 Using recorded material
3 Understanding connected speech

1 Choosing listening material for the classroom

Most classroom listening comprises two main sources: the teacher and other learners, and audio / video recordings and DVDs. Listening to you and other learners is probably the most genuine and motivating listening practice that learners can have, but it is the exposure to other types of listening material that is the focus of this chapter – recorded listening material that you choose and take in to the classroom.

Broadly speaking, this material can be divided into four types:

1 unscripted 'real world' English, e.g. a TV chat show interview, or perhaps a conversation you recorded at the home of some English-speaking friends
2 scripted 'real world' English, e.g. a TV news broadcast, or a radio play
3 unscripted recordings produced for the language classroom
4 scripted recordings produced for the language classroom

From this list, there are clearly two important factors:
- 'real world' English vs. English produced for the classroom
- unscripted vs. scripted English.

If our aim is to help learners understand English in the real world, then some would argue our priority should be exposure to real-world spoken English. Admittedly, learners will struggle with it at first, but we can compensate for the difficulty of the texts by making the tasks very simple, while at the same time developing the skills needed to deal with the main features of natural spoken English.

Most teachers would probably agree that real-world listening practice sounds good in theory, but their experience tells them that the majority of learners, and especially lower level learners, can become frustrated and demotivated by their inability to cope with the demands of such material. Our own experience has been that lower level learners can cope with certain songs or short TV extracts, but you have to be highly selective, and it isn't very easy to find appropriate material. It's true we can simplify the comprehension tasks we provide, but will the majority of learners be satisfied when they know they have not understood most of the recording? Worse still perhaps, if there is a very significant gap between the recorded material and the learners' current listening ability, there may not be sufficient understanding for learners to construct any meaningful interpretation of the text. In other words, they are so far out of their depth that they cannot use the text to build on their existing listening skills.

This is where listening material produced for the classroom, and specifically scripted listening material, has an advantage.
- It will be tailored to the level of the learners in terms of lexical difficulty and syntactic complexity.
- It can be written to include language you may want to teach.
- If it is well-scripted material it can approximate to natural spoken language, especially in routine and largely predictable conversation exchanges, e.g. some telephone calls and many short service encounters in shops, restaurants or hotels.

But even predictable conversations may not incorporate some of the features of natural spoken English you find in unscripted exchanges.

think![1]
Here is an unscripted recording of a common service encounter – asking for and giving directions in a hotel reception. The guest is American, the receptionist is British. Can you find any features in the conversation which would be unlikely if the conversation had been scripted? Think and then read on.

Guest I'm staying in room 101.
Rec Right.
G I need to get to Big Sound Studios.
R Oh, that's very near.
G Oh, OK.
R Erm, it's about a five-minute walk, erm, if you, if you want to walk. All you need to do is go to the end of the road here
G end of the road, OK
R when you get to the station
G yeah
R you need to turn left
G turn left
R and then the studios are just there, again, on the left, I mean, it's really not far.
G I don't need to take a cab.
R Oh, no, not at all.

from pre-intermediate **listening booklet**, tapescript 3.5 *p.12*

When conversations are scripted, the writer often includes hesitation devices such as *erm*, which are commonly found in natural speech, but in the unscripted conversation above, notice also the following:
- apparently needless repetition, e.g. *if you, if you*
- rather clumsy expression, e.g. *'you need to turn left and then the studios are just there, again, on the left.'*
- the fact that the guest asks for help not with a request (e.g. *Could you tell me how to get to Big Sound Studios?*), but with a statement (*I need to get to Big Sound Studios*), which the receptionist immediately recognises as a request.
- the indecisiveness of the receptionist. She knows she can't tell the guest what to do (*it's a five-minute walk, erm if you, if*

you want to walk), but clearly thinks walking is the best option by stressing its proximity (*oh that's very near ... all you need to do is ... I mean, it's really not far*).

– the fact that the guest interrupts and echoes the receptionist's instructions throughout.

We doubt these elements would have found their way into a scripted classroom dialogue that practises giving directions. Spontaneous spoken English is quite simply different from scripted language. It is messy, repetitive, often digresses, and usually looks very inelegant when written down. If learners are to cope with it, can we justify a diet of recorded listening material that distorts this reality and limits their exposure to it?

An approach we have used widely in **natural English** is to have a high percentage of spontaneous unscripted spoken text, but with compromises which make the texts more accessible to learners at different levels. We have done this by:

– using native speakers or very competent users of the language who naturally speak quite clearly and not too quickly
– giving these speakers guidelines about the content and length of text
– recording much more material than is necessary so that we can select what is most appropriate
– making use of recording technology to edit small sections of the text where necessary (e.g. cutting a difficult and unnecessary phrase or sentence)
– keeping the listening passages quite short to reduce the danger of overload.

> **Want to know more** about controlling the level of a listening passage? Go to **natural English** intermediate **teachers book**, **how to ...** teach listening, *p.151*

These measures rob texts of some of their authenticity – we might best describe the results as semi-authentic – but they can produce a text which retains almost all the features of natural spoken English yet remains achievable for lower level learners.

2 Using recorded material

Most of the listening material we take into the language classroom will be audio recordings which provide exposure to a range of voices and genres, e.g. casual conversation, interviews, service encounters, announcements, discussion, etc. They have the advantage that they can be replayed by the teacher to identify and address listening problems (more of this later), and they are a change of focus from listening to the teacher or other learners.

At the same time, there are drawbacks with audio recordings:

– they deny the listener important visual clues which are often present in real life listening, e.g. the speaker's body language
– they don't allow the listener the opportunity to interact with the speaker, e.g. to ask for repetition, seek clarification, and so on
– listening to a recording is usually less interesting and motivating than being in the presence of the speaker
– poor equipment or acoustics can undermine the effectiveness of using audio material.

> **think!**[2]
> Can you think of any other advantages or drawbacks of using audio recordings?
> go to **answer key** *p.180*.

using prediction

Audio materials on their own rarely give the listener any information about context, and they don't provide any visual clues. This makes it all the more important that there is a pre-listening phase with audio material in which learners gather as much information about the context as they would in a real life situation. For example, in **unit five** of the pre-intermediate **student's book**, the listening text is about how to use a study centre. First, the learners see the picture of a study centre below and describe what's in it (essential visual clues).

vocabulary study centre

1 Look at the picture for a minute. Then shut your book and tell a partner what you can remember.

   example   There's a computer in the room.

They are then told about the listening (essential scene-setting) and have an opportunity to predict the kinds of things they will hear described before they listen.

listen to this

tune in

1 These students are studying Italian. Their teacher is going to explain how to use the study centre. What do you think she will say? Tell your partner.

   example   You can use the photocopier.

2 [5.4] Listen. Which part of the study centre does she talk about first?

> from pre-intermediate **student's book**, unit five *p.46*

how to ... help learners understand natural speech

As a classroom activity, prediction has several virtues.

> **think!**[3]
> Can you think of two or three good reasons for asking learners to predict the content of a listening text? Note them down, then read on and compare your ideas.

- By asking learners to predict, we are encouraging them to activate their knowledge of the context. From this, they may go on to predict the content of the listening quite accurately. Successful prediction can contribute significantly to successful listening.
- Prediction is a skill we all use in our first language, but is often overlooked by learners when they are listening in a second language.
- Learners want to find out if their predictions are accurate, so the activity has served to motivate them for the listening passage.
- Prediction is best done as a cooperative activity in which learners discuss their predictions with a partner or in small groups. It becomes an interactive activity – speaking with a real communicative purpose – and the discussion may help them to refine their initial predictions and become more accurate.

> **Want to know more** about pre-listening activities?
> Go to intermediate **teacher's book, how to ...** teach listening
> *pp.151 and 152.*

tuning in

Even with a well-focused pre-listening phase, it can come as a shock to learners when they are pitched straight into an audio recording of unfamiliar voices. To ease this process, we have included a 'tune in' phase (as with other levels of the course) in which the learners have an opportunity to listen to a short section of the recording to adjust to the voice or voices before they listen to the whole passage. For example:

> ### tune in
>
> 1 (8.7) Jon met Nadia at a party last week. He decides to phone her. Listen to the beginning of the conversation. Tick ✓ the phrases you hear.
>
> ☐ Hi, Nadia.   ☐ It's Jon.
> ☐ Hello, Nadia.   ☐ This is Jon.
> ☐ I'm fine, how about you?   ☐ It was really great to see you.
> ☐ I'm OK, how about you?   ☐ It was really nice to see you.
>
> 2 What do you think Jon's going to say next? Tell the class.

> from pre-intermediate **student's book**, unit eight *p.78*

The comprehension task allows the teacher to find out if the learners understand Jon and Nadia's initial greetings. If they don't, the teacher is perhaps getting advance warning that the passage may prove difficult for the learners and might require more preparation. What might have been a very unrewarding listening experience can be rectified before it is too late. The teacher can also replay this section as many times as necessary, without giving away the rest of the conversation and spoiling it. The prediction activity afterwards (**exercise 2**), then prepares the ground for the next part of the recording.

grading tasks

With lower level learners it is important that the successful completion of a listening comprehension task doesn't depend too much on other skills. If learners struggle with a comprehension task, you need to know that the problem is related to their listening ability, and not their ability to read or write. So, if the task involves writing, keep it to a minimum. Here are some possible exercise types that reduce the need to write:

- circle the correct answer, from a choice of two or three
- put ticks or crosses in a box
- write T (true) or F (false) next to short statements
- choose the correct picture, from a choice of several
- put pictures in the correct order (commonly used to check understanding of a narrative)
- read a summary, then listen and underline any parts that are incorrect.

Many tasks involve reading, e.g. correcting mistakes in a summary. In this case, make sure you give learners sufficient time to read the summary before they listen and check that they understand it, e.g. deal with unknown lexis. If writing is required, perhaps with comprehension questions, or completing a table or grid, make it clear to learners that they only need to write short answers, not complete sentences.

If you sense that a particular passage will be at the very limit of your learners' listening ability, you can compensate by making the comprehension task easier. For example, **unit four** of the pre-intermediate **student's book** has an unscripted narrative about a shopping experience, which would be quite difficult for pre- intermediate learners without a supportive framework. After the initial **tune-in** activity, learners have the following tasks:

> ### listen carefully
>
> 2 Read the sentences from Jim's story. With your partner, write a possible word or phrase in each gap.
>
>   1 First he tried on a beautiful blue suit, but _____ .
>   2 Then he tried on a grey suit, but _____ .
>   3 The shop assistant was very _____ and brought Jim _____ .
>   4 Jim spent _____ trying them on, and finally he decided _____ .
>
> 3 Listen. Were you right?
>
> ### listening challenge
>
> 4 (4.6) Listen. Is the end of the story about:
>   the suit? the manager? the shop assistant?

> from pre-intermediate **student's book**, unit four *p.38*

In this case, the sentence beginnings actually provide the listener with the framework of the story, thus making it easier to follow; and the prediction activity should help the learners to narrow down the most likely endings.

testing vs. teaching

A common complaint with comprehension tasks – it could be levelled at all the tasks above – is that they 'test' listening rather than teach it. It's a criticism that is hard to deny, but also hard to avoid. In order to assess and improve our learners' listening ability, we need to know which parts of a text they understand and which parts they don't. Comprehension tasks give us at least some of that feedback, but they often don't answer the more important question: If learners haven't understood part of a text, <u>why</u> haven't they understood? With their knowledge and experience, teachers can sometimes make an informed guess, but not always. Asking the learners themselves is the most sensible option and certainly worth investigating. The drawback here is that learners can't always explain why they haven't understood something - and doing it on a regular basis may not be feasible with time constraints and a large class.

Here are several simple procedures you can use alongside a comprehension task to gain more information about the listening process and why your learners may be finding the text difficult.

- Monitor the learners discretely as they are doing tasks to assess their progress. This information can be the basis for the decision to replay the recording a second or third time.

- If you notice while monitoring that learners have different answers to certain parts of a task, put these answers on the board without saying which is correct. Play the passage, or the relevant part of it, again. Learners will be motivated to listen again – those with the correct answer can't be sure without listening a second time – and those who got it wrong first time round may be able to correct their mistake. If they can do this, they may also be able to explain why they were wrong the first time. This procedure is likely to tell them more about listening than simply being given the correct answers.

- Ask learners in pairs or small groups to compare and discuss their answers to the task before you give any correct answers. If you listen to these discussions carefully, you will sometimes uncover the reason for a breakdown in understanding. At the same time, the learners are all engaged in a worthwhile discussion in which they may gain insights from each other about the passage.

- If most learners are having problems with a particular segment or sentence, ask them to listen again and note down any words they can hear. Elicit these onto the board, with gaps for missing words. For example, if learners were unable to understand the sentence underlined below, they might hear *long, people,* and *the south*.

> L Well, now, people say that er, in the north it's much friendlier, and I think that probably is true. <u>It takes longer to get to know people in the south</u>, perhaps.
> E Yeah, yeah, I've heard that.

natural English pre-intermediate **listening booklet** 6.2 *p.20*

Write the words on the board with gaps:

___ _____ *long__* _____ ____ ____ ____ *people* ___ *the south*

Replay that extract as often as necessary so that learners can begin to identify more words and construct the meaning of the sentence. They may not get absolutely everything, but it should help them to decode the message and become more aware of features of connected speech (see **section 3** below).

As the focus is on developing the listening skill, it would be pointless for learners to read the tapescript while listening to the recording for the first time. However, after listening several times, let them listen with the tapescript. This procedure can help learners to identify not only <u>where</u> they had a problem but also <u>why</u> they had a problem. Let's look at some of these problems in more detail.

3 Understanding connected speech

There are many reasons why learners fail to understand parts of a spoken text, but one of the most common causes is illustrated by a scenario that many of you will be familiar with. Your learners have just listened to a passage of spoken text, and they find it more difficult than you anticipated. You play it again and still your learners are puzzled. Finally, you let them listen with the tapescript. This time the text is greeted with an assortment of groans: what the tapescript illustrates is that the text, or the vast majority of it, contains lexis the learners all know and understand in written form. However, as soon as these familiar words become part of a piece of connected speech, spoken at natural speed, they are not intelligible.

These problems will be identified as soon as learners are exposed to unscripted passages spoken at normal speed, but remedial training to develop this part of the listening skill can be undertaken successfully, and more economically, using short passages of scripted material. To be useful, the passages need to be long enough to contain chunks of language that will be uttered without a pause, e.g. a short sentence of at least six or eight words; and spoken at natural speed.

When learners learn a word, they may know how it is pronounced in isolation, but fail to recognize the same word in spoken English, e.g. *correct* /kəˈrekt/ in rapid speech is pronounced /krekt/. In connected speech, problems occur because of:

- **contractions**, e.g. *I'll* /aɪl/ instead of *I will* /aɪ wɪl/

- **weak forms**, e.g. /kən/ of *can* in weak form instead of /kæn/ of *can* in strong form

The way a word sounds can also be modified by the words that surround it. For example:

- **elision** (sounds are omitted), e.g. *round the corner* /raʊn ðə kɔːnə/ omitting the 'd' in round

- **assimilation** (sounds change), e.g. /n/ becoming /m/ in *ten people* /tem piːpl/

- **catenation** (linking the sounds of a word to the next word), e.g. *pick‿it‿up*

how to ... help learners understand natural speech

> ### think![4]
> Answer the questions in the chart.
>
> **weak forms**
>
> 1 Write the underlined words in phonemic script.
> We can _____ go for _____ coffee later.
> We were _____ younger than _____ the rest of _____ them _____ .
>
> **contractions**
>
> 2 What sound changes occur when the verbs are contracted?
> I will not do it   We would have gone *(two possibilities)*
>
> **elision**
>
> 3 Write the underlined words in phonemic script. Which two phonemic sounds disappear in these consonant clusters?
> roast _____   roast beef   must _____   mustn't forget
> dropped _____   she dropped the book
> cold _____   cold water
>
> **assimilation**
>
> 4 Write the underlined words in phonemic script.
> ten _____   ten people
> good _____   good book
> do _____   what do you think?
> would _____   What would you like?
>
> **catenation (linking)**
>
> 5 Pronounce the phrases. Where do sounds link between words?
> put‿it‿on   it's out of order
> her uncle   her mother and father
>
> go to **answer key** *p.180*

You can produce your own exercises to focus on these features of connected speech to suit your learners. Here are some ideas.

contractions and weak forms

1 count the words

A simple exercise you can try is to write a few short sentences containing contractions and weak forms suitable for your class. Tell learners they will hear a sentence, and with a partner, they should count the number of words. Make it clear whether you intend contractions, e.g. *can't*, to represent one word or two for the purpose of the exercise. Learners often enjoy the game-like element in this exercise.

2 mini dictations

These can also be extremely useful if your learners have problems identifying words in weak form or when sounds are omitted. For example you could record or read aloud sentences like the ones below in which the pronouns are pronounced naturally.

> Could you ask her /ə/ to give him /iːm/ a ring?
> Did you tell them /ðəm/ the phone number?
> Has he /ɪ/ given them /ðəm/ his address?

Whether learners misspell lexical items such as *address* is really of secondary importance as the aim here is to help them with decoding connected speech. Learners can compare answers, write them on the board, and you can use the sentences to deal remedially with any problems they had.

Want to know more? Read **Dictation**, Davis and Rinvolucri CUP

3 using the tapescript

Once you have used a recording for comprehension purposes, think about using the tapescript to focus on problems with perception. Below is a short semi-scripted dialogue in which a number of common weak forms are shown in bold. Learners listen to the recording again and focus on the schwa /ə/. You will need to pause the recording if you are doing this in class, and replay the first line a couple of times to enable them to hear the weak form. Another way of using this type of activity is to give learners the dialogue with the first few weak forms in bold, then play the recording and ask them to identify the remaining four. If your learners are familiar with phonemic script, you could write the weak and strong forms of the words in bold on the board in phonemic script, and ask them to listen and say which form they hear. Once they have identified them successfully, move on to practice, isolating and checking learners' pronunciation of the weak forms before they practise the whole dialogue.

> a Look at the words in bold in tapescript 3.2. These words are not stressed. Listen and notice the schwa /ə/.
>
> b Practise saying the dialogue. Remember to use the **schwa** /ə/.
> A **Have** you ever lived abroad?
> B Yeah, I have.
> A Where **was** that?
> B South America – I worked in Rio **for** a while.
> A And how long **were** you there?
> B About nine months – it **was** about ten years ago now.
> A Really? Did you like it?
> B Yeah, I loved it – it **was** fascinating. Completely different **from** Europe.

from pre-intermediate **listening booklet**, tapescript 3.2 *p.11*

elision and assimilation

Learners' problems with elision and assimilation are to some degree caused by interference from the written form; you can use this as a teaching tool. Here, you are aiming to show learners that what is written is not always pronounced.

1 using the tapescript

Ask learners to look at the sentences below (from the **natural English** box in **unit thirteen**, *p.126*). They have already dealt with the meaning of the questions, so you can use the recording again to highlight the elision of 't' in *What does …?*

> a When *t* is followed by a consonant, we often don't pronounce the *t*. Look at these examples from 13.3:
> What's /wɒs/ she like?
> What does /ˈwɒdəz/ she look like?
> What does /ˈwɒdəz/ she like doing?
>
> b Listen again and repeat.
>
> c Practise saying these sentences. You don't need to pronounce the underlined *t*.
> Wha*t* did you do last weekend?
> Wha*t* do you think of his latest film?
> Wha*t* does your best friend do?
> Wha*t* did you have for the first course?
> Wha*t* do most people think of the president?
> I saw him last Friday.
> It's the longest day.

from pre-intermediate **listening booklet** tapescript 13.3 *p.41*

2 gap fill dictations

Sound omissions and changes are very challenging for learners to decode, but a few combinations are very common and useful to focus on at low levels. For this, you can use a gap fill dictation.

> First, dictate the following natural segments. They won't make any sense, but they should intrigue learners. Let them write them in any way they like.
>
> /ˈgetʃuː/   /ˈmiːtʃuː/   /ˈwʊdʒə/   /ˈʃwiː/   /ˈkʊdʒə/   /dʒuː/
>
> Give them these gap fill sentences, and dictate the sentences containing the natural segments above. Learners can work with a partner.
> 1 What _____ like to do this evening?
> 2 Where _____ go in the evenings?
> 3 Shall I _____ at the cinema?
> 4 Can I _____ something to drink?
> 5 When _____ meet?
> 6 Excuse me, _____ pass me that paper?
>
> At the end, focus on the sounds of these segments in connected speech, and be sure to let learners know that this isn't lazy or incorrect speech; it's just natural.

catenation

1 noticing

Scripted and unscripted listening material can usually be exploited to encourage learners to notice linking between words. The following activity is based on an unscripted text which learners have already listened to with an accompanying comprehension task. They are shown graphically how sounds are linked, and listen to the model at the same time.

> Listen to 7.1. Notice how Tyler links the phrases below.
>   a few years‿ago
>   right‿in front‿of us.
>   the pilot ran‿over
>   she looked‿at me and she said, 'yes.'
>   we got‿out‿of the helicopter
>   we sat‿in the field‿and finished‿our picnic
>
> When a word ends in a consonant sound, and the next word begins with a vowel sound, we often link them in this way. Listen again and practise saying the phrases.

*from pre-intermediate **listening booklet**, tapescript 7.1 p.23*

You can also isolate a short section of a text and ask learners to indicate where the linking will occur. Practice will help to reinforce the idea that linking is a common feature of spoken English.

2 intensive listening activities

As a more challenging task, use a text which might incorporate various features of connected speech and you can do **intensive listening** activities, such as the one below. This text includes examples of weak forms and linking which learners have to actively listen for to fill the gaps. They can check with the tapescript. (Answers: them /ðəm/ home, them /ðəm/ here, at /ət/ the /ðə/ desk, take‿out, taking it‿out)

5.4 intensive listening

> Cover tapescript 5.4. Listen again and complete the gaps.
>
> Now, you can borrow most of the books here, and take _____ _____, but you can't take the dictionaries home. If you want to use the dictionaries, you have to use _____ _____. Remember that. Now, you have to write your name in the book _____ _____ _____
> – you write your name, the name of the book you want to _____ _____, and the date you're _____ _____ _____, OK?

*from pre-intermediate **listening booklet**, tapescript 5.4 p.16*

> **try it out** rhymes
>
> Rhymes are fun and a useful medium for highlighting and practising features of connected speech. Learners can learn and recite them (they are something that we tend to memorize in our own language, so this is quite a natural activity). You can focus on specific points. Here is a very nice example from *English Pronunciation in Use*:
>
> **Show where you can join a word ending with a consonant sound to a word starting with a vowel sound using this symbol: ‿ (There are eight in total). Then listen and practise saying the poem.**
>
> There was an‿old man called Greg,
> Who tried to break open an egg.
> He kicked it around,
> But fell on the ground,
> And found that he'd broken a leg.
>
> You could also use simple song lyrics in this way, particularly those popular with your learners.

*from **English Pronunciation in Use** by Mark Hancock p.85*

Conclusion

In this chapter we have looked at:
- the differences between scripted and unscripted audio material
- the advantages and disadvantages of using audio recordings
- approaches and techniques for pre-listening and while-listening stages
- the problems learners experience decoding connected speech, and some activities to help them

Helping learners to understand spoken English is a difficult task for teachers, largely because the listening process is not visible or easily accessible. We hope that the approaches and ideas in this chapter will have given you some practical and concrete strategies to use with your learners.

how to ... help learners understand natural speech

follow up

Field J 2003 *Promoting perception: lexical segmentation in L2 listening* in ELTJ vol. 57/4

Field J 1998 *The changing face of listening* in English Teaching Professional (6 Jan)

Kelly G 2000 *How to teach pronunciation* Longmont

Hancock M 2003 *English Pronunciation in Use* Cambridge University Press

White G 1998 *Listening* Oxford University Press

---

answer key

think![2] *p.175*

Advantages
- They are readily available and relatively cheap.
- They can be used to provide a consistent pronunciation model, and some non-native teachers like to have the support of a native-speaker model for their learners.
- They can be a source of cultural information.
- They allow learners to listen to a dialogue: two people interacting.

Disadvantages
- Finding your place on the cassette can be fiddly and irritating, especially when you need to rewind and play a section again. (This is less of a problem with CDs.)
- Usually, everyone has to listen at the same pace; learners have little control, unless they are studying in a listening centre or language laboratory.
- Audio recordings often come with a tapescript; sometimes learners read them in advance or while listening.

think![4] *p.178*

1 can, /kən/, for /fə/, were /wə/, than /ðən/, of /əv/, them /ðəm/
  Modal verbs *can*, *could*, *shall*, *should*, *would*, and *will* all have weak forms, as do forms of the auxiliary verbs *be*, *do* and *have*. For a full list of weak forms, see John Field (2002).

2 full form: will not /wɪl nɒt/, contracted form: won't /wəʊnt/;
  full form: we would have gone /wiː wʊd hæv gɒn/;
  weak forms: we'd have gone /wiːd əv gɒn/ we would've gone /wiː wʊdəv gɒn/.

3 roast beef /rəʊs biːf/
  mustn't forget /mʌsn fəget/
  dropped the book /drɒp ðə bʊk/
  cold water /kəʊl wɔːtə/
  The 't' and 'd' sounds disappear

4 ten people /tem piːpl/, good book /gʊb bʊk/ do you /ðʒuː/, would you /wʊdʒuː/

5 out‿of‿order   her‿uncle   her mother‿and father

language reference key

unit one

1.1
1 Is he a doctor?
2 Does he live with his parents?
3 Has he got a car?
4 Did he go to Italy last year?
5 Can he understand German?
6 Are they married?
7 Have they got any children?
8 Do they like skiing?
9 Did they stay at home last night?
10 Were they at university in the 1990s?

1.2
1 Where's he from? / Where does he come from?
2 When / What time did you get up?
3 Why did he go / come to England / America?
4 How much is it? / How much does it cost?
5 How old is she?

1.3
1 with
2 How
3 for / at
4 Was
5 What

1.4
1 don't like
2 Do you watch
3 speaks
4 does he go
5 doesn't drive

1.5
1 boys'
2 sisters'
3 children's
4 women's
5 brothers'

1.6
1 Mark's brother
2 the name of the film
3 Petra's husband
4 my sister's computer
5 the middle of the country

1.7
1 When did they ~~returned~~ return?
2 She ~~seen~~ saw him last week.
3 We ~~studyed~~ studied this grammar yesterday.
4 correct
5 What time did he ~~left~~ leave the party?
6 We ~~stoped~~ stopped work at five o'clock.
7 I ~~drived~~ drove home last night.
8 He ~~putted~~ put his coat on.
9 correct
10 He didn't ~~went~~ go to school today.

1.8
1 yesterday
2 ago
3 last
4 in
5 at

unit two

2.1
1 I had a drink after I finished work.
2 Did you have breakfast at home today?
3 Do you usually have lunch outside?
4 We often have a snack when we are hungry.
5 She had dinner with friends yesterday.

2.2
1 is
2 an
3 some
4 some
5 is
6 some
7 is
8 are
9 a
10 some

2.3
1 U
2 C
3 U
4 U
5 U
6 U
7 C
8 U
9 C
10 U

2.4
1 much
2 a lot of
3 any
4 a lot of
5 many
6 a lot of
7 any
8 many
9 much
10 a lot of

2.5
1 feel very warm
2 gets angry
3 smell very nice
4 seems nice
5 tasted very salty

2.6
1 delicious
2 slowly / carefully
3 angry
4 well / badly
5 cold

unit three

3.1
1 been
2 worked
3 driven
4 seen
5 won

3.2
1 Have you ever played tennis?
2 She has visited Italy three times.
3 I've never seen The Taj Mahal.
4 She hasn't been to a football match.
5 Has he ever lost his passport?

3.3
1 went
2 Have you ever lived
3 didn't come
4 has never used
5 Did they stay

unit four

4.1
1 these
2 that
3 this
4 that
5 these

4.2
A Would you like a cake?
B Oh, thanks.
A This **one** looks very nice.
B Which **one**?
A This **one** here.
B Yes, but I'm going to have that **one**.

4.3
1 I'll help you. / I'll carry that for you.
2 I'll get you an aspirin.
3 I'll get you a drink / glass of water.
4 I'll show / take you.
5 I'll get / answer it.

4.4
1 the TV / radio / stereo, etc.
2 –
3 my son / bicycle / suitcase, etc.
4 your coat / jacket, etc.
5 –

4.5
1 I'll look after the children.
2 correct
3 Please turn it off.
3 correct
5 I'm looking for my pen.

4.6
1 correct
2 incorrect (This drink is *very* cold – lovely!)
3 incorrect (We did well in the test, but it was *very* difficult.)
4 correct
5 incorrect (He's only 12; he's *too* young to drive a car.)

4.7
1 too much
2 too many
3 too much
4 too
5 too many
6 too many
7 too much
8 too

unit five

5.1
1 You have to
2 I don't have to
3 Do I have to
4 I didn't have to
5 Did you have to

5.2
1 I've got to work late today.
2 Have we got to return the books?
3 He hasn't got to go back this evening.
4 What time have you got to be there?
5 She's got to phone her mother.

5.3
1 can't
2 have to
3 don't have to
4 can
5 can't
6 Can
7 don't have to
8 can't
9 can
10 have to; can

Photocopiable © Oxford University Press 2005   181

5.4
1. go to work
2. go to university
3. go (in)to hospital
4. go to school
5. go to church

unit six

6.1
1. Maria comes from ~~the~~ South America.
2. correct
3. He lives near ~~the~~ Red Square.
4. The capital of ~~the~~ France is Paris.
5. The north-east ~~the~~ coast is very cold.
6. I've been to ~~the~~ Mount Kilimanjaro.
7. correct
8. Have you been to ~~the~~ Cairo?
9. correct
10. ~~The~~ Russia is in ~~the~~ Europe.

6.2
1. longer / the longest
2. more dangerous / the most dangerous
3. happier / the happiest
4. safer / the safest
5. fatter / the fattest
6. more traditional / the most traditional
7. wetter / the wettest
8. more interesting / the most interesting
9. better / the best
10. more useful / the most useful

6.3
1. the most interesting
2. the cheapest
3. the most crowded
4. the hottest
5. the best

6.4
1. more
2. the
3. in
4. than
5. easier

6.5
1. is going to
2. Is she going to
3. aren't going to
4. 're going to
5. 'm going to

6.6
1. Will it rain tomorrow?
2. Is he going to be a footballer?
3. I am not going to finish this tonight.
4. We probably won't arrive home before seven o'clock.
5. People might work at home in the future.

unit seven

7.1
1. started a journey
2. arrived
3. stopped working
4. left the ground
5. continued

7.2
1. ~~Were~~ Was he working?
2. They ~~wasn't~~ weren't having dinner.
3. She was ~~puting~~ putting on her coat.
4. correct
5. Was the doctor leaving?

7.3
1. B
2. A
3. A

7.4
1. were studying; arrived
2. was walking; found
3. phoned; was working
4. were waiting; left
5. lost; was shopping

unit eight

8.1
1. I might ~~to~~ see them this evening.
2. ~~Do~~ Would you like to go swimming this weekend?
3. What time are you going to see them?
4. correct
5. I'd like to watch the match tomorrow.

8.2
1. am
2. wouldn't
3. isn't
4. might
5. would

8.3
1. –
2. the
3. –
4. the
5. –

8.4
1. She went to Ibiza ~~the~~ last week.
2. I'll see you in ~~the~~ June.
3. I'd like to go on holiday ~~the~~ next month.
4. correct
5. I took my final exams ~~the~~ last year.

8.5
1. 's working
2. are you seeing
3. aren't going
4. 'm having
5. isn't meeting

8.6
You can use the present continuous or be going to in sentences 1, 2, 3, and 5. In sentence 4, you cannot say 'I'm looking for a job in January'.

unit nine

9.1
1. since seven o'clock
2. for about a week
3. for ten minutes
4. since last week
5. for a day or two

9.2
1. A is correct.
2. B is correct.

9.3
1. Gill has had long hair since 2004.
2. I haven't seen him for three months.
3. How long have you lived in Morocco?
4. She's (has) been a photographer for a few years.
5. I've known Carol since last year.

9.4
1. d
2. e
3. c
4. a
5. b

unit ten

10.1 Phrases 2, 3, and 5 are correct.

10.2
1. interesting
2. embarrassed
3. worried
4. excited
5. relaxing

10.3
1. a
2. my
3. a
4. – ('a stomach ache' is also possible)
5. my
6. – ('the flu' is also possible)

10.4
1. me
2. my teacher
3. to your mother
4. the school
5. to Michael

unit eleven

11.1
1. will / call
2. won't / 's
3. see / will
4. will / go
5. 's / might go

11.2
1. I really like Joe. I will / 'll go to his party if he invites me.
2. If you take your coat, you won't feel cold.
3. I'm not sure, but he might go to school tomorrow if he feels better.
4. If you book the tickets today, they might be cheaper.
5. What will / 'll happen if you are late?

unit twelve

12.1
1. same
2. same
3. different

12.2
1. correct
2. Did you ~~used~~ use to go to Rome a lot?
3. My brother ~~used to live~~ lived in that flat for a year. OR My brother used to live in that flat ~~for a year~~.
4. correct
5. I used to go out every evening when I was at university.

unit thirteen

13.1
1. went / would get
2. played / would ('d) lose
3. Would you still work / won
4. were / would ask
5. were / wouldn't spend

13.2
1. But they don't live near us, so we don't see / aren't going to see them every weekend.
2. But I haven't got / don't have a car, so I'm not going to drive there.
3. But I don't like my flat, so I'm not going to stay there.

13.3
1. listening
2. eating
3. going
4. having
5. working

13.4
1. who
2. which
3. who
4. who
5. which

182   Photocopiable © Oxford University Press 2005

unit fourteen

14.1
1 A
2 P
3 P
4 A
5 P

14.2
1 Computer parts are made here.
2 The food is sent to the market.
3 The man was taken to the station.
4 The children were sent home early.
5 The car was sold yesterday.

14.3
credit card   bus stop
car park   post office
pop star   washing machine

14.4
1 Could I borrow your dictionary (please)?
2 Could you (possibly) open the window?
3 Could I (possibly) speak to you after class?
4 Could you take my book to the classroom (please)?
5 Could you (possibly) help me with my homework?

OXFORD
UNIVERSITY PRESS

Great Clarendon Street, Oxford OX2 6DP

Oxford University Press is a department of the University of Oxford.
It furthers the University's objective of excellence in research, scholarship,
and education by publishing worldwide in

Oxford   New York

Auckland Cape Town Dar es Salaam Hong Kong Karachi
Kuala Lumpur Madrid Melbourne Mexico City Nairobi
New Delhi Shanghai Taipei Toronto

With offices in

Argentina Austria Brazil Chile Czech Republic France Greece
Guatemala Hungary Italy Japan Poland Portugal Singapore
South Korea Switzerland Thailand Turkey Ukraine Vietnam

OXFORD and OXFORD ENGLISH are registered trade marks of
Oxford University Press in the UK and in certain other countries

© Oxford University Press 2005

The moral rights of the author have been asserted

Database right Oxford University Press (maker)

First published 2005

2009 2008 2007 2006 2005
10 9 8 7 6 5 4 3 2 1

All rights reserved. No part of this publication may be reproduced,
stored in a retrieval system, or transmitted, in any form or by any means,
without the prior permission in writing of Oxford University Press (with
the sole exception of photocopying carried out under the conditions stated
in the paragraph headed 'Photocopying'), or as expressly permitted by law, or
under terms agreed with the appropriate reprographics rights organization.
Enquiries concerning reproduction outside the scope of the above should
be sent to the ELT Rights Department, Oxford University Press, at the
address above

You must not circulate this book in any other binding or cover
and you must impose this same condition on any acquirer

Photocopying

The Publisher grants permission for the photocopying of those pages marked
'photocopiable' according to the following conditions. Individual purchasers
may make copies for their own use or for use by classes that they teach.
School purchasers may make copies for use by staff and students, but this
permission does not extend to additional schools or branches

Under no circumstances may any part of this book be photocopied for resale

Any websites referred to in this publication are in the public domain and
their addresses are provided by Oxford University Press for information only.
Oxford University Press disclaims any responsibility for the content

ISBN-13: 978 0 19 438868 9
ISBN-10: 0 19 438868 9

Printed and bound by Grafiasa S. A. in Portugal

ACKNOWLEDGEMENTS

Cover illustration © Claire Bretécher 2005

Illustrations by: Emma Dodd pp.157, 162; Mark Duffin p.175

*The Publisher would like to thank the following for permission to reproduce
photographs:* Alamy p. 175 (group of friends/ImageState), 146 (group of
students/Jacky Chapman/Janine Wiedel Photography); Getty Images cover, 1
(man and woman smiling), p.155 (man leaning/Seth Joe/Taxi), Zefa Picture
Library p.146 (pair of students/Masterfile/Pierre Tremblay).